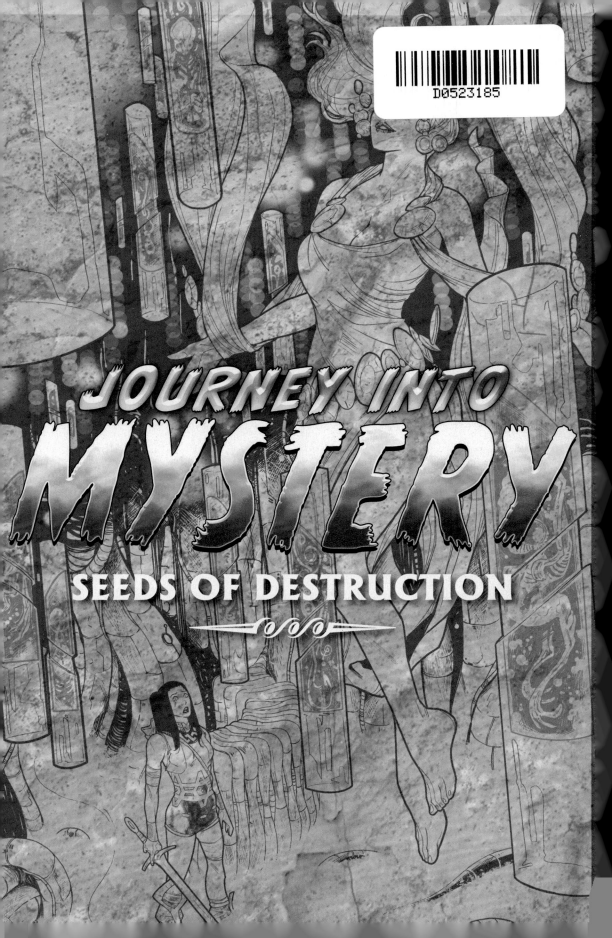

JOURNEY INTO MYSTERY

SEEDS OF DESTRUCTION

COLLECTION EDITOR
CORY LEVINE

ASSISTANT EDITORS
**ALEX STARBUCK
NELSON RIBEIRO**

EDITORS,
SPECIAL PROJECTS
**JENNIFER GRÜNWALD
MARK D. BEAZLEY**

SENIOR EDITOR,
SPECIAL PROJECTS
JEFF YOUNGQUIST

SVP OF PRINT & DIGITAL
PUBLISHING SALES
DAVID GABRIEL

BOOK DESIGN
**JEFF POWELL
CORY LEVINE**

EDITOR IN CHIEF
AXEL ALONSO

CHIEF CREATIVE OFFICER
JOE QUESADA

PUBLISHER
DAN BUCKLEY

EXECUTIVE PRODUCER
ALAN FINE

JOURNEY INTO MYSTERY FEATURING SIF VOL. 2: SEEDS
OF DESTRUCTION. Contains material originally published
in magazine form as JOURNEY INTO MYSTERY 651-655.
First printing 2013. ISBN# 978-0-7851-8447-8. Published
by MARVEL WORLDWIDE, INC., a subsidiary of MARVEL
ENTERTAINMENT, LLC. OFFICE OF PUBLICATION: 135 West
50th Street, New York, NY 10020. Copyright © 2013 Marvel
Characters, Inc. All rights reserved. All characters featured in
this issue and the distinctive names and likenesses thereof,
and all related indicia are trademarks of Marvel Characters,
Inc. No similarity between any of the names, characters,
persons, and/or institutions in this magazine with those
of any living or dead person or institution is intended, and
any such similarity which may exist is purely coincidental.
Printed in Canada. ALAN FINE, EVP - Office of the President,
Marvel Worldwide, Inc. and EVP & CMO Marvel Characters
B.V.; DAN BUCKLEY, Publisher & President - Print, Animation
& Digital Divisions; JOE QUESADA, Chief Creative Officer;
TOM BREVOORT, SVP of Publishing; DAVID BOGART, SVP of
Operations & Procurement, Publishing; C.B. CEBULSKI, SVP of
Creator & Content Development; DAVID GABRIEL, SVP of Print
& Digital Publishing Sales; JIM O'KEEFE, VP of Operations
& Logistics; DAN CARR, Executive Director of Publishing
Technology; SUSAN CRESPI, Editorial Operations Manager;
ALEX MORALES, Publishing Operations Manager; STAN LEE,
Chairman Emeritus. For information regarding advertising in
Marvel Comics or on Marvel.com, please contact Niza Disla,
Director of Marvel Partnerships, at ndisla@marvel.com. For
Marvel subscription inquiries, please call 800-217-9158.
**Manufactured between 8/30/2013 and 10/7/2013 by
SOLISCO PRINTERS, SCOTT, QC, CANADA.**

10 9 8 7 6 5 4 3 2 1

JOURNEY INTO MYSTERY

SEEDS OF DESTRUCTION

WRITER
KATHRYN IMMONEN

ARTISTS
PEPE LARRAZ (#651)
VALERIO SCHITI (#652-655)

COLOR ARTIST
JORDIE BELLAIRE

LETTERER
VC'S CLAYTON COWLES

COVER ARTIST
JEFF DEKAL

ASSISTANT EDITOR
JACOB THOMAS

EDITOR
LAUREN SANKOVITCH

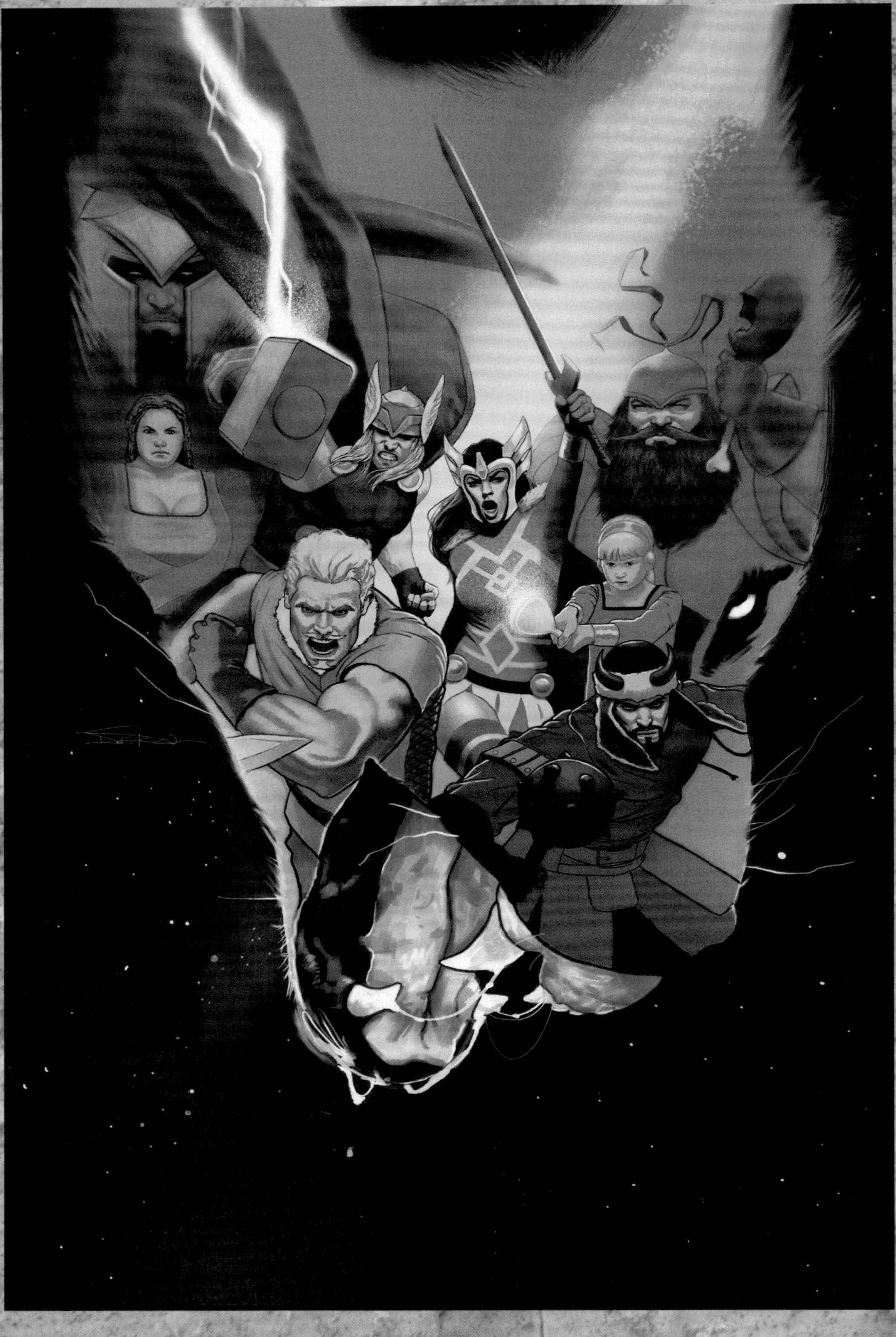

#651

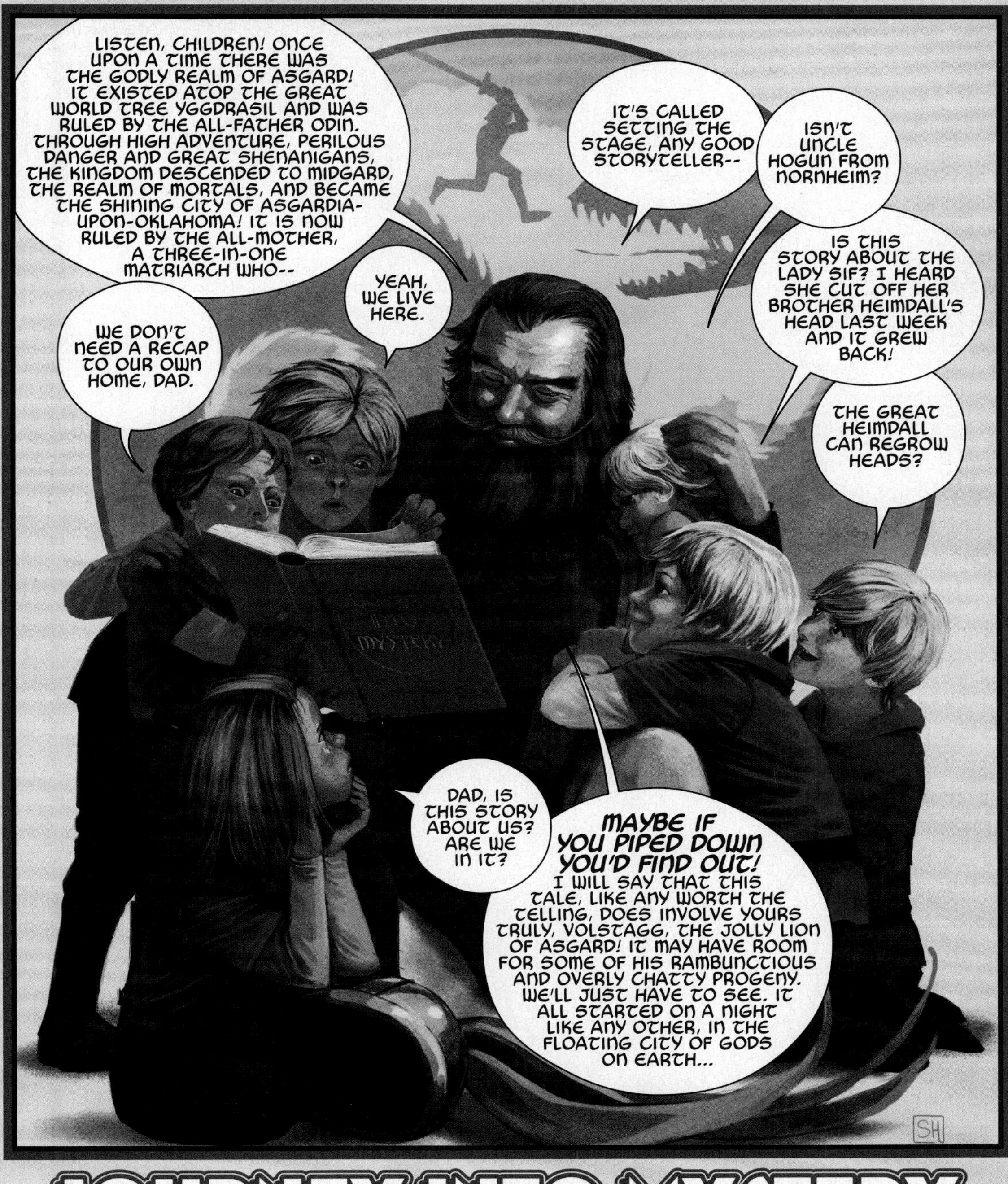
LISTEN, CHILDREN! ONCE UPON A TIME THERE WAS THE GODLY REALM OF ASGARD! IT EXISTED ATOP THE GREAT WORLD TREE YGGDRASIL AND WAS RULED BY THE ALL-FATHER ODIN. THROUGH HIGH ADVENTURE, PERILOUS DANGER AND GREAT SHENANIGANS, THE KINGDOM DESCENDED TO MIDGARD, THE REALM OF MORTALS, AND BECAME THE SHINING CITY OF ASGARDIA-UPON-OKLAHOMA! IT IS NOW RULED BY THE ALL-MOTHER, A THREE-IN-ONE MATRIARCH WHO--
IT'S CALLED SETTING THE STAGE, ANY GOOD STORYTELLER--
ISN'T UNCLE HOGUN FROM NORNHEIM?
YEAH, WE LIVE HERE.
WE DON'T NEED A RECAP TO OUR OWN HOME, DAD.
IS THIS STORY ABOUT THE LADY SIF? I HEARD SHE CUT OFF HER BROTHER HEIMDALL'S HEAD LAST WEEK AND IT GREW BACK!
THE GREAT HEIMDALL CAN REGROW HEADS?
MYSTERY
DAD, IS THIS STORY ABOUT US? ARE WE IN IT?
MAYBE IF YOU PIPED DOWN YOU'D FIND OUT! I WILL SAY THAT THIS TALE, LIKE ANY WORTH THE TELLING, DOES INVOLVE YOURS TRULY, VOLSTAGG, THE JOLLY LION OF ASGARD! IT MAY HAVE ROOM FOR SOME OF HIS RAMBUNCTIOUS AND OVERLY CHATTY PROGENY. WE'LL JUST HAVE TO SEE. IT ALL STARTED ON A NIGHT LIKE ANY OTHER, IN THE FLOATING CITY OF GODS ON EARTH...
SH

JOURNEY INTO MYSTERY

A CHILD'S GARDEN OF VERSES

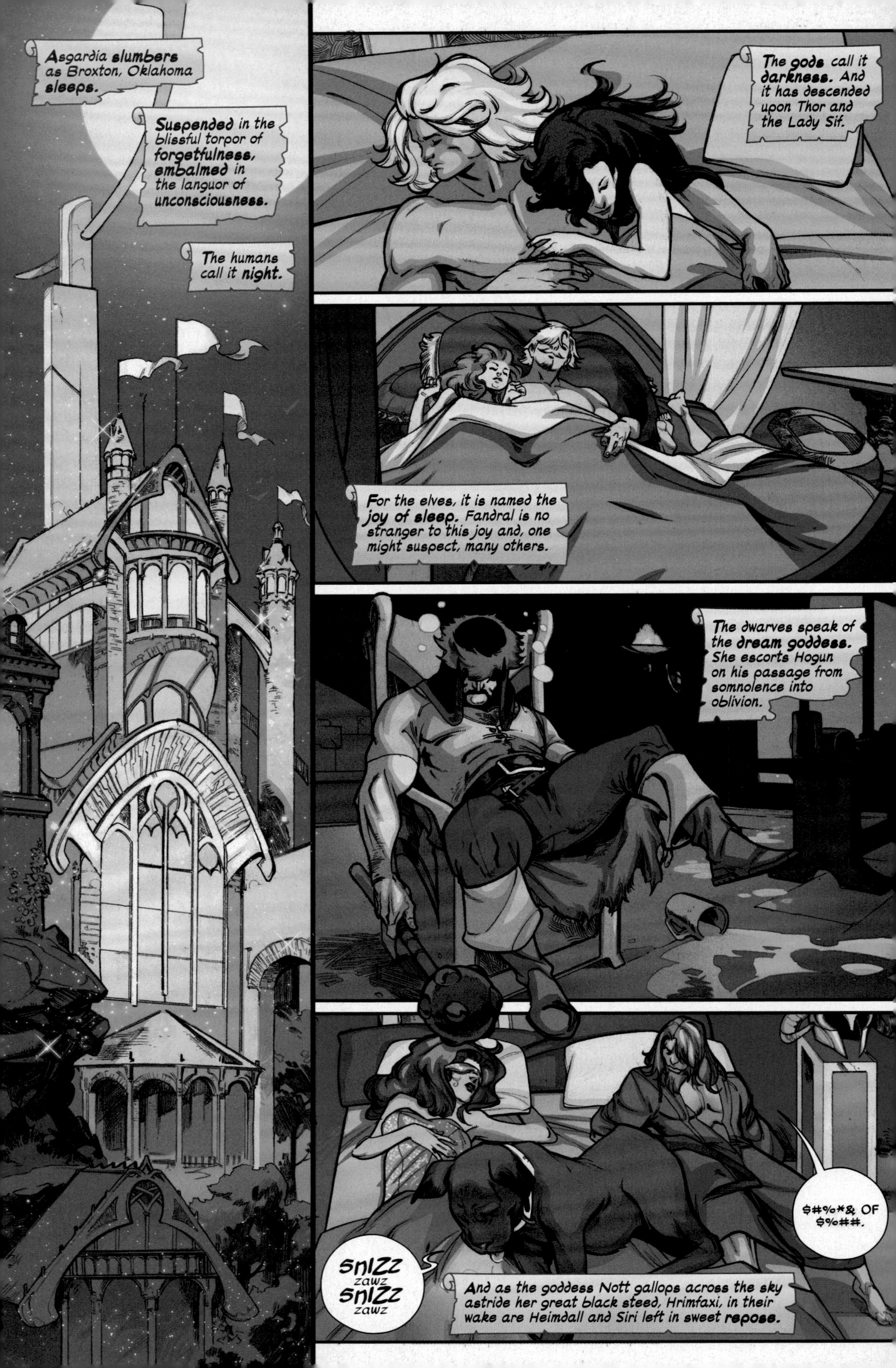

Asgardia slumbers as Broxton, Oklahoma sleeps.
Suspended in the blissful torpor of forgetfulness, embalmed in the languor of unconsciousness.
The humans call it night.
The gods call it darkness. And it has descended upon Thor and the Lady Sif.
For the elves, it is named the joy of sleep. Fandral is no stranger to this joy and, one might suspect, many others.
The dwarves speak of the dream goddess. She escorts Hogun on his passage from somnolence into oblivion.
$#%*& OF $%##.
SNIZZ zawz SNIZZ zawz
And as the goddess Nott gallops across the sky astride her great black steed, Hrimfaxi, in their wake are Heimdall and Siri left in sweet repose.

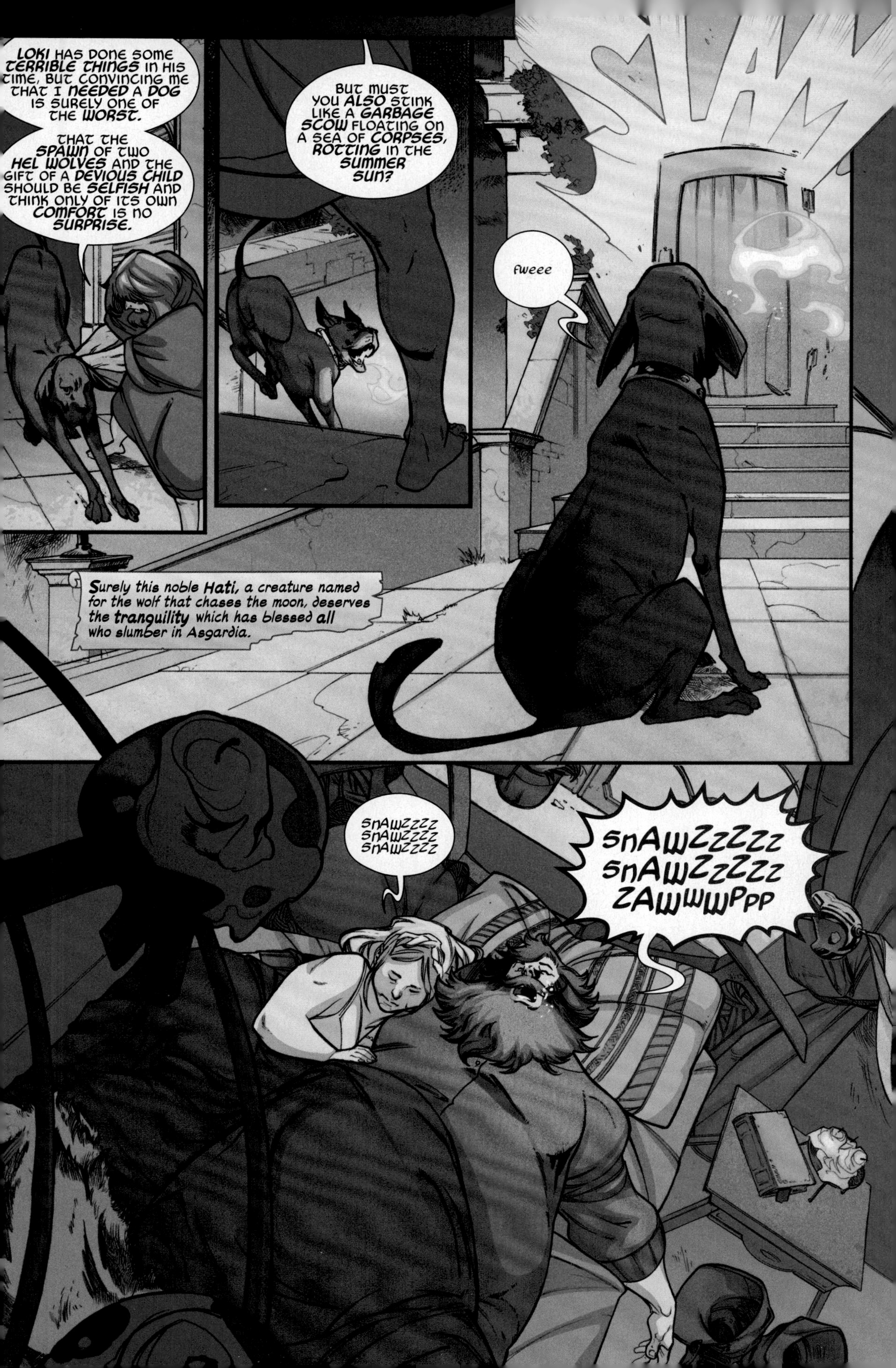
LOKI HAS DONE SOME TERRIBLE THINGS IN HIS TIME, BUT CONVINCING ME THAT I NEEDED A DOG IS SURELY ONE OF THE WORST.
THAT THE SPAWN OF TWO HEL WOLVES AND THE GIFT OF A DEVIOUS CHILD SHOULD BE SELFISH AND THINK ONLY OF ITS OWN COMFORT IS NO SURPRISE.
BUT MUST YOU ALSO STINK LIKE A GARBAGE SCOW FLOATING ON A SEA OF CORPSES, ROTTING IN THE SUMMER SUN?
SLAM
fweee
Surely this noble Hati, a creature named for the wolf that chases the moon, deserves the tranquility which has blessed all who slumber in Asgardia.
SNAWZZZZ SNAWZZZZ SNAWZZZZ
SNAWZZZZZZ SNAWZZZZZZ ZAWWWPPP

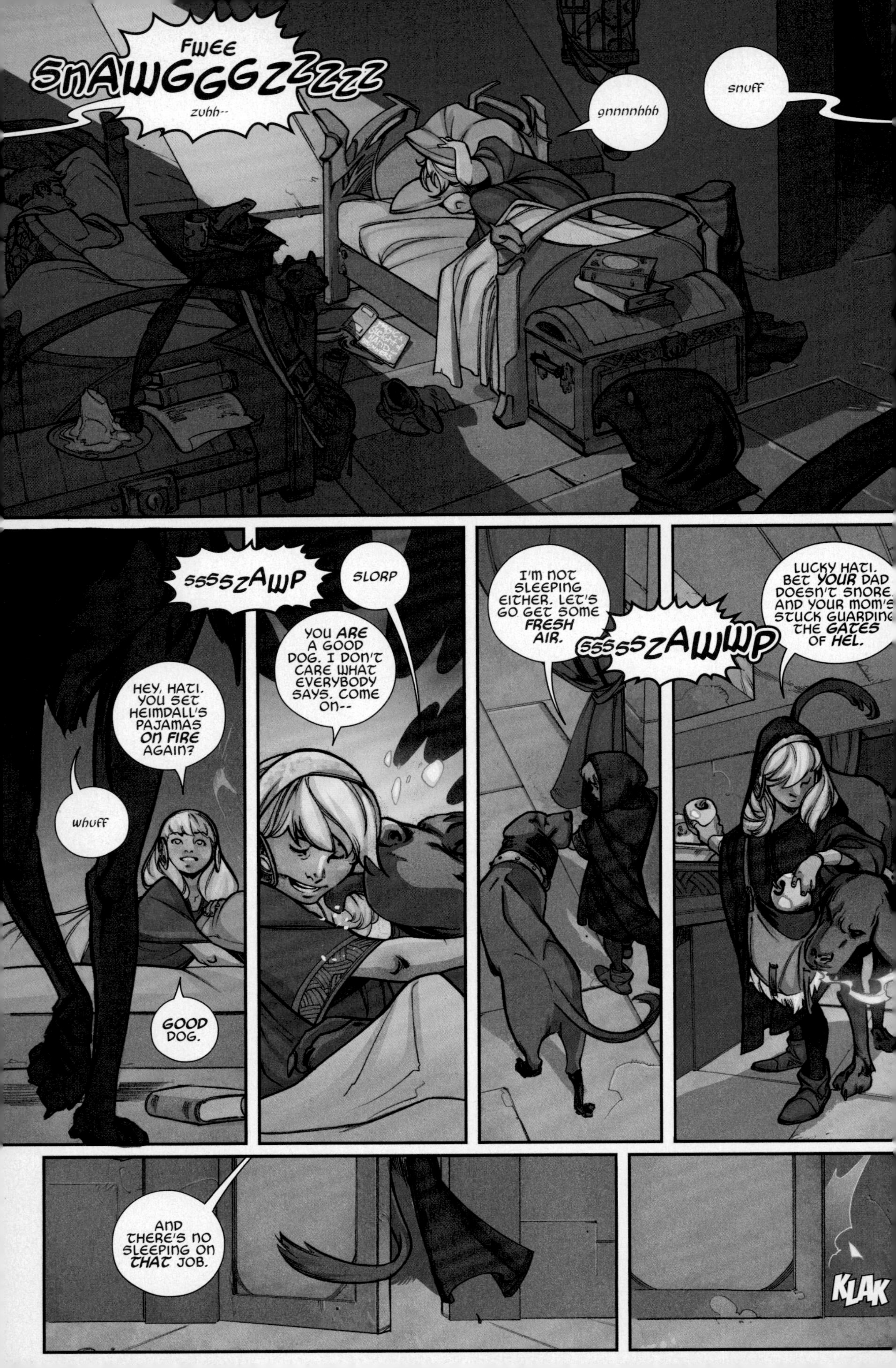
FWEE
SNAWGGGZZZZZ
zuhh--
gnnnnhhh
snuff
SSSSZAWP
HEY, HATI. YOU SET HEIMDALL'S PAJAMAS ON FIRE AGAIN?
whuff
GOOD DOG.
SLORP
YOU ARE A GOOD DOG. I DON'T CARE WHAT EVERYBODY SAYS. COME ON--
I'M NOT SLEEPING EITHER. LET'S GO GET SOME FRESH AIR.
SSSSSZAWWP
LUCKY HATI. BET YOUR DAD DOESN'T SNORE. AND YOUR MOM'S STUCK GUARDING THE GATES OF HEL.
AND THERE'S NO SLEEPING ON THAT JOB.
KLAK

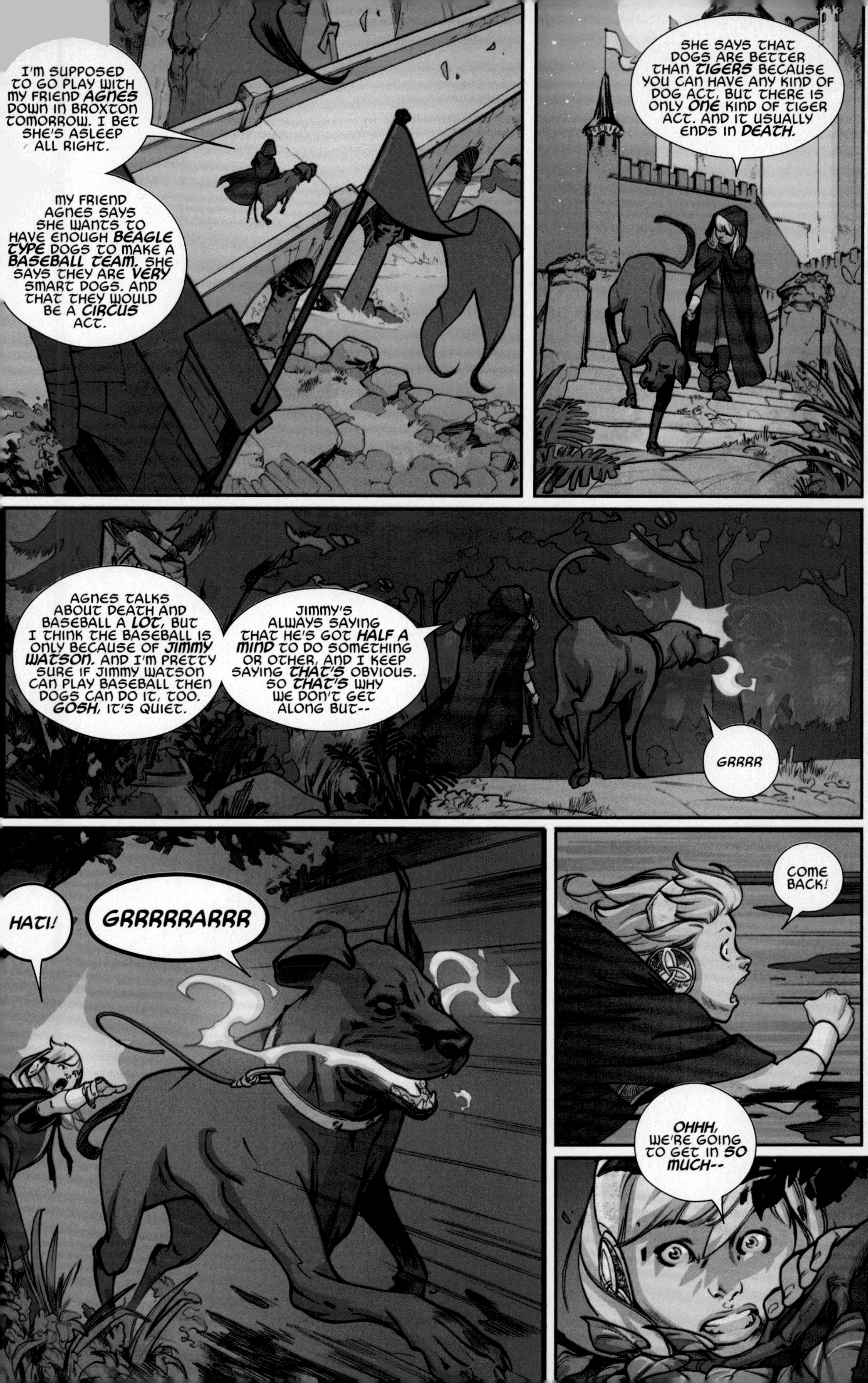

I'M SUPPOSED TO GO PLAY WITH MY FRIEND AGNES DOWN IN BROXTON TOMORROW. I BET SHE'S ASLEEP ALL RIGHT.
MY FRIEND AGNES SAYS SHE WANTS TO HAVE ENOUGH BEAGLE TYPE DOGS TO MAKE A BASEBALL TEAM. SHE SAYS THEY ARE VERY SMART DOGS. AND THAT THEY WOULD BE A CIRCUS ACT.
SHE SAYS THAT DOGS ARE BETTER THAN TIGERS BECAUSE YOU CAN HAVE ANY KIND OF DOG ACT, BUT THERE IS ONLY ONE KIND OF TIGER ACT. AND IT USUALLY ENDS IN DEATH.
AGNES TALKS ABOUT DEATH AND BASEBALL A LOT, BUT I THINK THE BASEBALL IS ONLY BECAUSE OF JIMMY WATSON. AND I'M PRETTY SURE IF JIMMY WATSON CAN PLAY BASEBALL THEN DOGS CAN DO IT, TOO. GOSH, IT'S QUIET.
JIMMY'S ALWAYS SAYING THAT HE'S GOT HALF A MIND TO DO SOMETHING OR OTHER, AND I KEEP SAYING THAT'S OBVIOUS. SO THAT'S WHY WE DON'T GET ALONG BUT--
GRRRR
HATI!
GRRRRRARRR
COME BACK!
OHHH, WE'RE GOING TO GET IN SO MUCH--

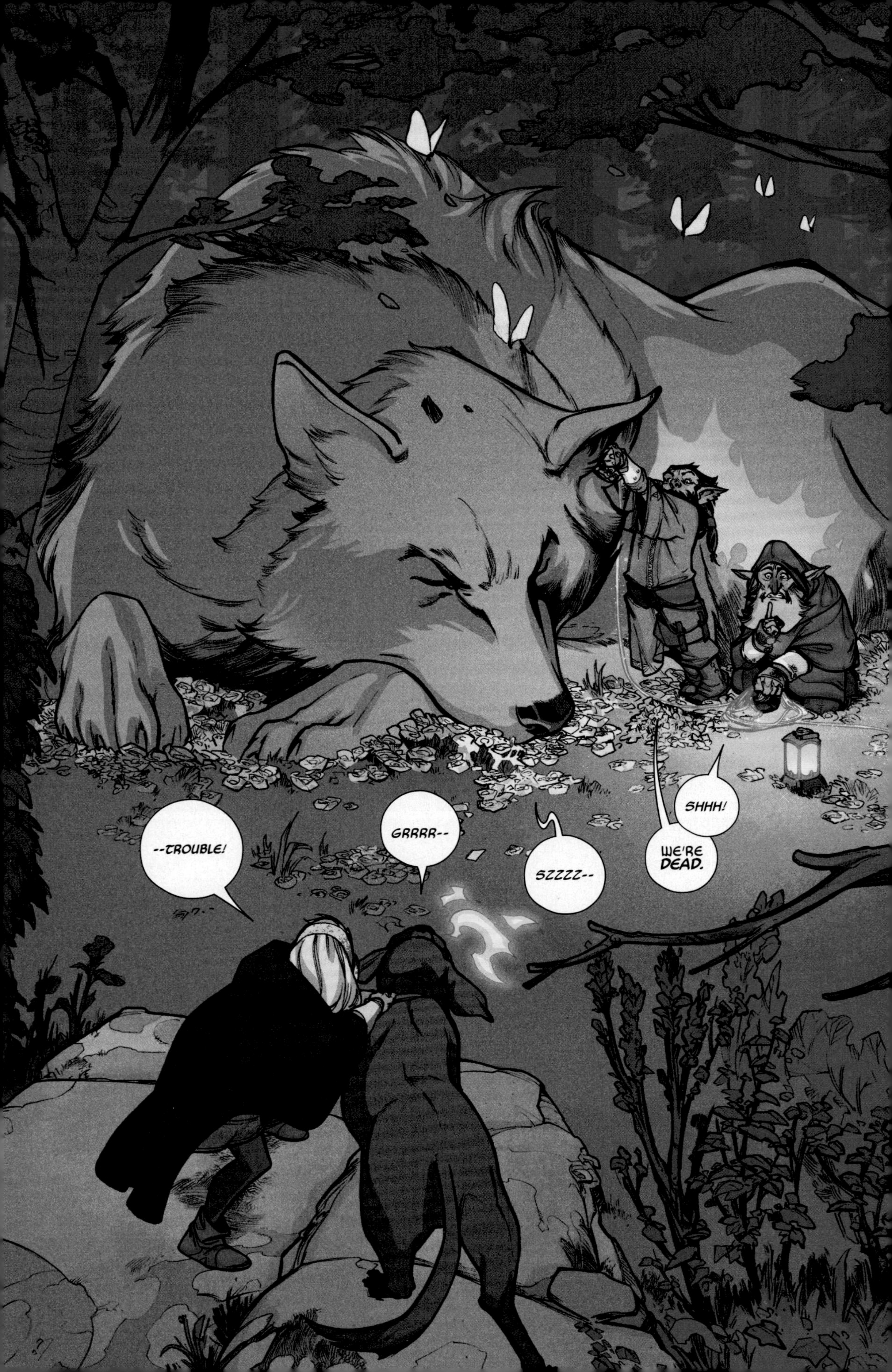
--TROUBLE!
GRRRR--
SZZZZ--
WE'RE DEAD.
SHHH!

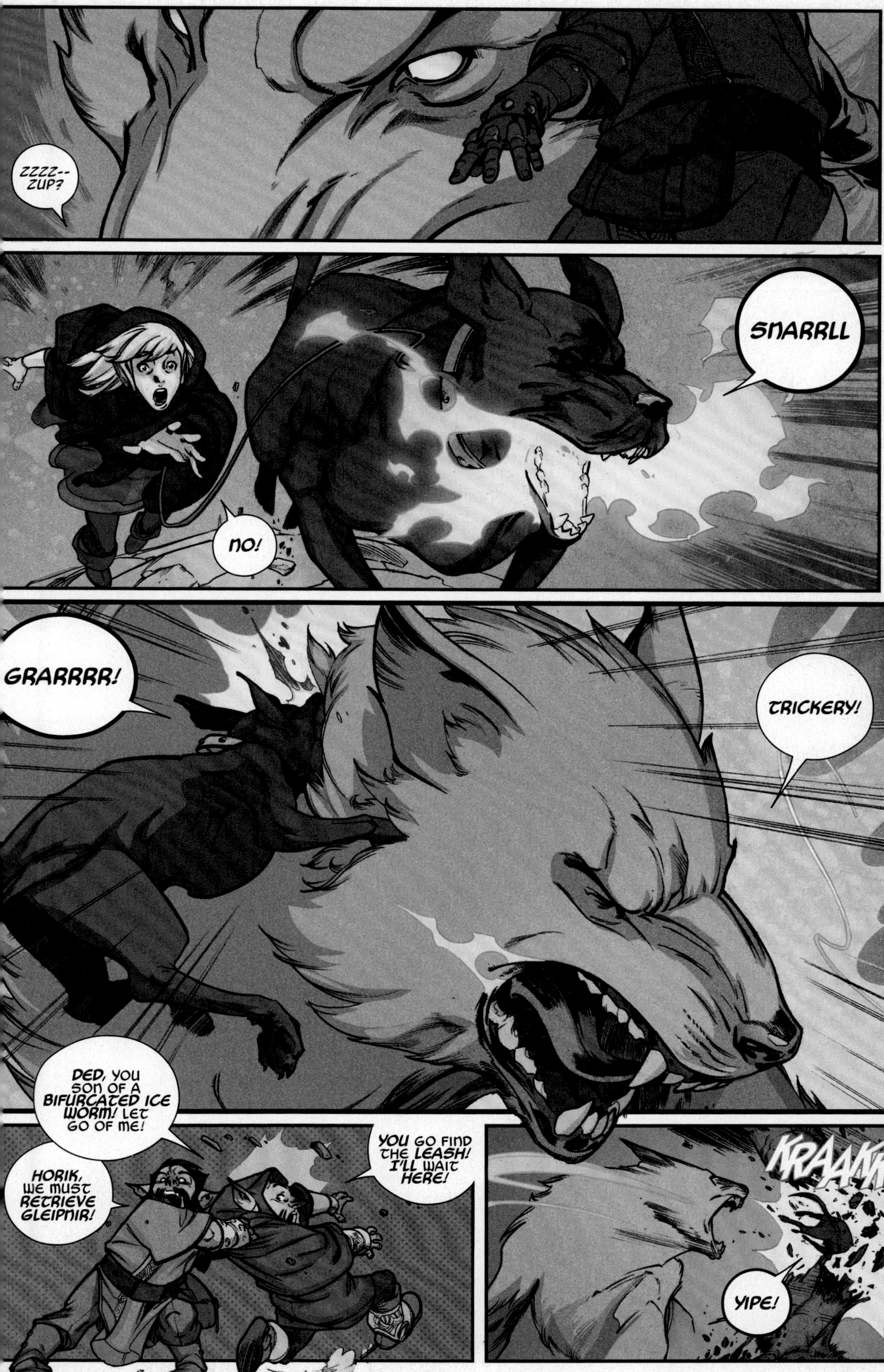
ZZZZ-- ZUP?
SNARRLL
NO!
GRARRRR!
TRICKERY!
DED, YOU SON OF A BIFURCATED ICE WORM! LET GO OF ME!
HORIK, WE MUST RETRIEVE GLEIPNIR!
YOU GO FIND THE LEASH! I'LL WAIT HERE!
KRAAKK
YIPE!

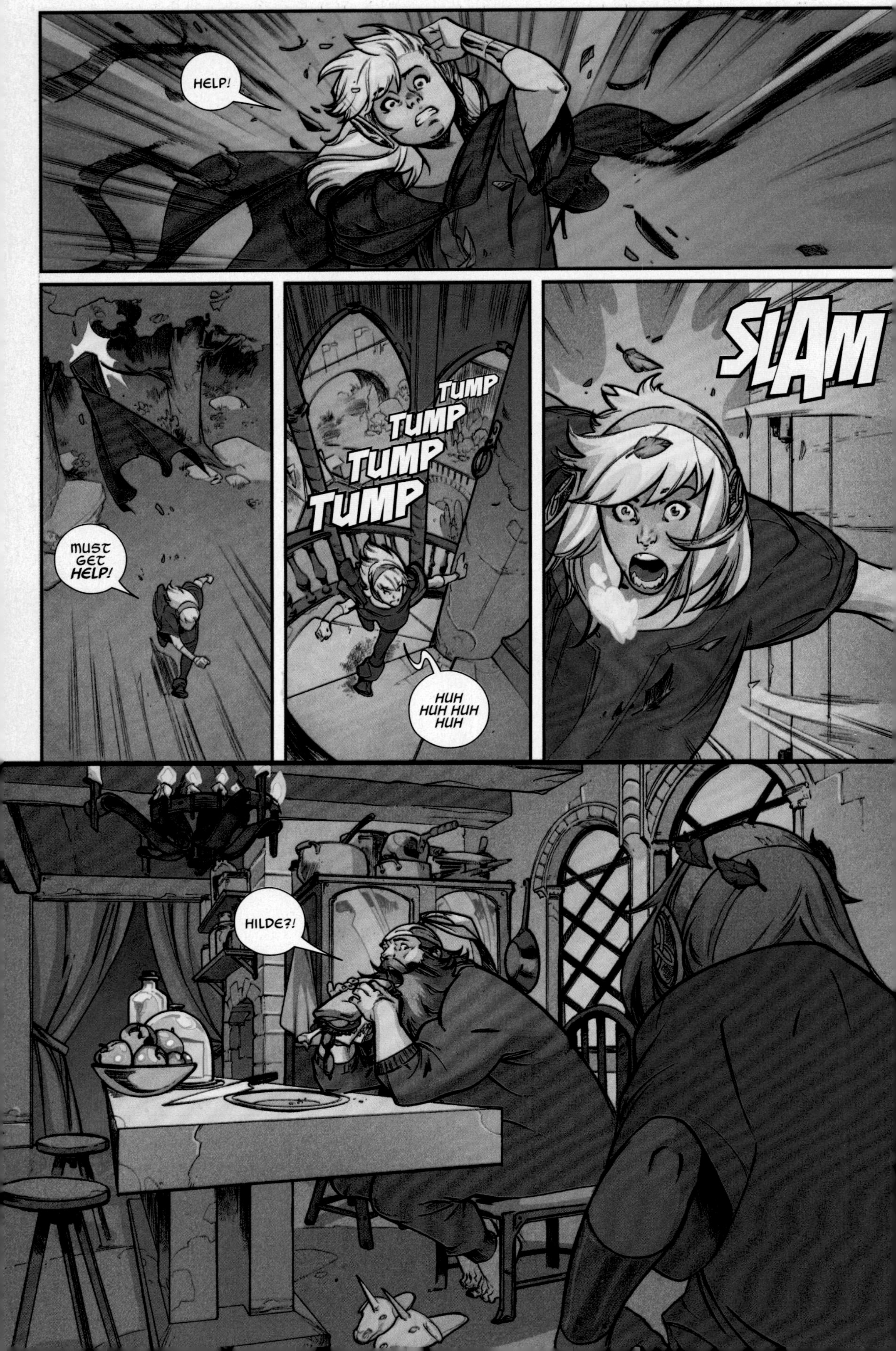
HELP!
MUST GET HELP!
TUMP
TUMP
TUMP
TUMP
HUH HUH HUH HUH
SLAM
HILDE?!

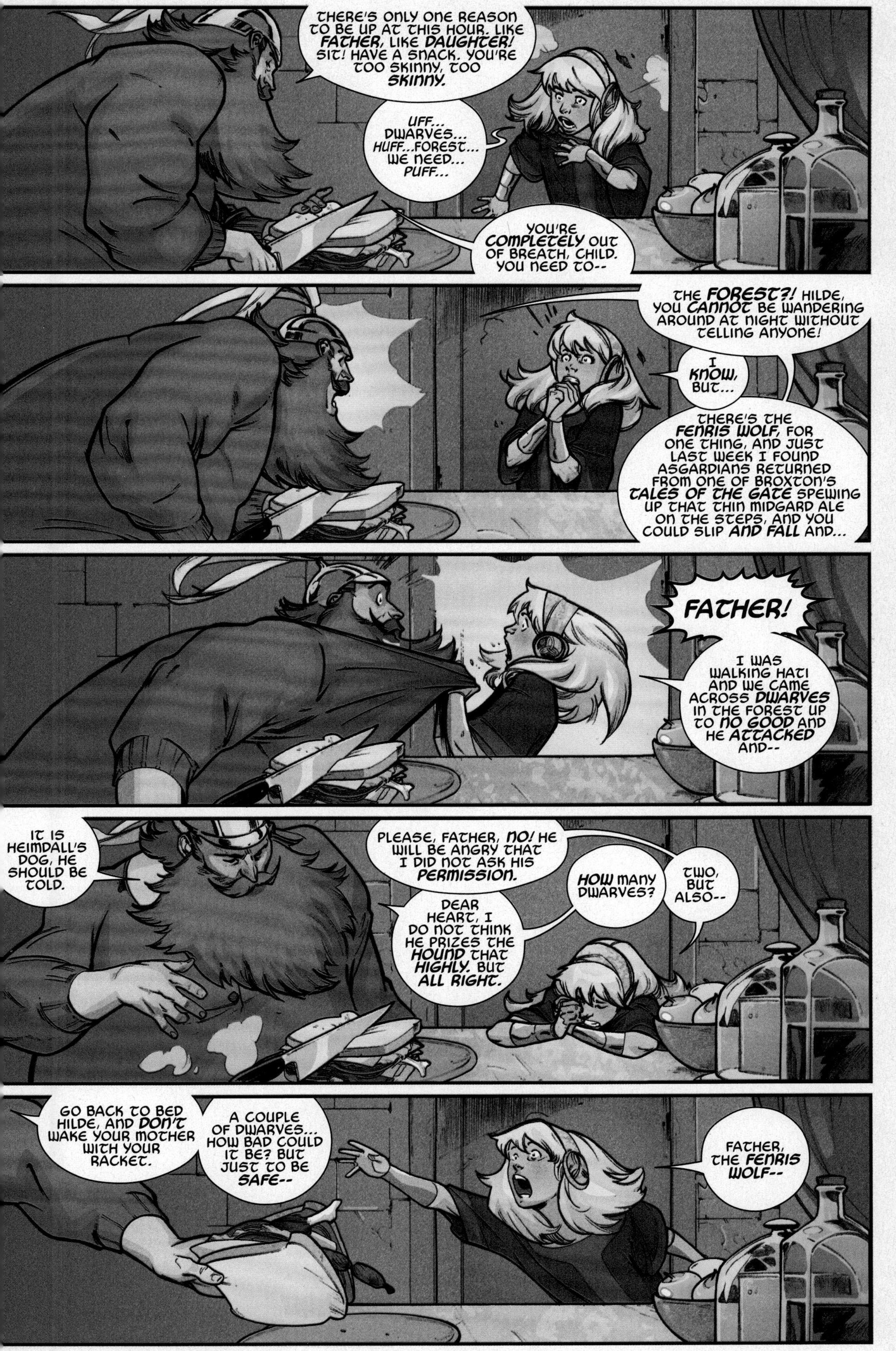
THERE'S ONLY ONE REASON TO BE UP AT THIS HOUR. LIKE FATHER, LIKE DAUGHTER! SIT! HAVE A SNACK. YOU'RE TOO SKINNY, TOO SKINNY.
UFF... DWARVES... HUFF...FOREST... WE NEED... PUFF...
YOU'RE COMPLETELY OUT OF BREATH, CHILD. YOU NEED TO--
THE FOREST?! HILDE, YOU CANNOT BE WANDERING AROUND AT NIGHT WITHOUT TELLING ANYONE!
I KNOW, BUT...
THERE'S THE FENRIS WOLF, FOR ONE THING, AND JUST LAST WEEK I FOUND ASGARDIANS RETURNED FROM ONE OF BROXTON'S TALES OF THE GATE SPEWING UP THAT THIN MIDGARD ALE ON THE STEPS, AND YOU COULD SLIP AND FALL AND...
FATHER!
I WAS WALKING HATI AND WE CAME ACROSS DWARVES IN THE FOREST UP TO NO GOOD AND HE ATTACKED AND--
IT IS HEIMDALL'S DOG, HE SHOULD BE TOLD.
PLEASE, FATHER, NO! HE WILL BE ANGRY THAT I DID NOT ASK HIS PERMISSION.
DEAR HEART, I DO NOT THINK HE PRIZES THE HOUND THAT HIGHLY. BUT ALL RIGHT.
HOW MANY DWARVES?
TWO, BUT ALSO--
GO BACK TO BED HILDE, AND DON'T WAKE YOUR MOTHER WITH YOUR RACKET.
A COUPLE OF DWARVES... HOW BAD COULD IT BE? BUT JUST TO BE SAFE--
FATHER, THE FENRIS WOLF--

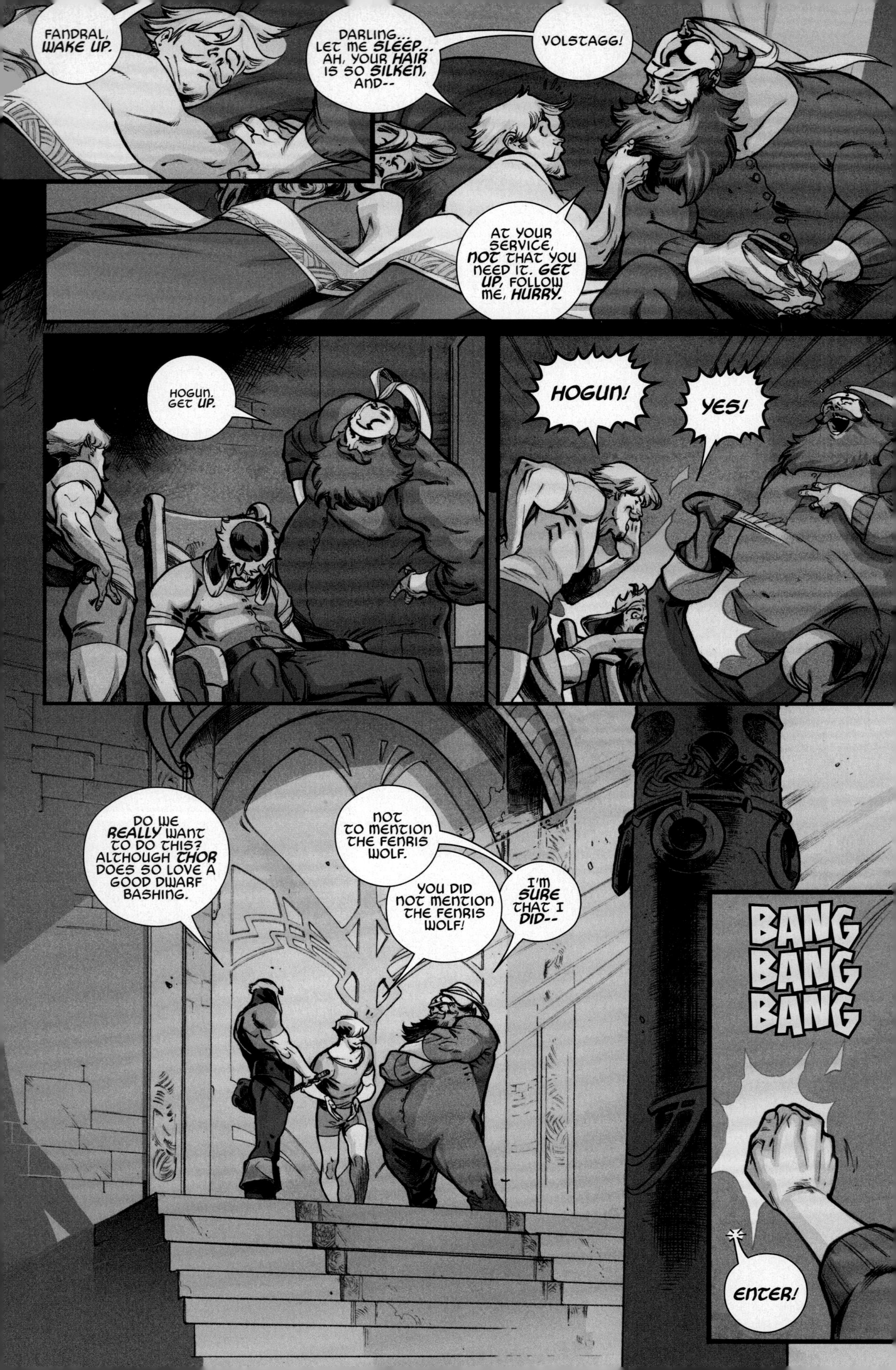
FANDRAL, WAKE UP.
DARLING... LET ME SLEEP... AH, YOUR HAIR IS SO SILKEN, AND--
VOLSTAGG!
AT YOUR SERVICE, NOT THAT YOU NEED IT. GET UP, FOLLOW ME, HURRY.
HOGUN. GET UP.
HOGUN!
YES!
DO WE REALLY WANT TO DO THIS? ALTHOUGH THOR DOES SO LOVE A GOOD DWARF BASHING.
NOT TO MENTION THE FENRIS WOLF.
YOU DID NOT MENTION THE FENRIS WOLF!
I'M SURE THAT I DID--
BANG BANG BANG
ENTER!

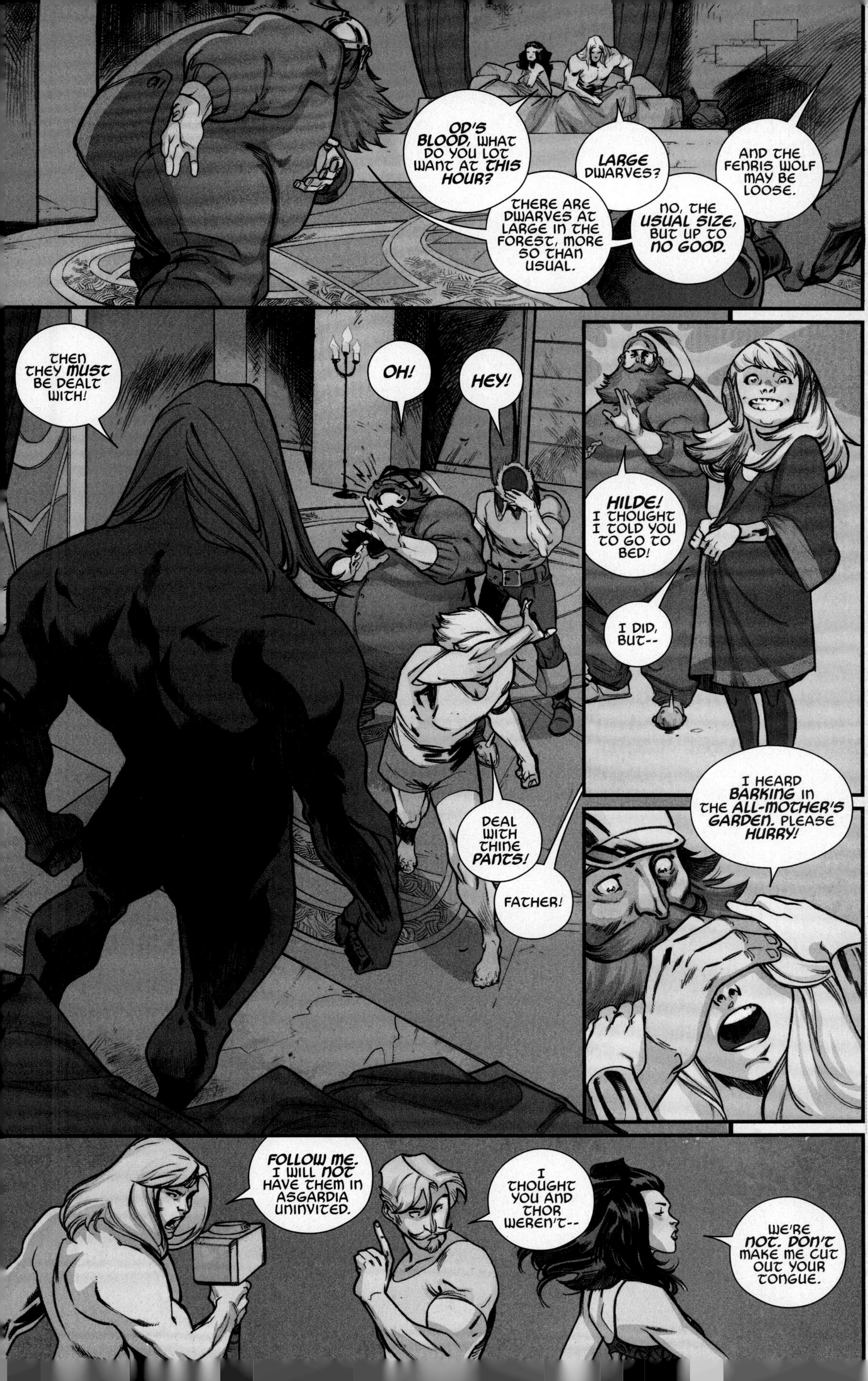

OD'S BLOOD, WHAT DO YOU LOT WANT AT THIS HOUR?
THERE ARE DWARVES AT LARGE IN THE FOREST, MORE SO THAN USUAL.
LARGE DWARVES?
NO, THE USUAL SIZE, BUT UP TO NO GOOD.
AND THE FENRIS WOLF MAY BE LOOSE.
THEN THEY MUST BE DEALT WITH!
OH!
HEY!
DEAL WITH THINE PANTS!
FATHER!
HILDE! I THOUGHT I TOLD YOU TO GO TO BED!
I DID, BUT--
I HEARD BARKING IN THE ALL-MOTHER'S GARDEN. PLEASE HURRY!
FOLLOW ME. I WILL NOT HAVE THEM IN ASGARDIA UNINVITED.
I THOUGHT YOU AND THOR WEREN'T--
WE'RE NOT. DON'T MAKE ME CUT OUT YOUR TONGUE.

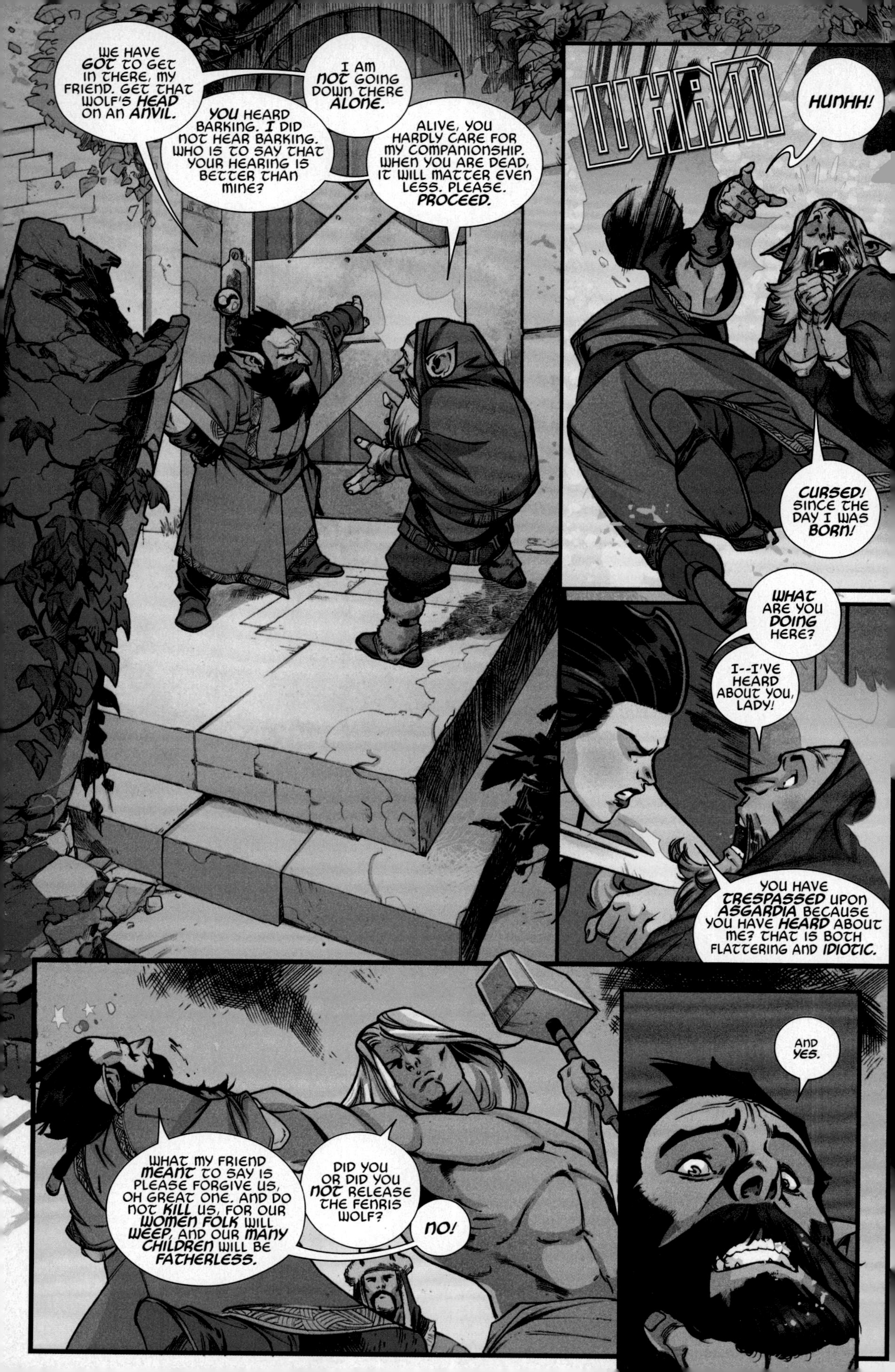
WE HAVE GOT TO GET IN THERE, MY FRIEND. GET THAT WOLF'S HEAD ON AN ANVIL.
I AM NOT GOING DOWN THERE ALONE.
YOU HEARD BARKING. I DID NOT HEAR BARKING. WHO IS TO SAY THAT YOUR HEARING IS BETTER THAN MINE?
ALIVE, YOU HARDLY CARE FOR MY COMPANIONSHIP. WHEN YOU ARE DEAD, IT WILL MATTER EVEN LESS. PLEASE. PROCEED.
WHAM
HUNHH!
CURSED! SINCE THE DAY I WAS BORN!
WHAT ARE YOU DOING HERE?
I--I'VE HEARD ABOUT YOU, LADY!
YOU HAVE TRESPASSED UPON ASGARDIA BECAUSE YOU HAVE HEARD ABOUT ME? THAT IS BOTH FLATTERING AND IDIOTIC.
DID YOU OR DID YOU NOT RELEASE THE FENRIS WOLF?
NO!
WHAT MY FRIEND MEANT TO SAY IS PLEASE FORGIVE US, OH GREAT ONE. AND DO NOT KILL US, FOR OUR WOMEN FOLK WILL WEEP, AND OUR MANY CHILDREN WILL BE FATHERLESS.
AND YES.

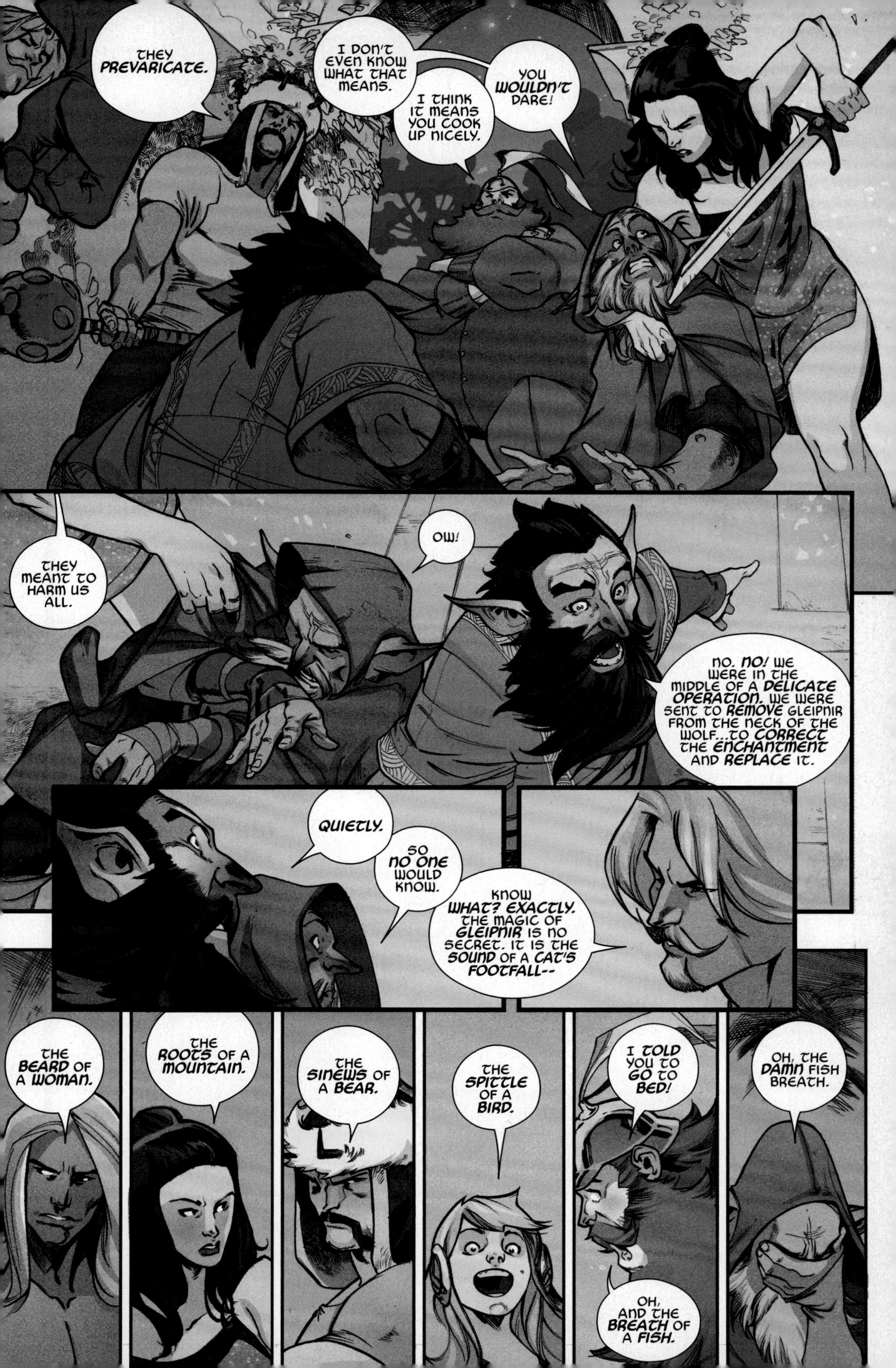
THEY PREVARICATE.
I DON'T EVEN KNOW WHAT THAT MEANS.
I THINK IT MEANS YOU COOK UP NICELY.
YOU WOULDN'T DARE!
THEY MEANT TO HARM US ALL.
OW!
NO. NO! WE WERE IN THE MIDDLE OF A DELICATE OPERATION. WE WERE SENT TO REMOVE GLEIPNIR FROM THE NECK OF THE WOLF...TO CORRECT THE ENCHANTMENT AND REPLACE IT.
QUIETLY.
SO NO ONE WOULD KNOW.
KNOW WHAT? EXACTLY. THE MAGIC OF GLEIPNIR IS NO SECRET. IT IS THE SOUND OF A CAT'S FOOTFALL--
THE BEARD OF A WOMAN.
THE ROOTS OF A MOUNTAIN.
THE SINEWS OF A BEAR.
THE SPITTLE OF A BIRD.
I TOLD YOU TO GO TO BED!
OH, AND THE BREATH OF A FISH.
OH, THE DAMN FISH BREATH.

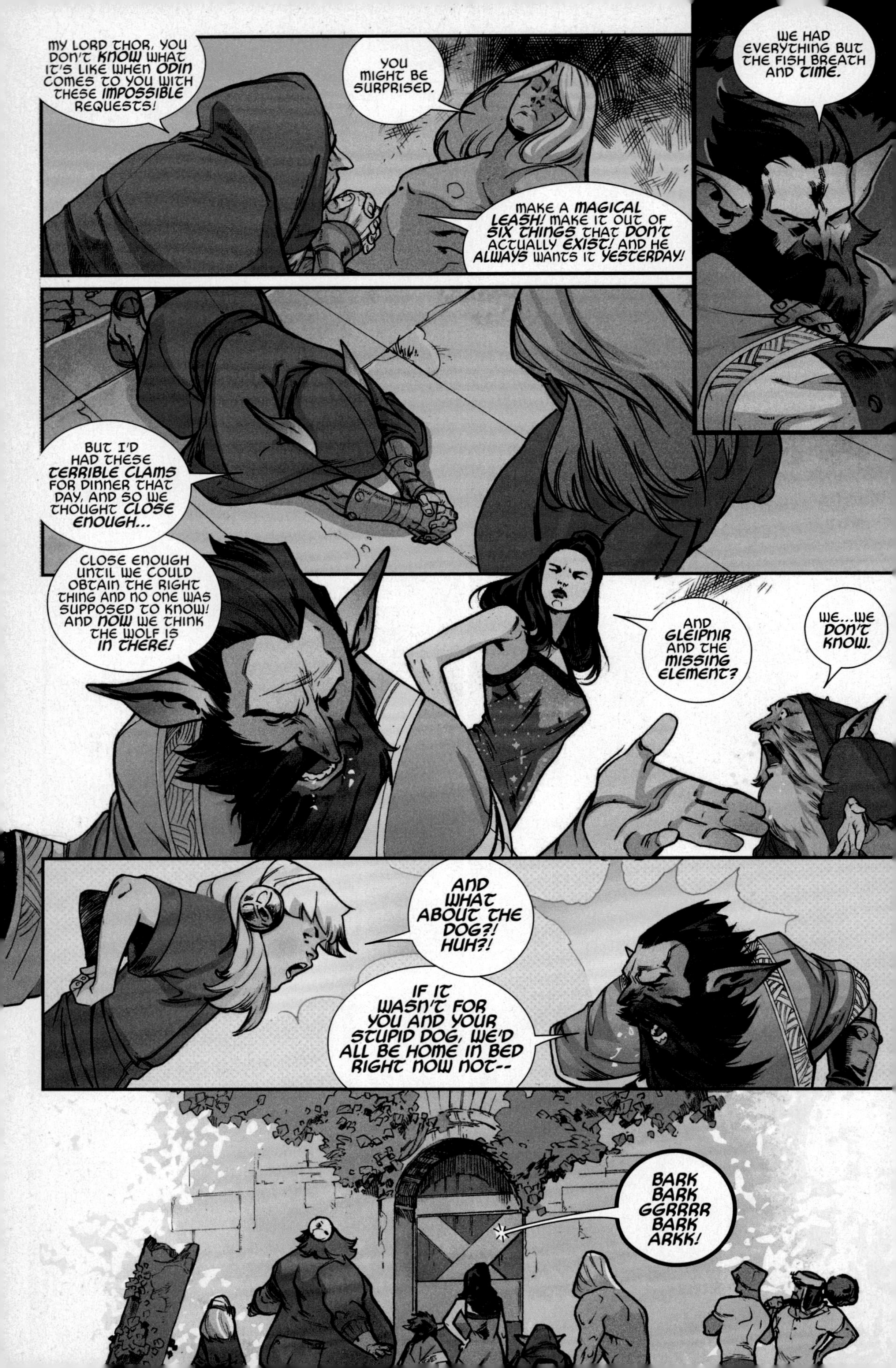
MY LORD THOR, YOU DON'T KNOW WHAT IT'S LIKE WHEN ODIN COMES TO YOU WITH THESE IMPOSSIBLE REQUESTS!
YOU MIGHT BE SURPRISED.
MAKE A MAGICAL LEASH! MAKE IT OUT OF SIX THINGS THAT DON'T ACTUALLY EXIST! AND HE ALWAYS WANTS IT YESTERDAY!
WE HAD EVERYTHING BUT THE FISH BREATH AND TIME.
BUT I'D HAD THESE TERRIBLE CLAMS FOR DINNER THAT DAY, AND SO WE THOUGHT CLOSE ENOUGH...
CLOSE ENOUGH UNTIL WE COULD OBTAIN THE RIGHT THING AND NO ONE WAS SUPPOSED TO KNOW! AND NOW WE THINK THE WOLF IS IN THERE!
AND GLEIPNIR AND THE MISSING ELEMENT?
WE...WE DON'T KNOW.
AND WHAT ABOUT THE DOG?! HUH?!
IF IT WASN'T FOR YOU AND YOUR STUPID DOG, WE'D ALL BE HOME IN BED RIGHT NOW NOT--
BARK BARK GGRRRR BARK ARKK!

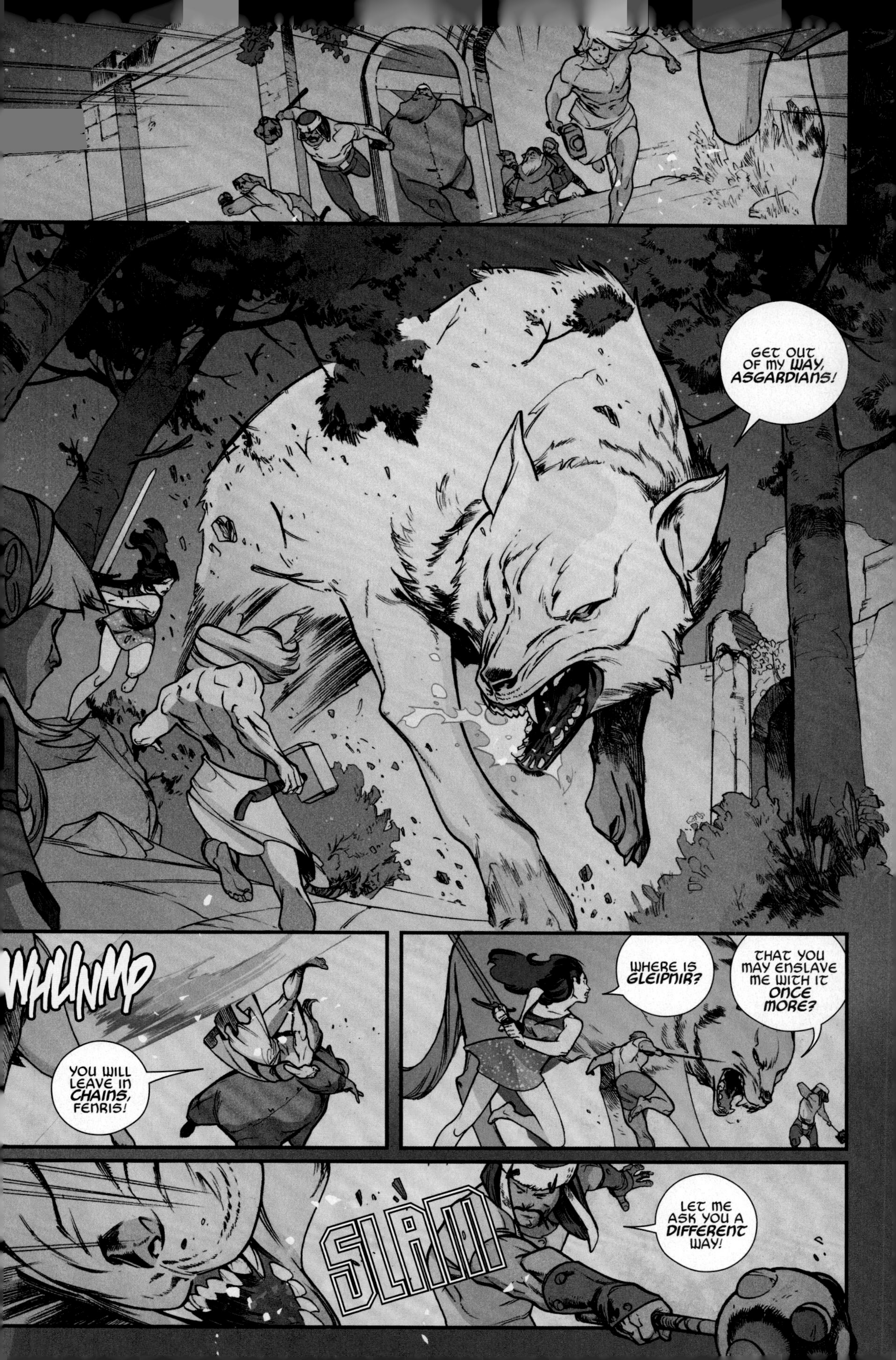
GET OUT OF MY WAY, ASGARDIANS!
WHUNMP
YOU WILL LEAVE IN CHAINS, FENRIS!
WHERE IS GLEIPNIR?
THAT YOU MAY ENSLAVE ME WITH IT ONCE MORE?
SLAM
LET ME ASK YOU A DIFFERENT WAY!

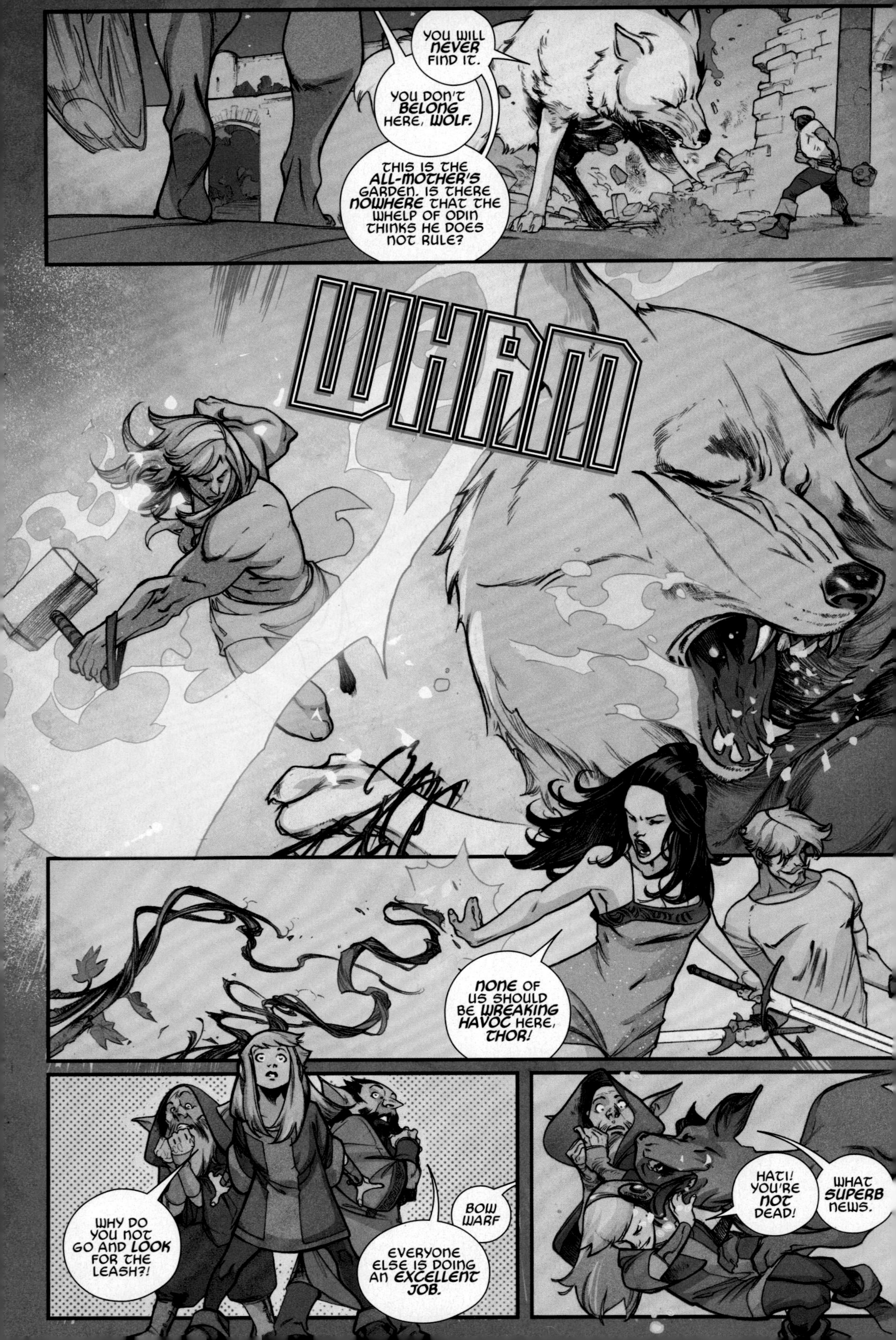
YOU WILL NEVER FIND IT.
YOU DON'T BELONG HERE, WOLF.
THIS IS THE ALL-MOTHER'S GARDEN. IS THERE NOWHERE THAT THE WHELP OF ODIN THINKS HE DOES NOT RULE?
WHAM
NONE OF US SHOULD BE WREAKING HAVOC HERE, THOR!
WHY DO YOU NOT GO AND LOOK FOR THE LEASH?!
BOW WARF
EVERYONE ELSE IS DOING AN EXCELLENT JOB.
HATI! YOU'RE NOT DEAD!
WHAT SUPERB NEWS.

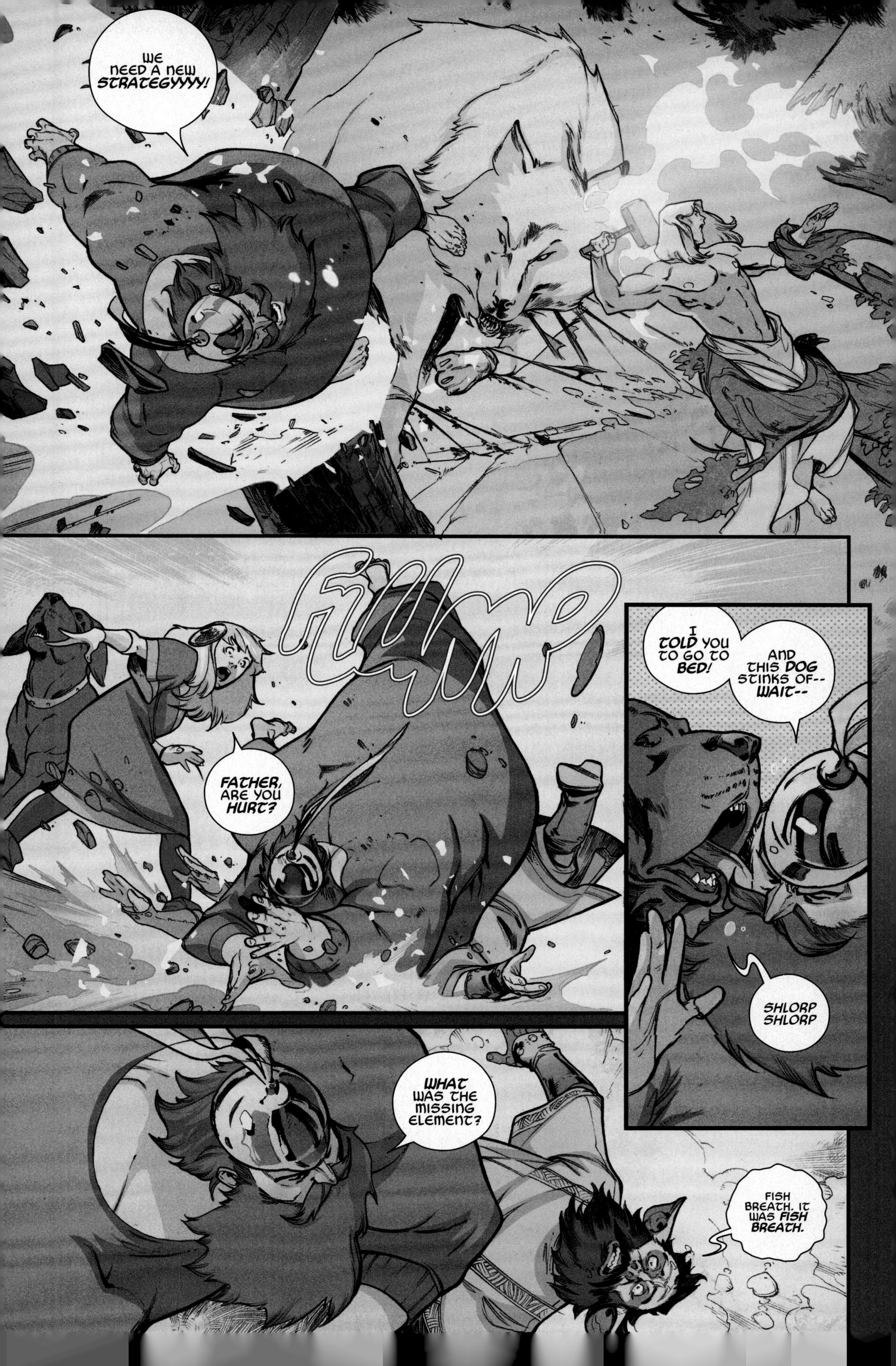
WE NEED A NEW STRATEGYYYY!
FATHER, ARE YOU HURT?
I TOLD YOU TO GO TO BED!
AND THIS DOG STINKS OF-- WAIT--
SHLORP SHLORP
WHAT WAS THE MISSING ELEMENT?
FISH BREATH. IT WAS FISH BREATH.

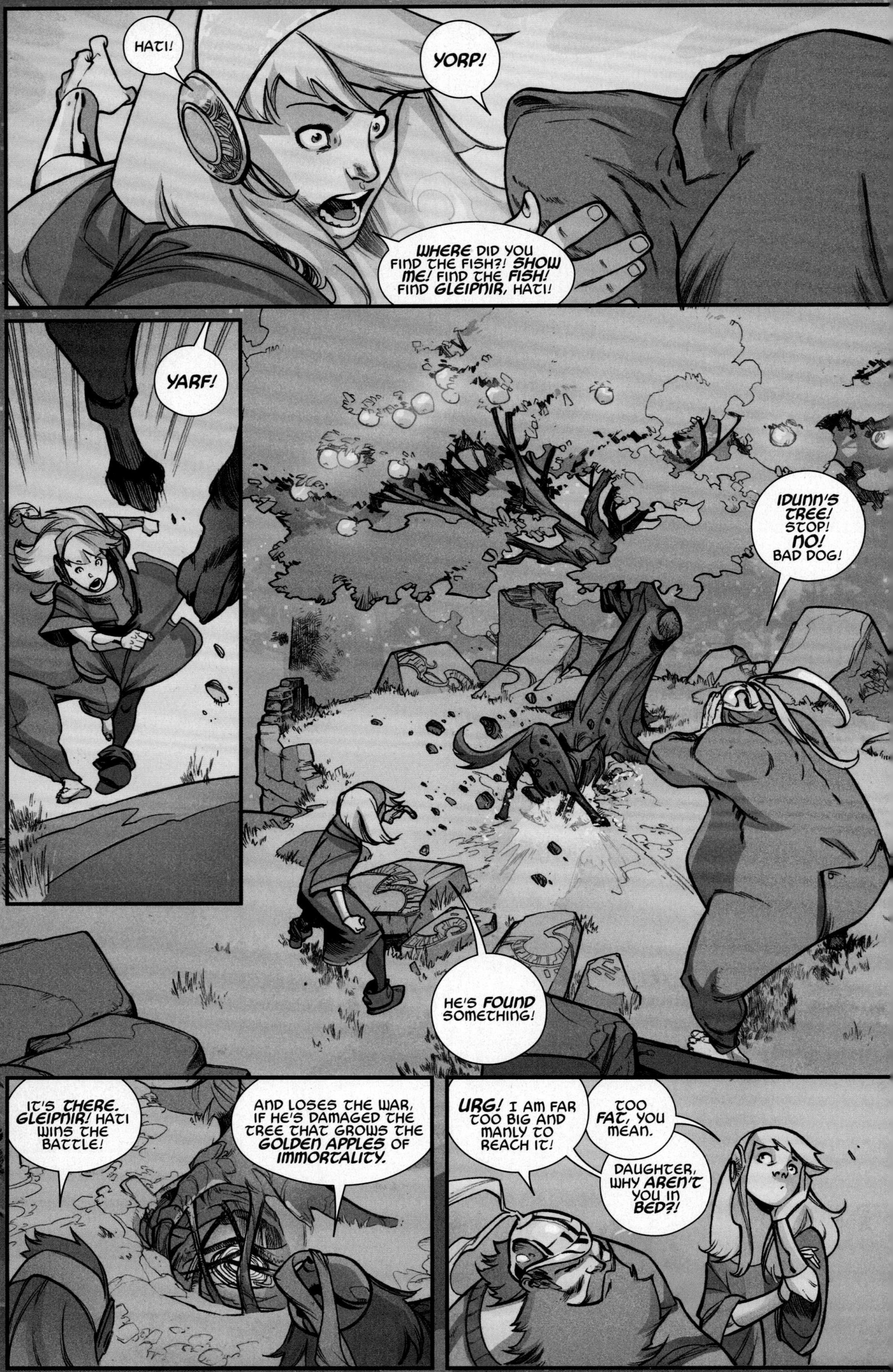
HATI!
YORP!
WHERE DID YOU FIND THE FISH?! SHOW ME! FIND THE FISH! FIND GLEIPNIR, HATI!
YARF!
IDUNN'S TREE! STOP! NO! BAD DOG!
HE'S FOUND SOMETHING!
IT'S THERE. GLEIPNIR! HATI WINS THE BATTLE!
AND LOSES THE WAR, IF HE'S DAMAGED THE TREE THAT GROWS THE GOLDEN APPLES OF IMMORTALITY.
URG! I AM FAR TOO BIG AND MANLY TO REACH IT!
TOO FAT, YOU MEAN.
DAUGHTER, WHY AREN'T YOU IN BED?!

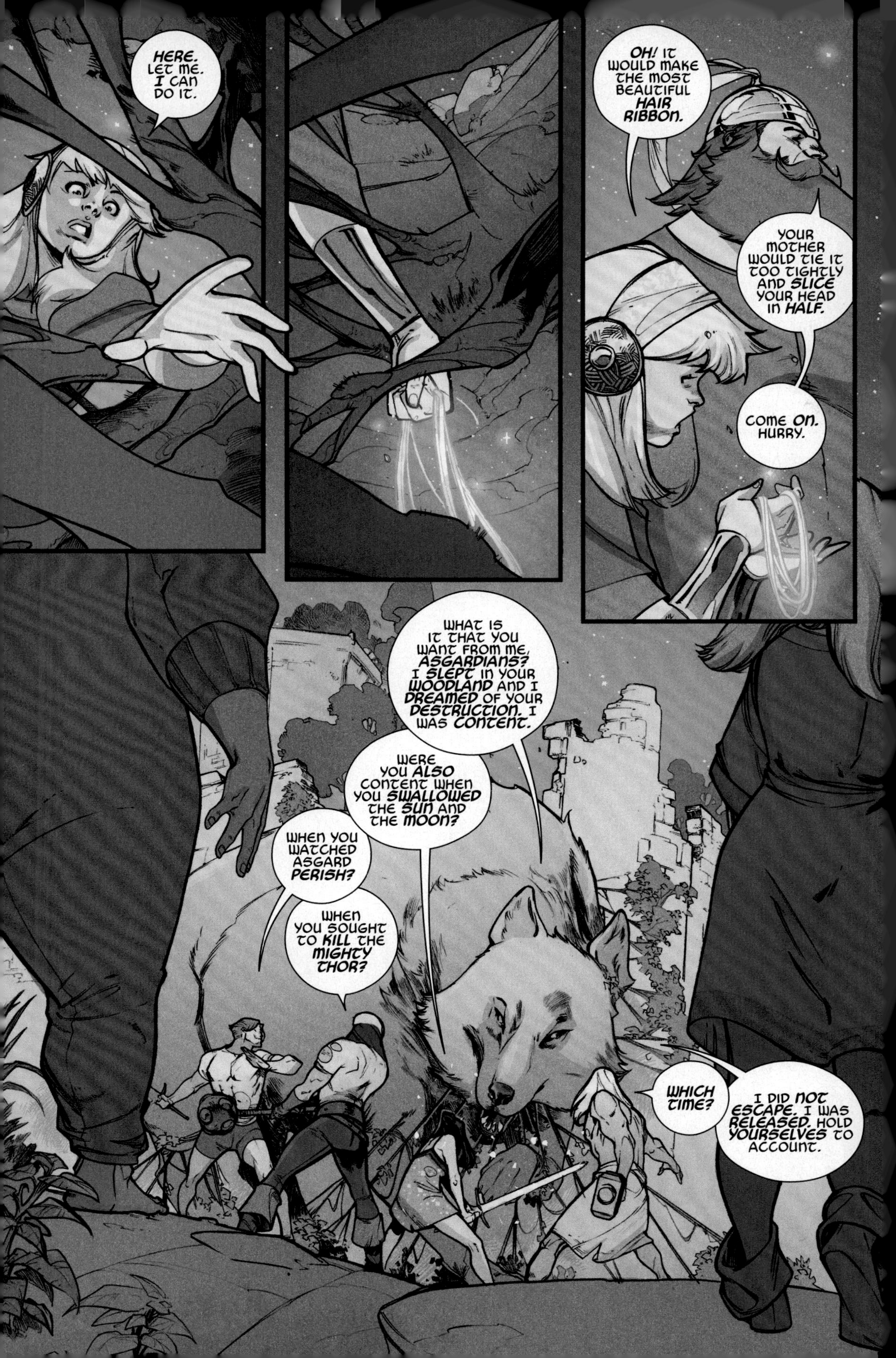
HERE. LET ME. I CAN DO IT.
OH! IT WOULD MAKE THE MOST BEAUTIFUL HAIR RIBBON.
YOUR MOTHER WOULD TIE IT TOO TIGHTLY AND SLICE YOUR HEAD IN HALF.
COME ON. HURRY.
WHAT IS IT THAT YOU WANT FROM ME, ASGARDIANS? I SLEPT IN YOUR WOODLAND AND I DREAMED OF YOUR DESTRUCTION. I WAS CONTENT.
WERE YOU ALSO CONTENT WHEN YOU SWALLOWED THE SUN AND THE MOON?
WHEN YOU WATCHED ASGARD PERISH?
WHEN YOU SOUGHT TO KILL THE MIGHTY THOR?
WHICH TIME?
I DID NOT ESCAPE. I WAS RELEASED. HOLD YOURSELVES TO ACCOUNT.

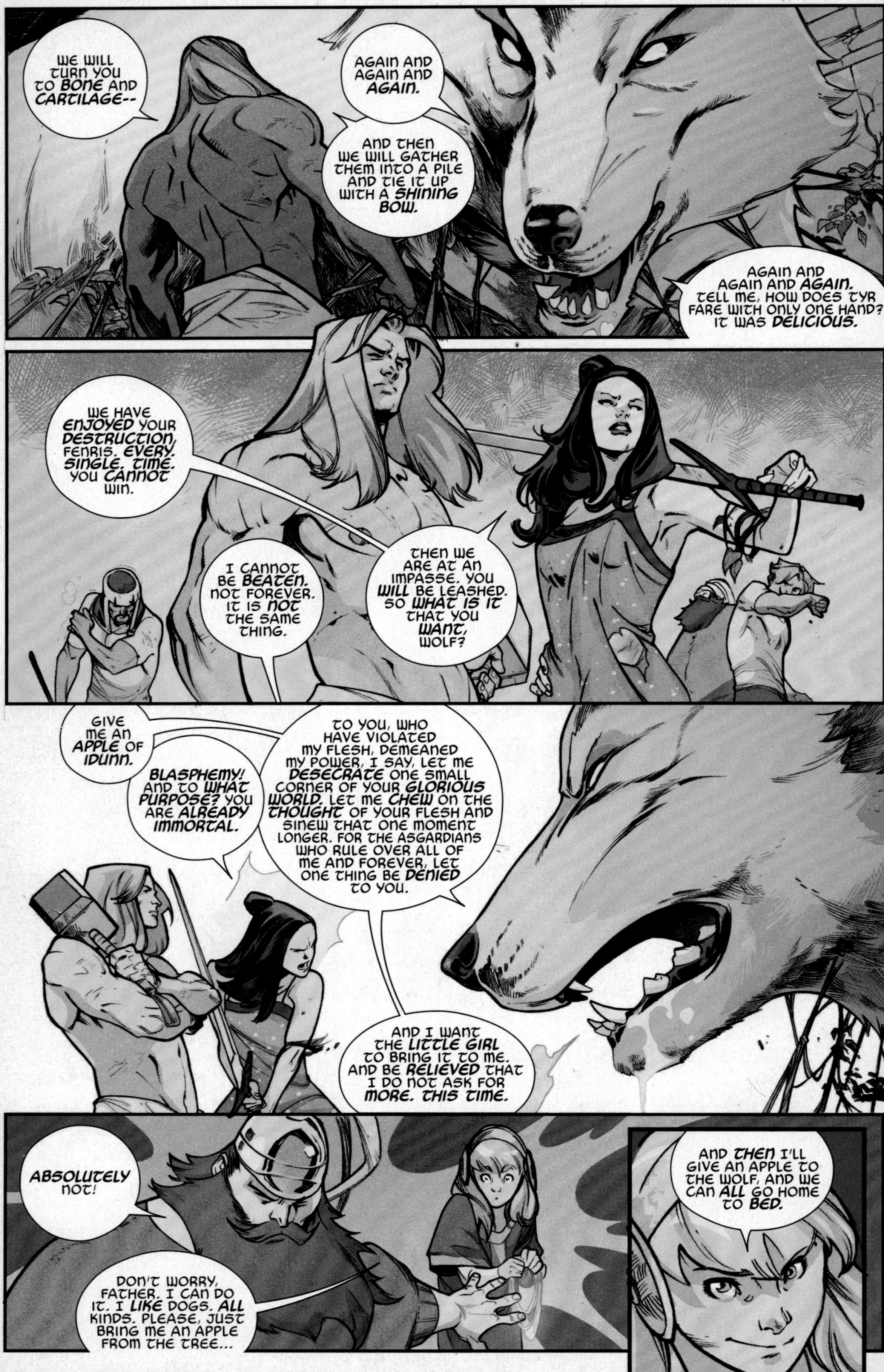
WE WILL TURN YOU TO BONE AND CARTILAGE--
AGAIN AND AGAIN AND AGAIN.
AND THEN WE WILL GATHER THEM INTO A PILE AND TIE IT UP WITH A SHINING BOW.
AGAIN AND AGAIN AND AGAIN. TELL ME, HOW DOES TYR FARE WITH ONLY ONE HAND? IT WAS DELICIOUS.
WE HAVE ENJOYED YOUR DESTRUCTION, FENRIS. EVERY. SINGLE. TIME. YOU CANNOT WIN.
I CANNOT BE BEATEN. NOT FOREVER. IT IS NOT THE SAME THING.
THEN WE ARE AT AN IMPASSE. YOU WILL BE LEASHED. SO WHAT IS IT THAT YOU WANT, WOLF?
GIVE ME AN APPLE OF IDUNN.
BLASPHEMY! AND TO WHAT PURPOSE? YOU ARE ALREADY IMMORTAL.
TO YOU, WHO HAVE VIOLATED MY FLESH, DEMEANED MY POWER, I SAY, LET ME DESECRATE ONE SMALL CORNER OF YOUR GLORIOUS WORLD. LET ME CHEW ON THE THOUGHT OF YOUR FLESH AND SINEW THAT ONE MOMENT LONGER. FOR THE ASGARDIANS WHO RULE OVER ALL OF ME AND FOREVER, LET ONE THING BE DENIED TO YOU.
AND I WANT THE LITTLE GIRL TO BRING IT TO ME. AND BE RELIEVED THAT I DO NOT ASK FOR MORE. THIS TIME.
ABSOLUTELY NOT!
DON'T WORRY, FATHER. I CAN DO IT. I LIKE DOGS. ALL KINDS. PLEASE, JUST BRING ME AN APPLE FROM THE TREE...
AND THEN I'LL GIVE AN APPLE TO THE WOLF, AND WE CAN ALL GO HOME TO BED.

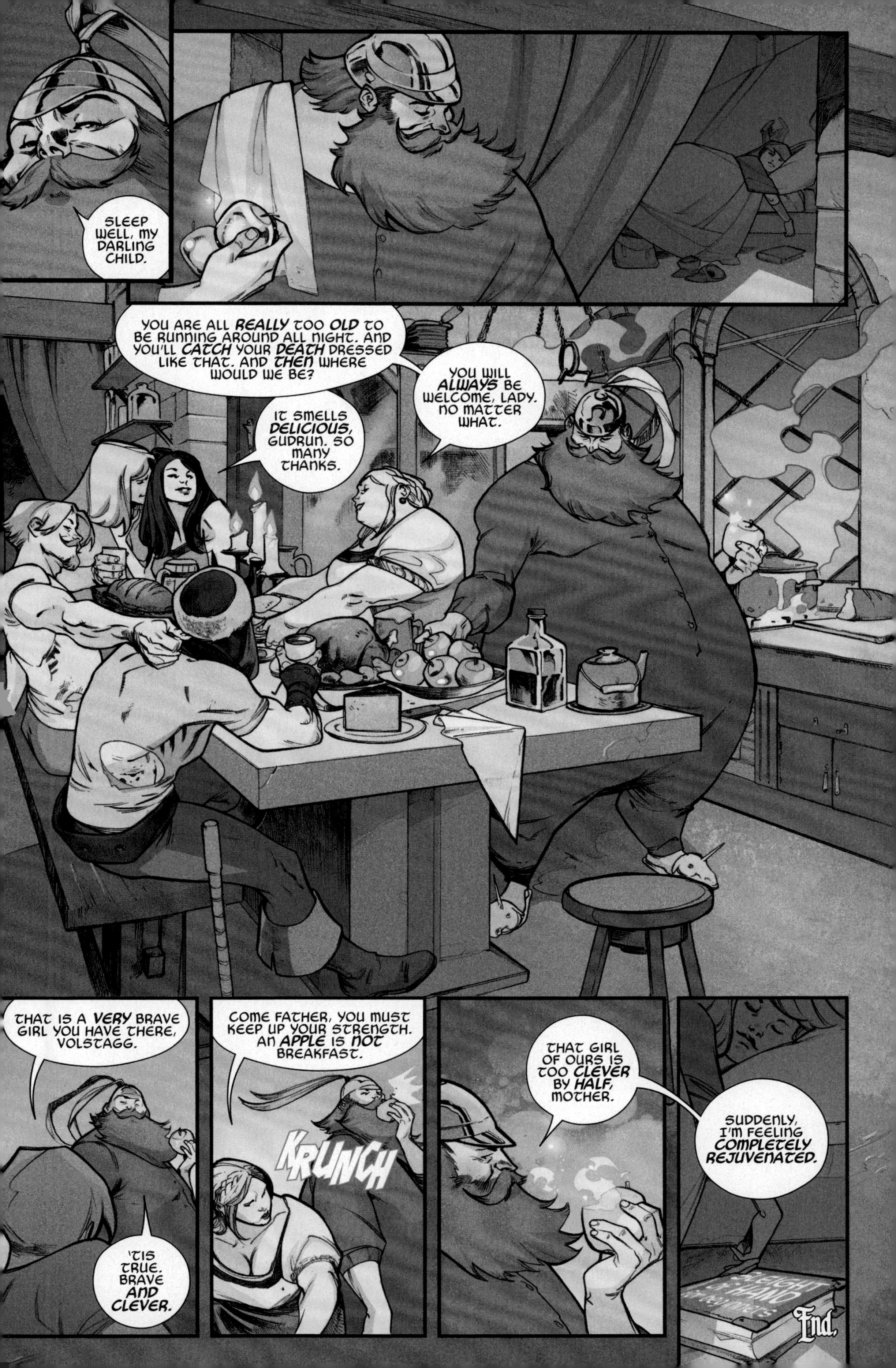
SLEEP WELL, MY DARLING CHILD.
YOU ARE ALL REALLY TOO OLD TO BE RUNNING AROUND ALL NIGHT. AND YOU'LL CATCH YOUR DEATH DRESSED LIKE THAT. AND THEN WHERE WOULD WE BE?
YOU WILL ALWAYS BE WELCOME, LADY. NO MATTER WHAT.
IT SMELLS DELICIOUS, GUDRUN. SO MANY THANKS.
THAT IS A VERY BRAVE GIRL YOU HAVE THERE, VOLSTAGG.
'TIS TRUE. BRAVE AND CLEVER.
COME FATHER, YOU MUST KEEP UP YOUR STRENGTH. AN APPLE IS NOT BREAKFAST.
KRUNCH
THAT GIRL OF OURS IS TOO CLEVER BY HALF, MOTHER.
SUDDENLY, I'M FEELING COMPLETELY REJUVENATED.
End.

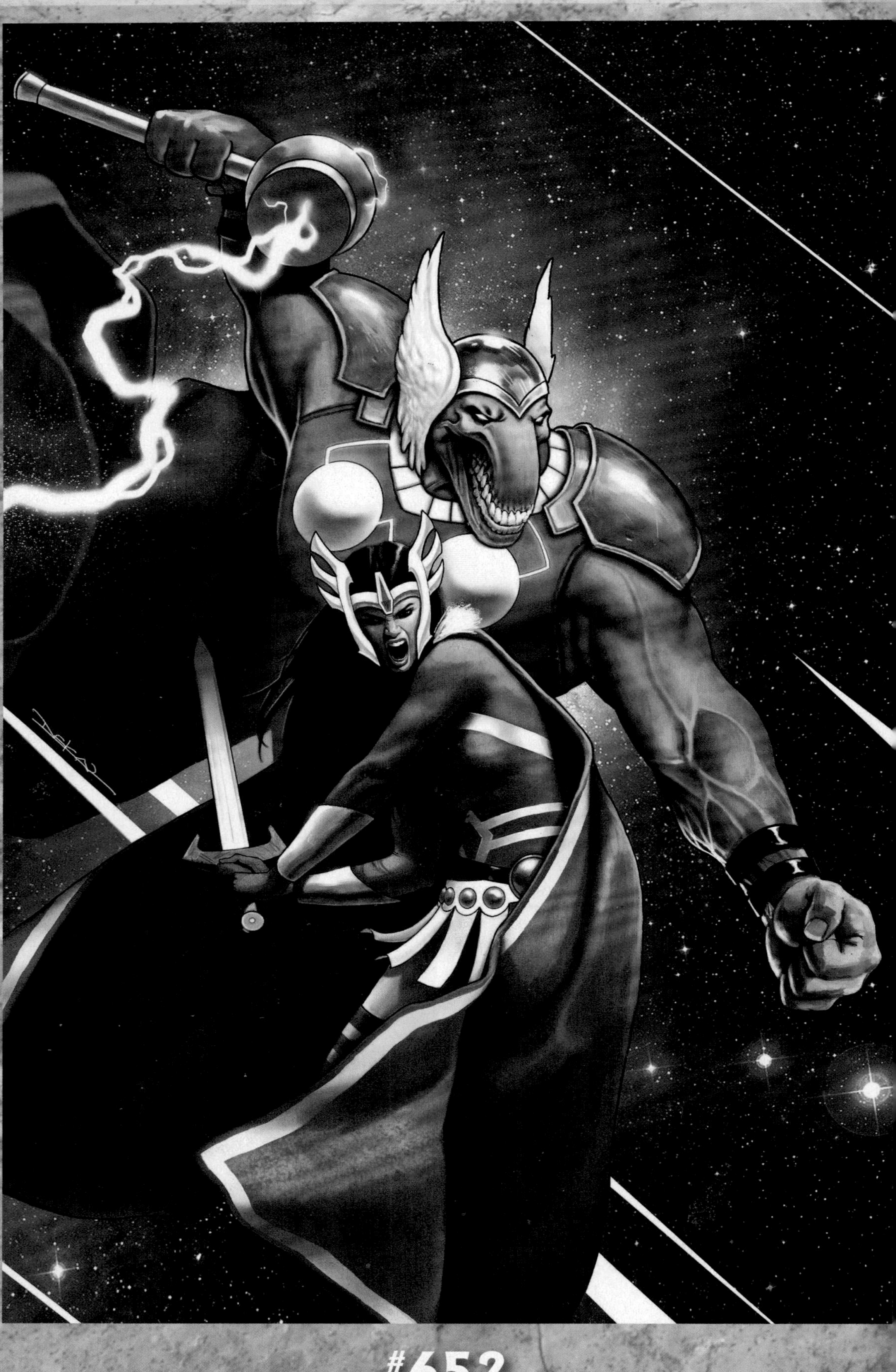

#652

I AM *SIF*. I *KNOW* WHO I AM. FROM WHENCE I CAME. AND FOR WHAT *PURPOSE*.

I CAN NAME THE *NINE REALMS* AND *ALL* WHO RESIDE THERE.

AND WHOM I HAVE *SLAIN* THERE. AND IN WHAT *MANNER*.

I HAVE FOUGHT *MONSTERS* THAT WOULD NOT *BLEED*.

MEN WHO WOULD NOT *SUBMIT*.

I HAVE VENTURED *FURTHER* THAN MOST WOULD *DARE*.

AND DARED *ENOUGH* TO BOAST FOR A *LIFETIME*.

I *KNOW* WHO I AM. AND FOR WHAT *PURPOSE* I WAS *MADE*.

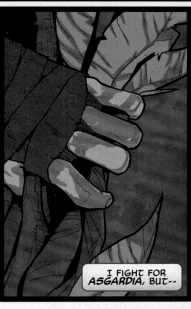

I FIGHT FOR *ASGARDIA*, BUT--

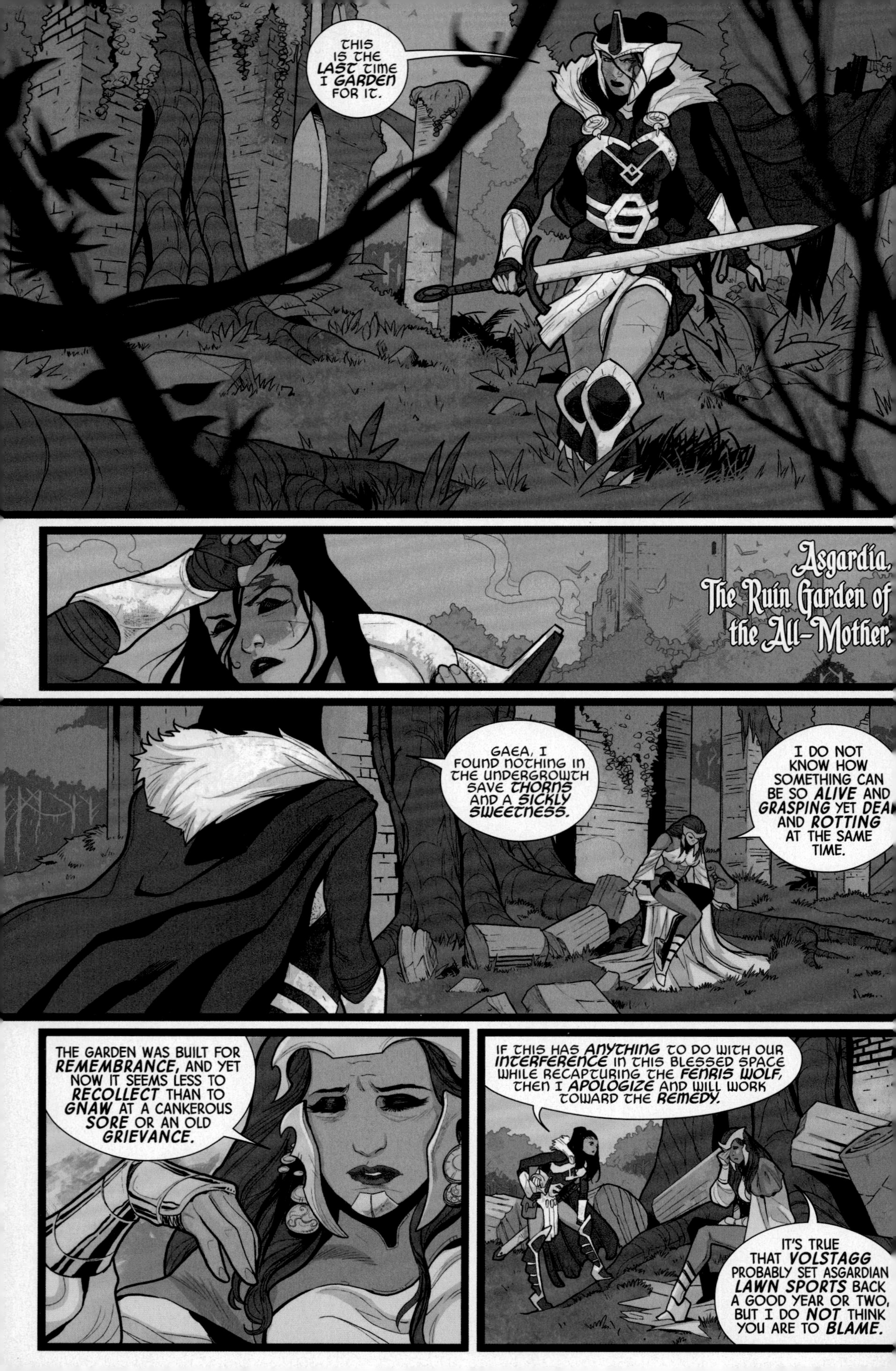
THIS IS THE LAST TIME I GARDEN FOR IT.
Asgardia, The Ruin Garden of the All-Mother.
GAEA, I FOUND NOTHING IN THE UNDERGROWTH SAVE THORNS AND A SICKLY SWEETNESS.
I DO NOT KNOW HOW SOMETHING CAN BE SO ALIVE AND GRASPING YET DEAD AND ROTTING AT THE SAME TIME.
THE GARDEN WAS BUILT FOR REMEMBRANCE, AND YET NOW IT SEEMS LESS TO RECOLLECT THAN TO GNAW AT A CANKEROUS SORE OR AN OLD GRIEVANCE.
IF THIS HAS ANYTHING TO DO WITH OUR INTERFERENCE IN THIS BLESSED SPACE WHILE RECAPTURING THE FENRIS WOLF, THEN I APOLOGIZE AND WILL WORK TOWARD THE REMEDY.
IT'S TRUE THAT VOLSTAGG PROBABLY SET ASGARDIAN LAWN SPORTS BACK A GOOD YEAR OR TWO, BUT I DO NOT THINK YOU ARE TO BLAME.

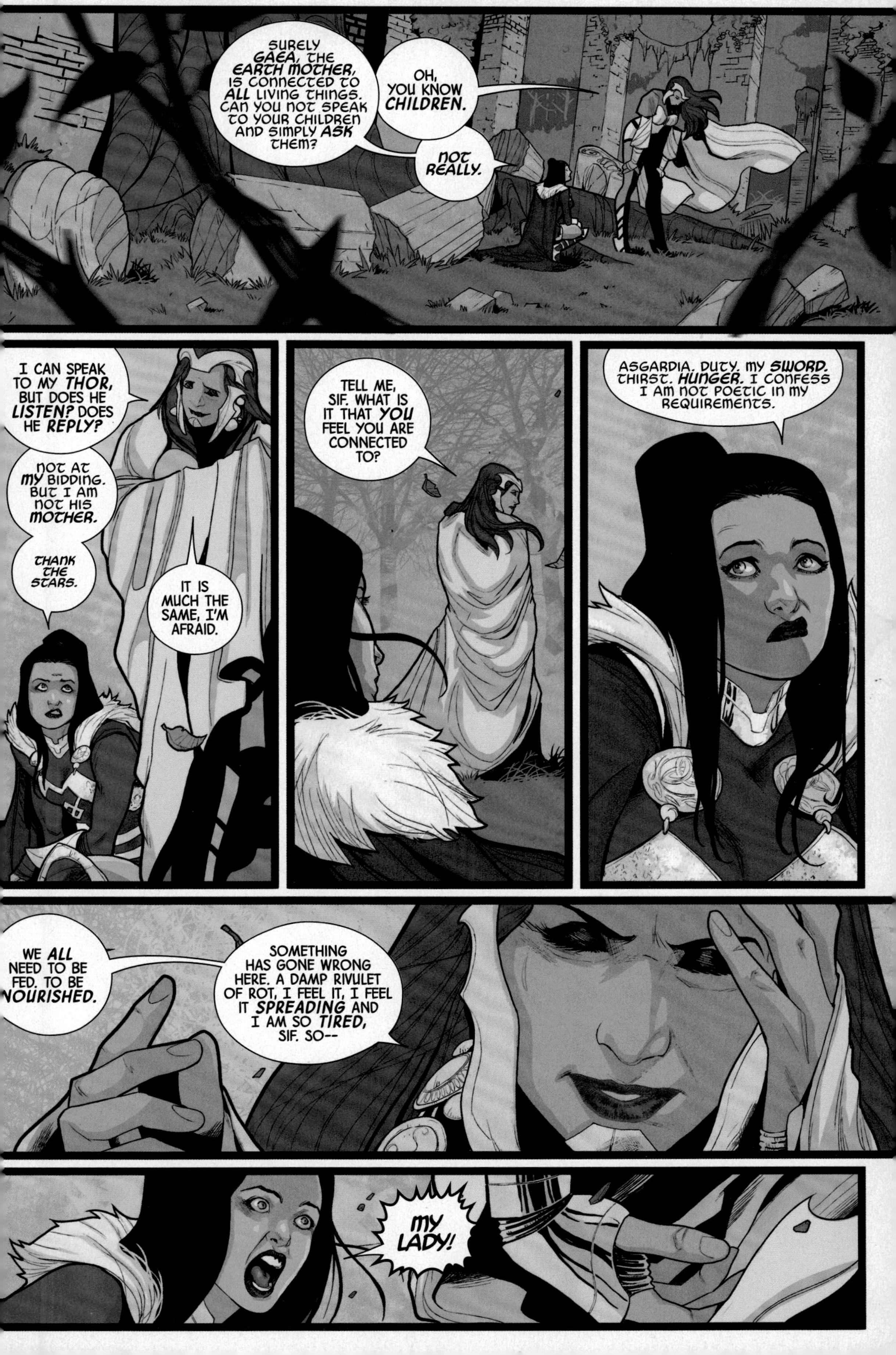
SURELY GAEA, THE EARTH MOTHER, IS CONNECTED TO ALL LIVING THINGS. CAN YOU NOT SPEAK TO YOUR CHILDREN AND SIMPLY ASK THEM?
OH, YOU KNOW CHILDREN.
NOT REALLY.
I CAN SPEAK TO MY THOR, BUT DOES HE LISTEN? DOES HE REPLY?
NOT AT MY BIDDING. BUT I AM NOT HIS MOTHER.
THANK THE STARS.
IT IS MUCH THE SAME, I'M AFRAID.
TELL ME, SIF. WHAT IS IT THAT YOU FEEL YOU ARE CONNECTED TO?
ASGARDIA. DUTY. MY SWORD. THIRST. HUNGER. I CONFESS I AM NOT POETIC IN MY REQUIREMENTS.
WE ALL NEED TO BE FED. TO BE NOURISHED.
SOMETHING HAS GONE WRONG HERE. A DAMP RIVULET OF ROT, I FEEL IT, I FEEL IT SPREADING AND I AM SO TIRED, SIF. SO--
MY LADY!

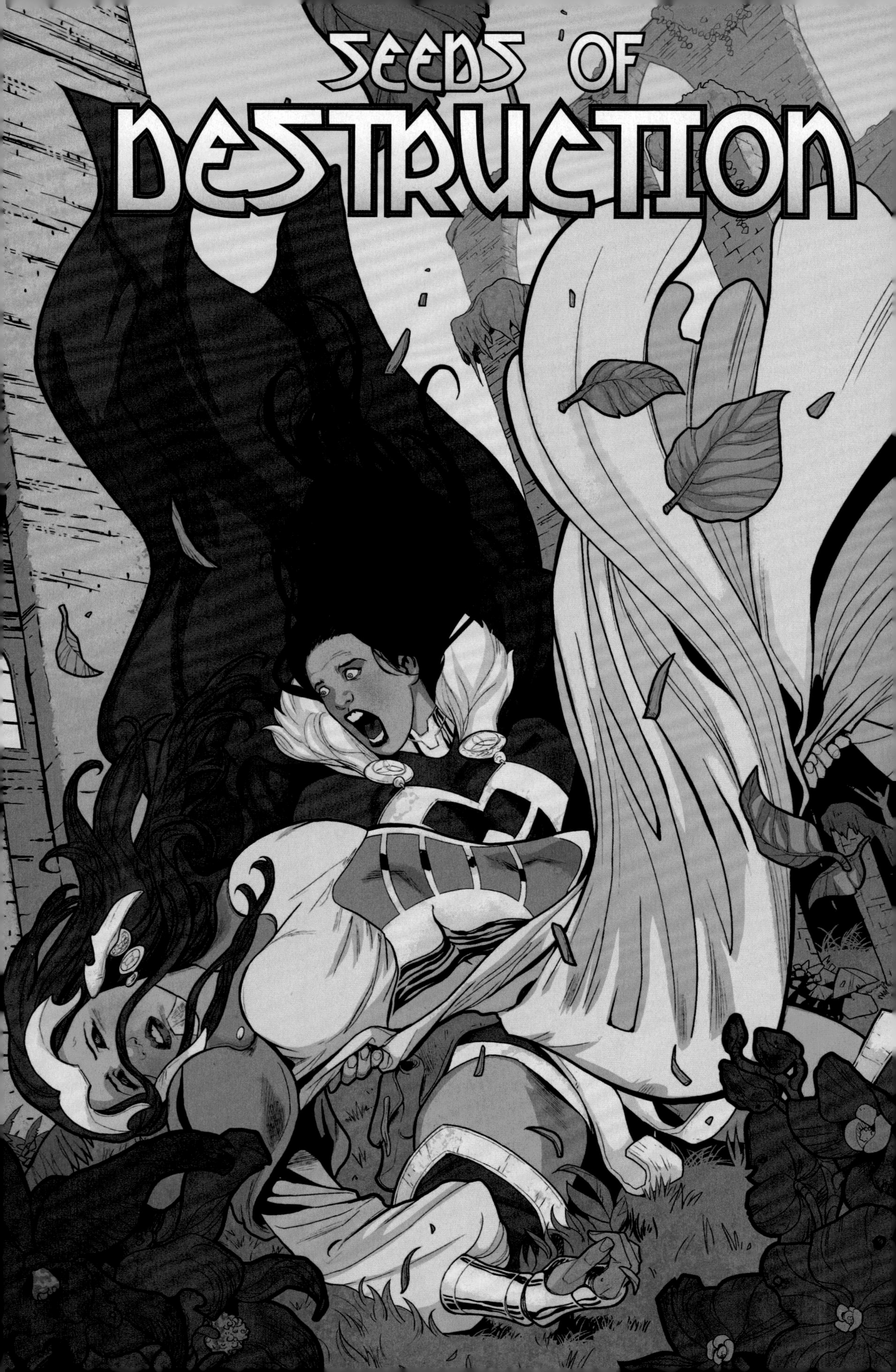
SEEDS OF
DESTRUCTION

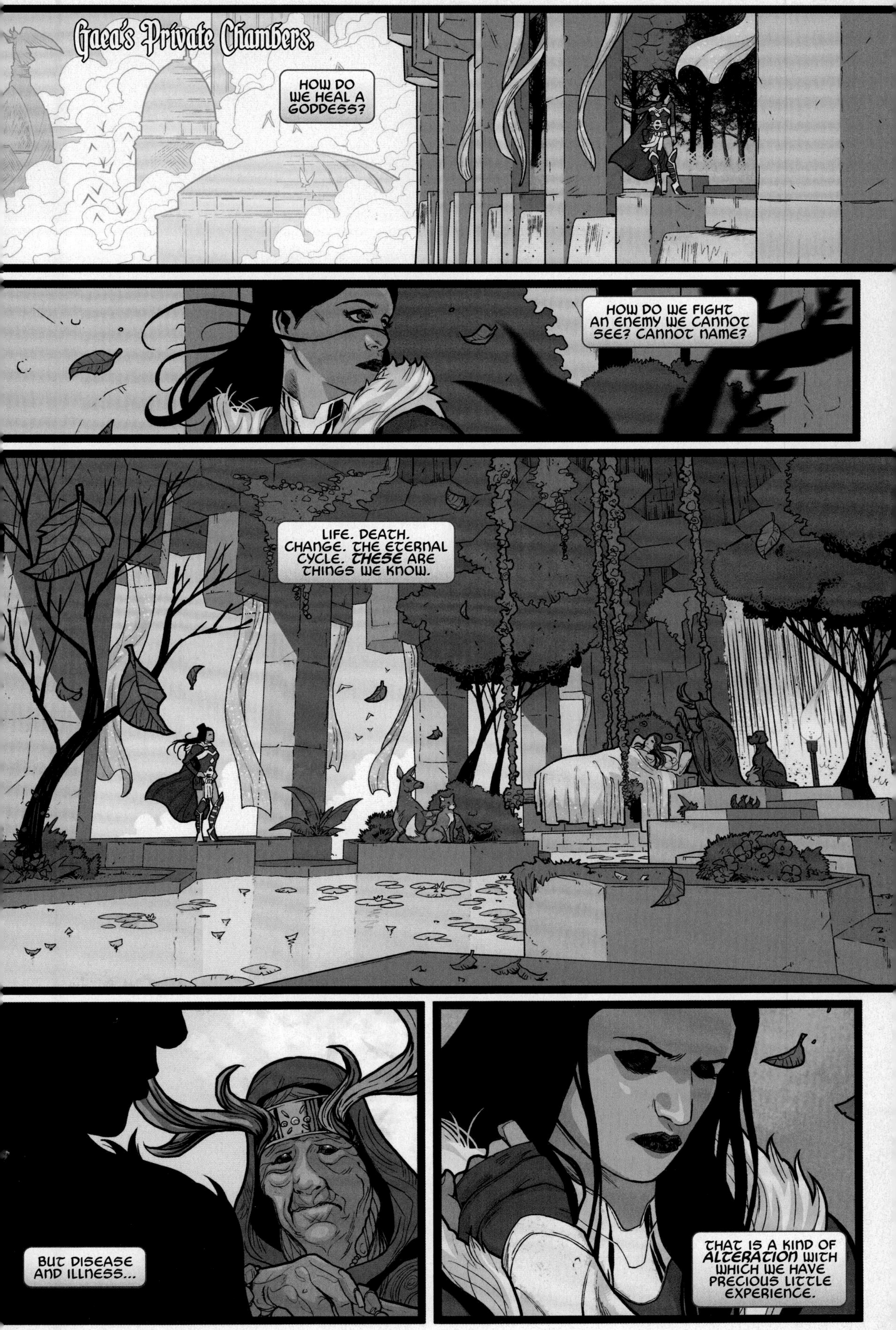
Gaea's Private Chambers.
HOW DO WE HEAL A GODDESS?
HOW DO WE FIGHT AN ENEMY WE CANNOT SEE? CANNOT NAME?
LIFE. DEATH. CHANGE. THE ETERNAL CYCLE. THESE ARE THINGS WE KNOW.
BUT DISEASE AND ILLNESS...
THAT IS A KIND OF ALTERATION WITH WHICH WE HAVE PRECIOUS LITTLE EXPERIENCE.

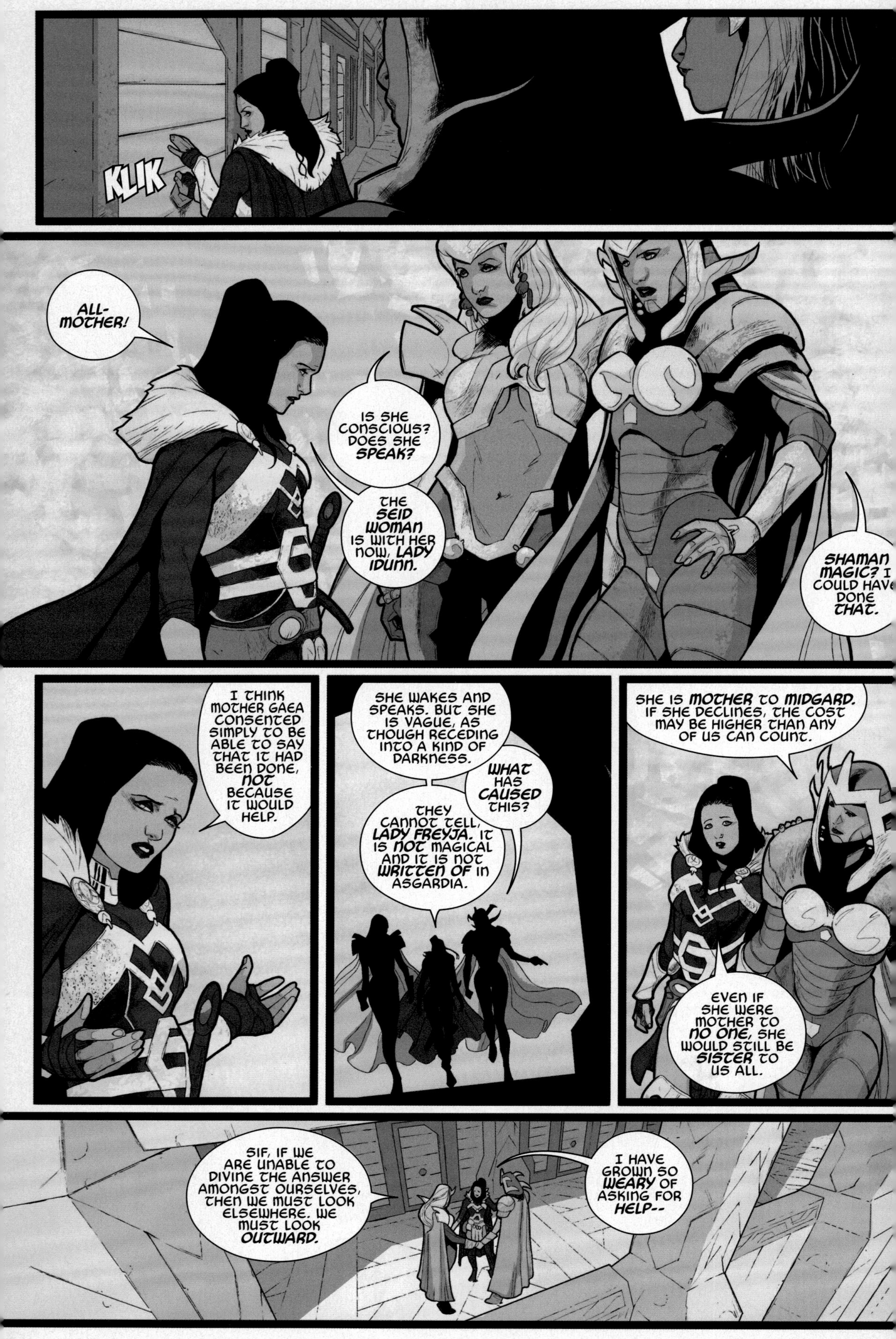
KLIK
ALL-MOTHER!
IS SHE CONSCIOUS? DOES SHE SPEAK?
THE SEID WOMAN IS WITH HER NOW, LADY IDUNN.
SHAMAN MAGIC? I COULD HAVE DONE THAT.
I THINK MOTHER GAEA CONSENTED SIMPLY TO BE ABLE TO SAY THAT IT HAD BEEN DONE, NOT BECAUSE IT WOULD HELP.
SHE WAKES AND SPEAKS. BUT SHE IS VAGUE, AS THOUGH RECEDING INTO A KIND OF DARKNESS.
WHAT HAS CAUSED THIS?
THEY CANNOT TELL, LADY FREYJA. IT IS NOT MAGICAL AND IT IS NOT WRITTEN OF IN ASGARDIA.
SHE IS MOTHER TO MIDGARD. IF SHE DECLINES, THE COST MAY BE HIGHER THAN ANY OF US CAN COUNT.
EVEN IF SHE WERE MOTHER TO NO ONE, SHE WOULD STILL BE SISTER TO US ALL.
SIF, IF WE ARE UNABLE TO DIVINE THE ANSWER AMONGST OURSELVES, THEN WE MUST LOOK ELSEWHERE. WE MUST LOOK OUTWARD.
I HAVE GROWN SO WEARY OF ASKING FOR HELP--

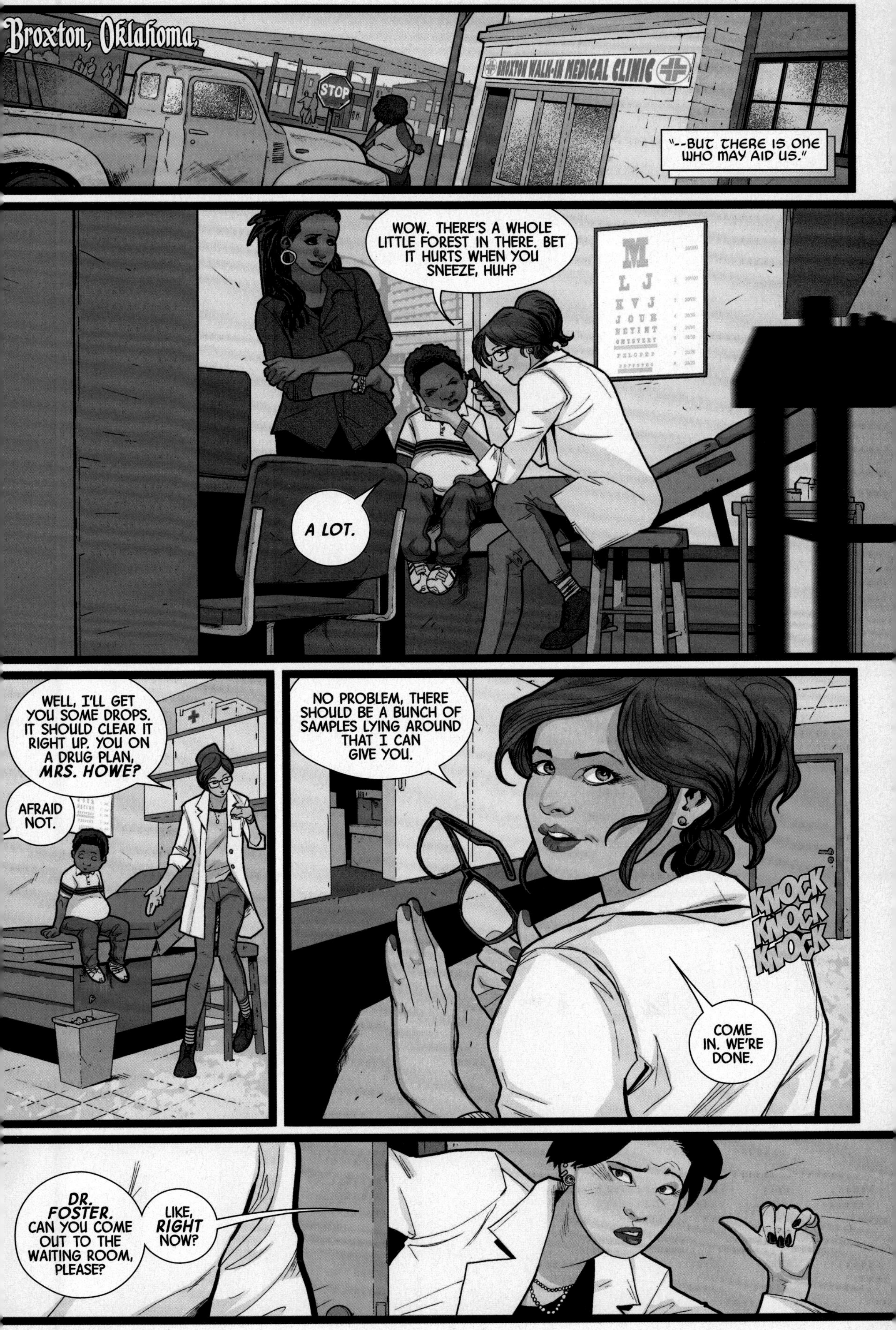
Broxton, Oklahoma.
BROXTON WALK-IN MEDICAL CLINIC
STOP
"--BUT THERE IS ONE WHO MAY AID US."
WOW. THERE'S A WHOLE LITTLE FOREST IN THERE. BET IT HURTS WHEN YOU SNEEZE, HUH?
A LOT.
WELL, I'LL GET YOU SOME DROPS. IT SHOULD CLEAR IT RIGHT UP. YOU ON A DRUG PLAN, MRS. HOWE?
AFRAID NOT.
NO PROBLEM, THERE SHOULD BE A BUNCH OF SAMPLES LYING AROUND THAT I CAN GIVE YOU.
KNOCK KNOCK KNOCK
COME IN. WE'RE DONE.
DR. FOSTER. CAN YOU COME OUT TO THE WAITING ROOM, PLEASE?
LIKE, RIGHT NOW?

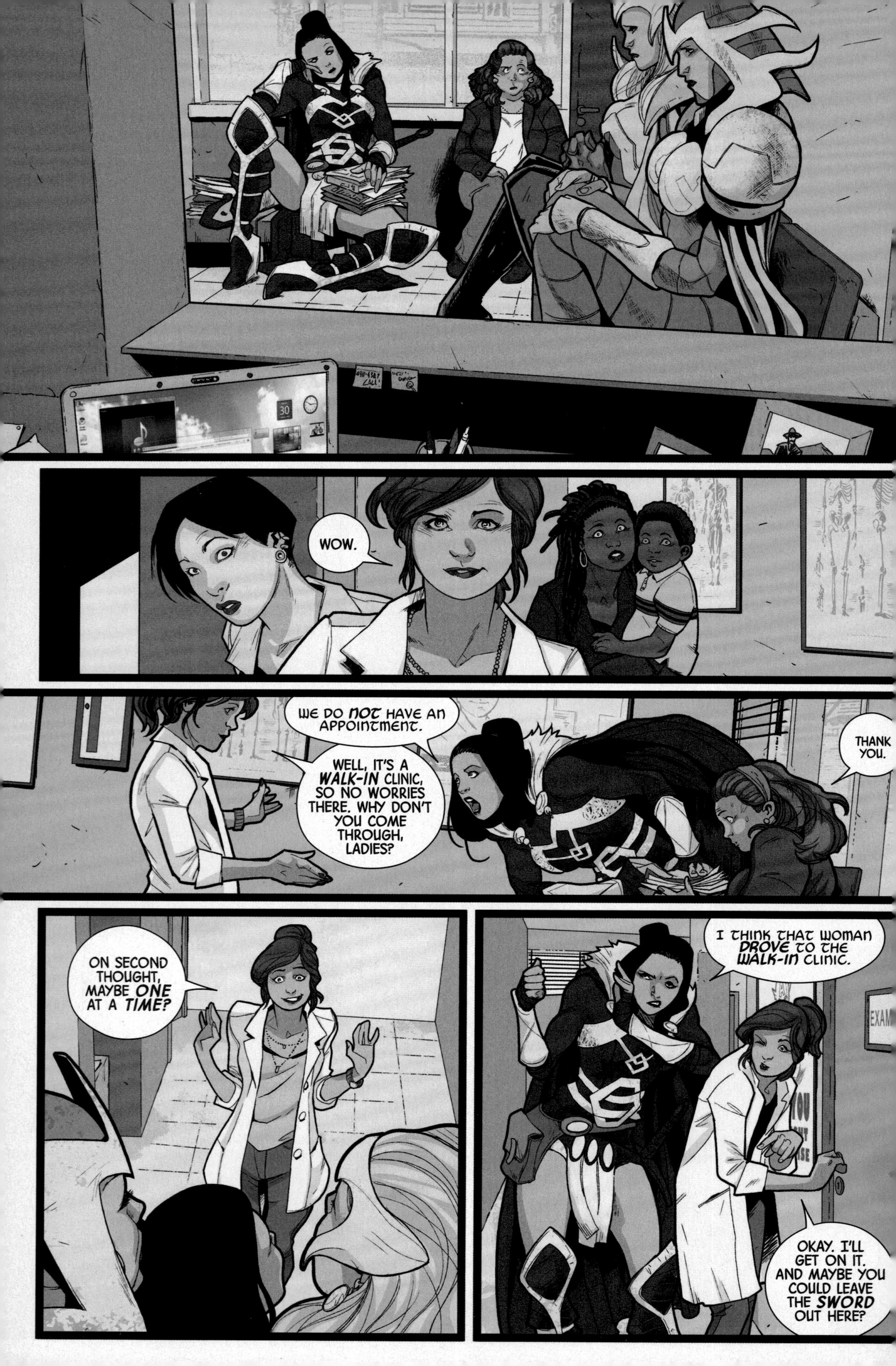
WOW.
WE DO NOT HAVE AN APPOINTMENT.
WELL, IT'S A WALK-IN CLINIC, SO NO WORRIES THERE. WHY DON'T YOU COME THROUGH, LADIES?
THANK YOU.
ON SECOND THOUGHT, MAYBE ONE AT A TIME?
I THINK THAT WOMAN DROVE TO THE WALK-IN CLINIC.
OKAY. I'LL GET ON IT. AND MAYBE YOU COULD LEAVE THE SWORD OUT HERE?
EXAM

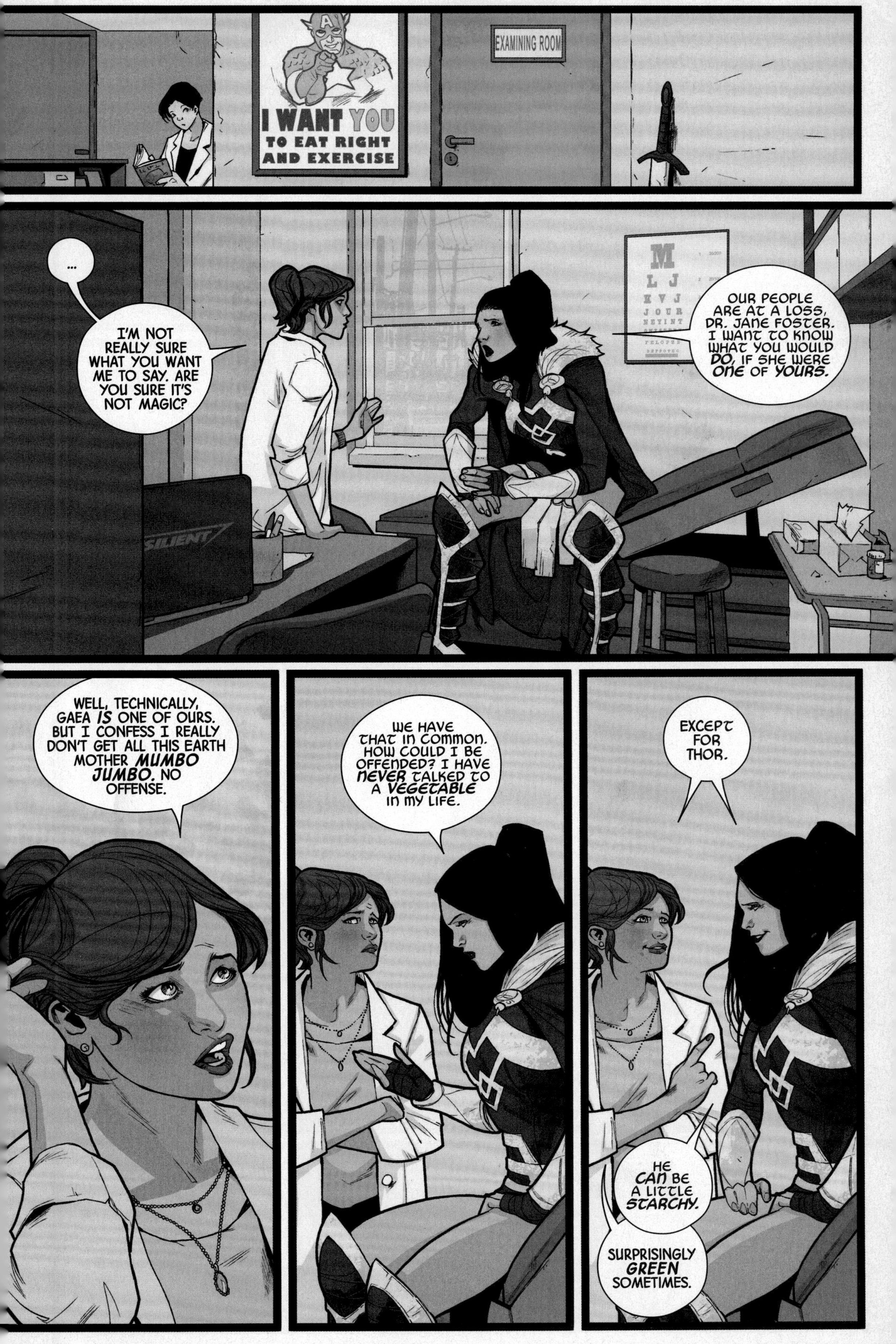
I WANT YOU
TO EAT RIGHT
AND EXERCISE
EXAMINING ROOM
...
I'M NOT REALLY SURE WHAT YOU WANT ME TO SAY. ARE YOU SURE IT'S NOT MAGIC?
OUR PEOPLE ARE AT A LOSS, DR. JANE FOSTER. I WANT TO KNOW WHAT YOU WOULD DO, IF SHE WERE ONE OF YOURS.
WELL, TECHNICALLY, GAEA IS ONE OF OURS. BUT I CONFESS I REALLY DON'T GET ALL THIS EARTH MOTHER MUMBO JUMBO. NO OFFENSE.
WE HAVE THAT IN COMMON. HOW COULD I BE OFFENDED? I HAVE NEVER TALKED TO A VEGETABLE IN MY LIFE.
EXCEPT FOR THOR.
HE CAN BE A LITTLE STARCHY.
SURPRISINGLY GREEN SOMETIMES.

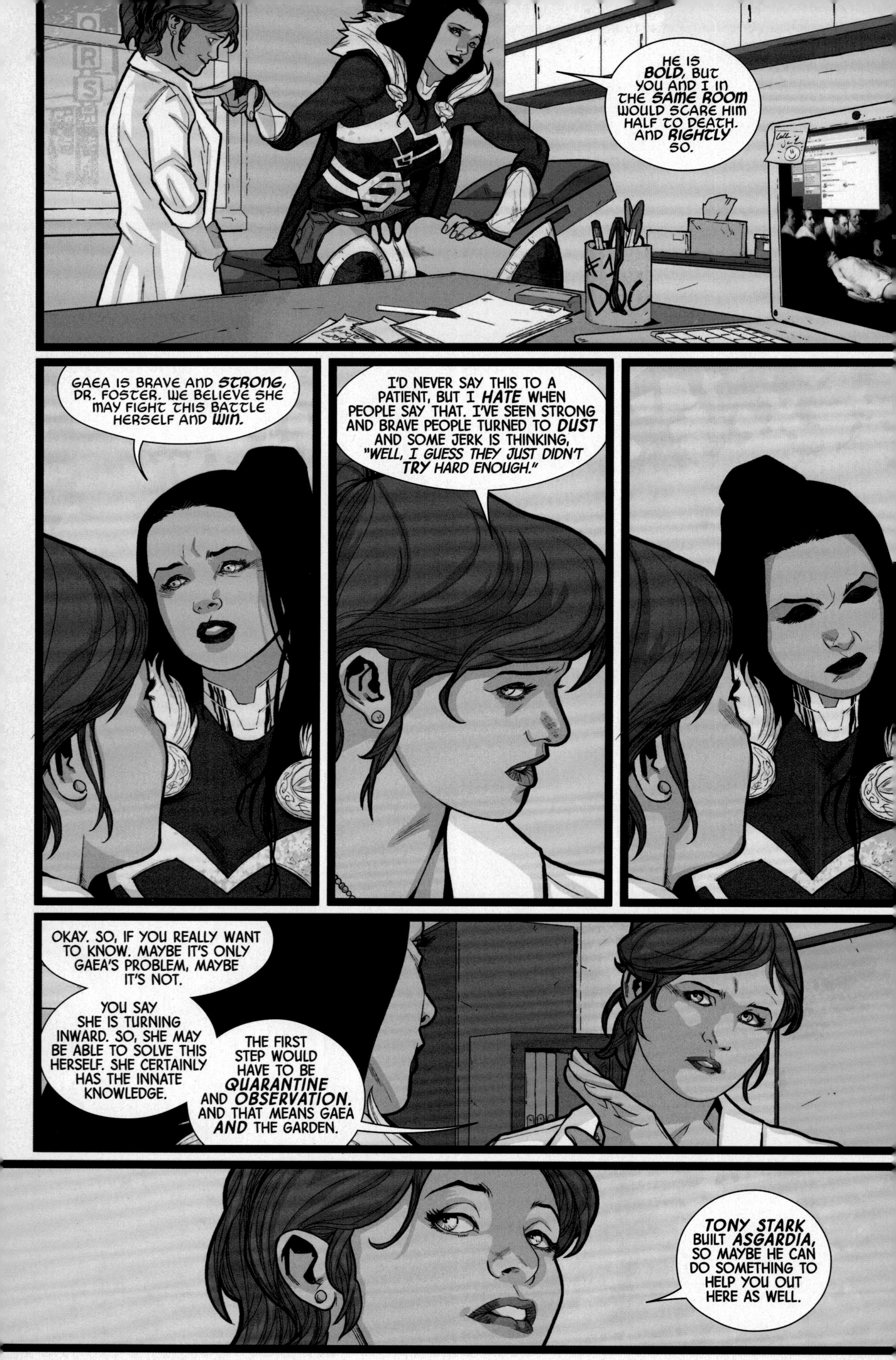
HE IS BOLD, BUT YOU AND I IN THE SAME ROOM WOULD SCARE HIM HALF TO DEATH. AND RIGHTLY SO.
#1 DOC
GAEA IS BRAVE AND STRONG, DR. FOSTER. WE BELIEVE SHE MAY FIGHT THIS BATTLE HERSELF AND WIN.
I'D NEVER SAY THIS TO A PATIENT, BUT I HATE WHEN PEOPLE SAY THAT. I'VE SEEN STRONG AND BRAVE PEOPLE TURNED TO DUST AND SOME JERK IS THINKING, "WELL, I GUESS THEY JUST DIDN'T TRY HARD ENOUGH."
OKAY. SO, IF YOU REALLY WANT TO KNOW. MAYBE IT'S ONLY GAEA'S PROBLEM, MAYBE IT'S NOT.
YOU SAY SHE IS TURNING INWARD. SO, SHE MAY BE ABLE TO SOLVE THIS HERSELF. SHE CERTAINLY HAS THE INNATE KNOWLEDGE.
THE FIRST STEP WOULD HAVE TO BE QUARANTINE AND OBSERVATION. AND THAT MEANS GAEA AND THE GARDEN.
TONY STARK BUILT ASGARDIA, SO MAYBE HE CAN DO SOMETHING TO HELP YOU OUT HERE AS WELL.

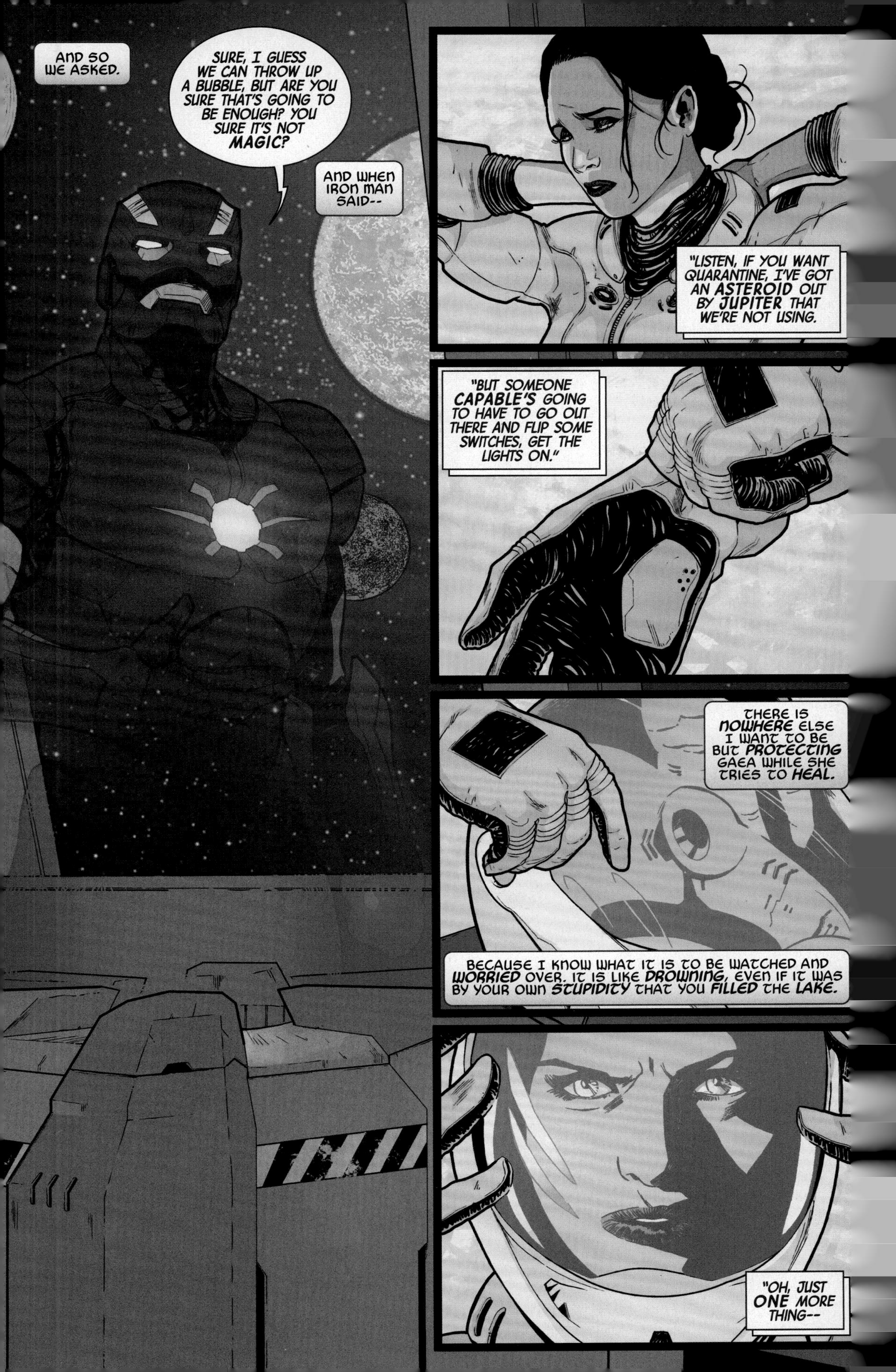
AND SO WE ASKED.
SURE, I GUESS WE CAN THROW UP A BUBBLE, BUT ARE YOU SURE THAT'S GOING TO BE ENOUGH? YOU SURE IT'S NOT MAGIC?
AND WHEN IRON MAN SAID--
"LISTEN, IF YOU WANT QUARANTINE, I'VE GOT AN ASTEROID OUT BY JUPITER THAT WE'RE NOT USING.
"BUT SOMEONE CAPABLE'S GOING TO HAVE TO GO OUT THERE AND FLIP SOME SWITCHES, GET THE LIGHTS ON."
THERE IS NOWHERE ELSE I WANT TO BE BUT PROTECTING GAEA WHILE SHE TRIES TO HEAL.
BECAUSE I KNOW WHAT IT IS TO BE WATCHED AND WORRIED OVER. IT IS LIKE DROWNING, EVEN IF IT WAS BY YOUR OWN STUPIDITY THAT YOU FILLED THE LAKE.
"OH, JUST ONE MORE THING--

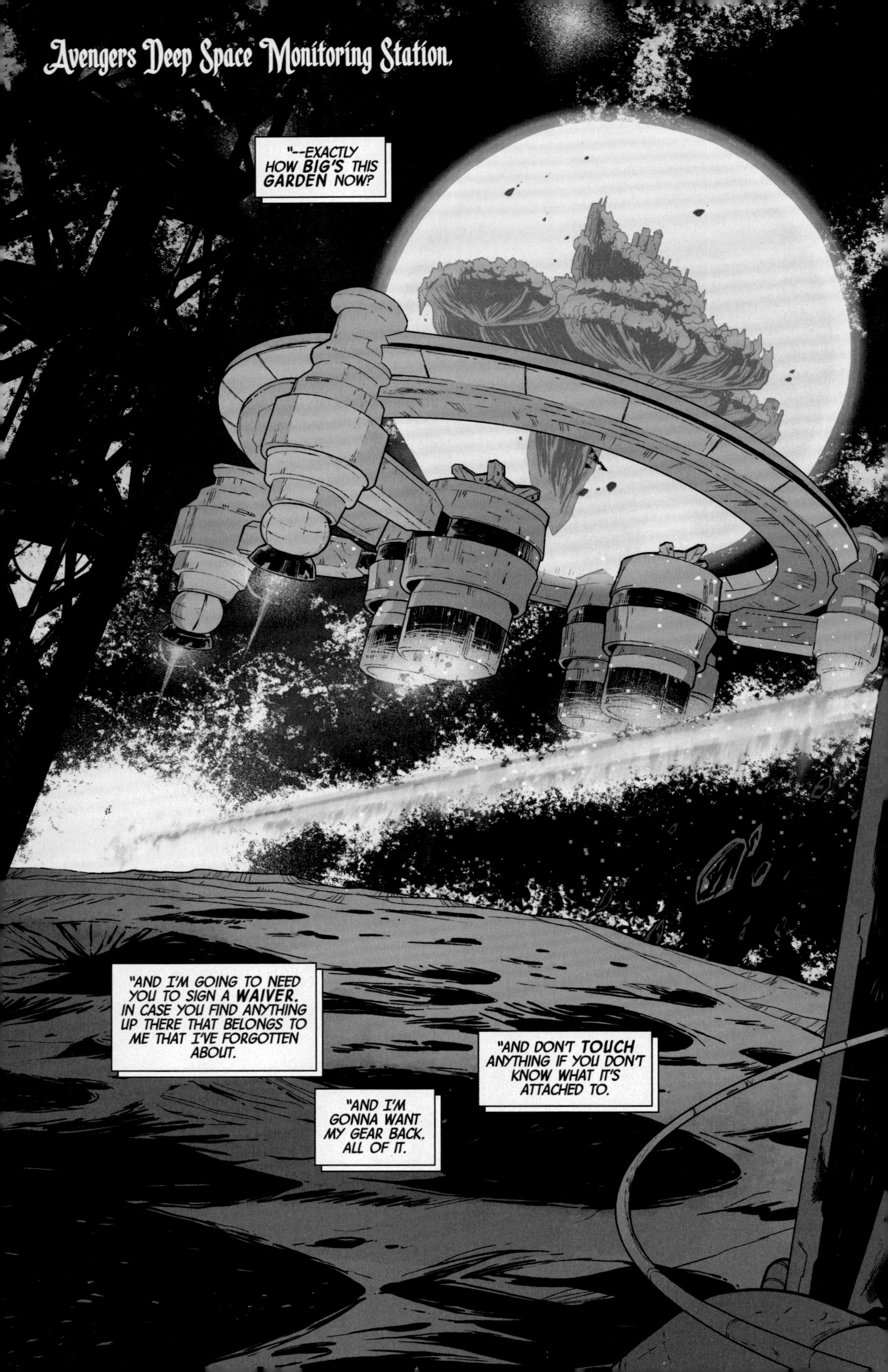
Avengers Deep Space Monitoring Station.
"--EXACTLY HOW BIG'S THIS GARDEN NOW?
"AND I'M GOING TO NEED YOU TO SIGN A WAIVER. IN CASE YOU FIND ANYTHING UP THERE THAT BELONGS TO ME THAT I'VE FORGOTTEN ABOUT.
"AND DON'T TOUCH ANYTHING IF YOU DON'T KNOW WHAT IT'S ATTACHED TO.
"AND I'M GONNA WANT MY GEAR BACK. ALL OF IT.

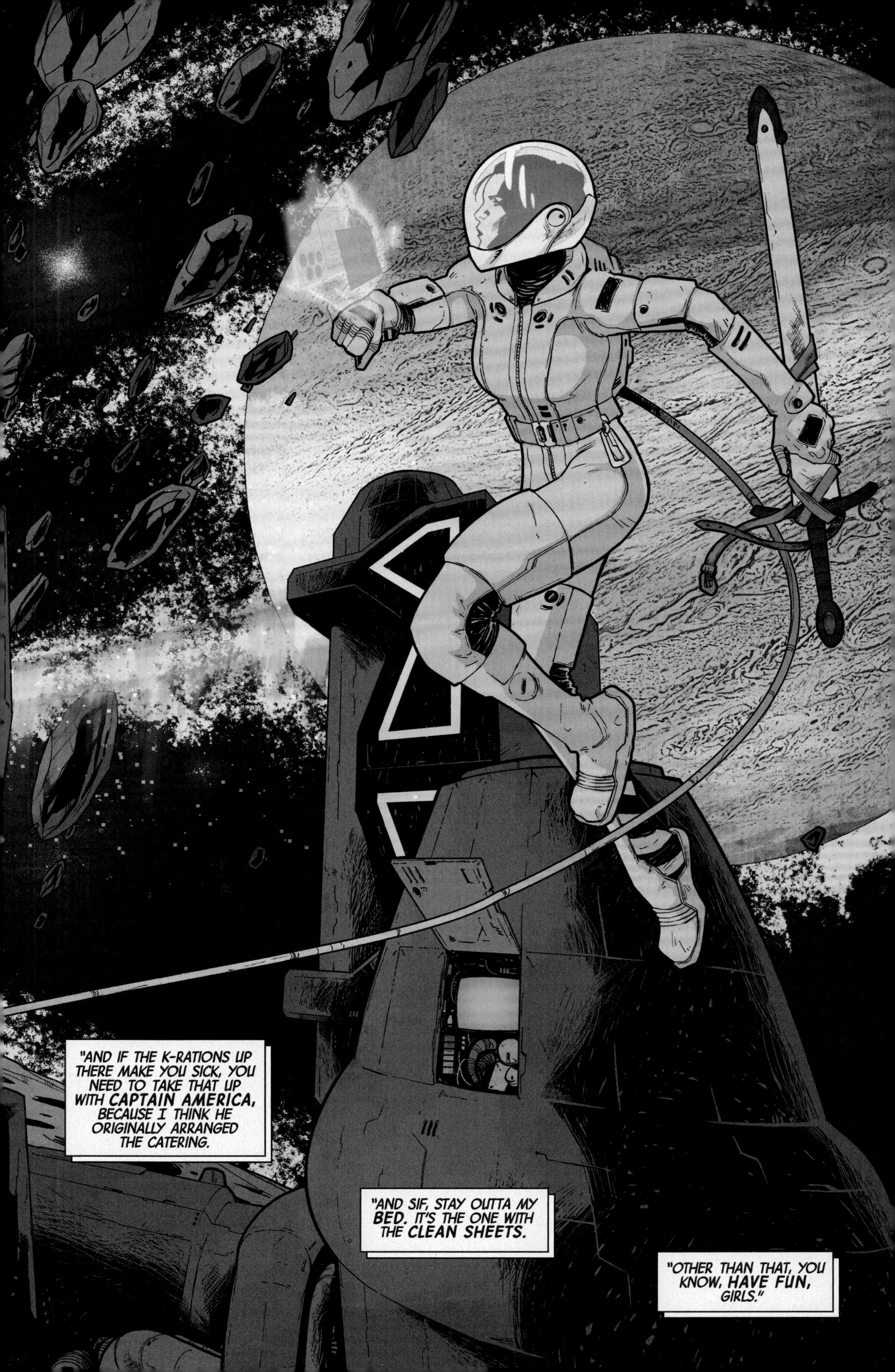
"AND IF THE K-RATIONS UP THERE MAKE YOU SICK, YOU NEED TO TAKE THAT UP WITH CAPTAIN AMERICA, BECAUSE I THINK HE ORIGINALLY ARRANGED THE CATERING.
"AND SIF, STAY OUTTA MY BED. IT'S THE ONE WITH THE CLEAN SHEETS.
"OTHER THAN THAT, YOU KNOW, HAVE FUN, GIRLS."

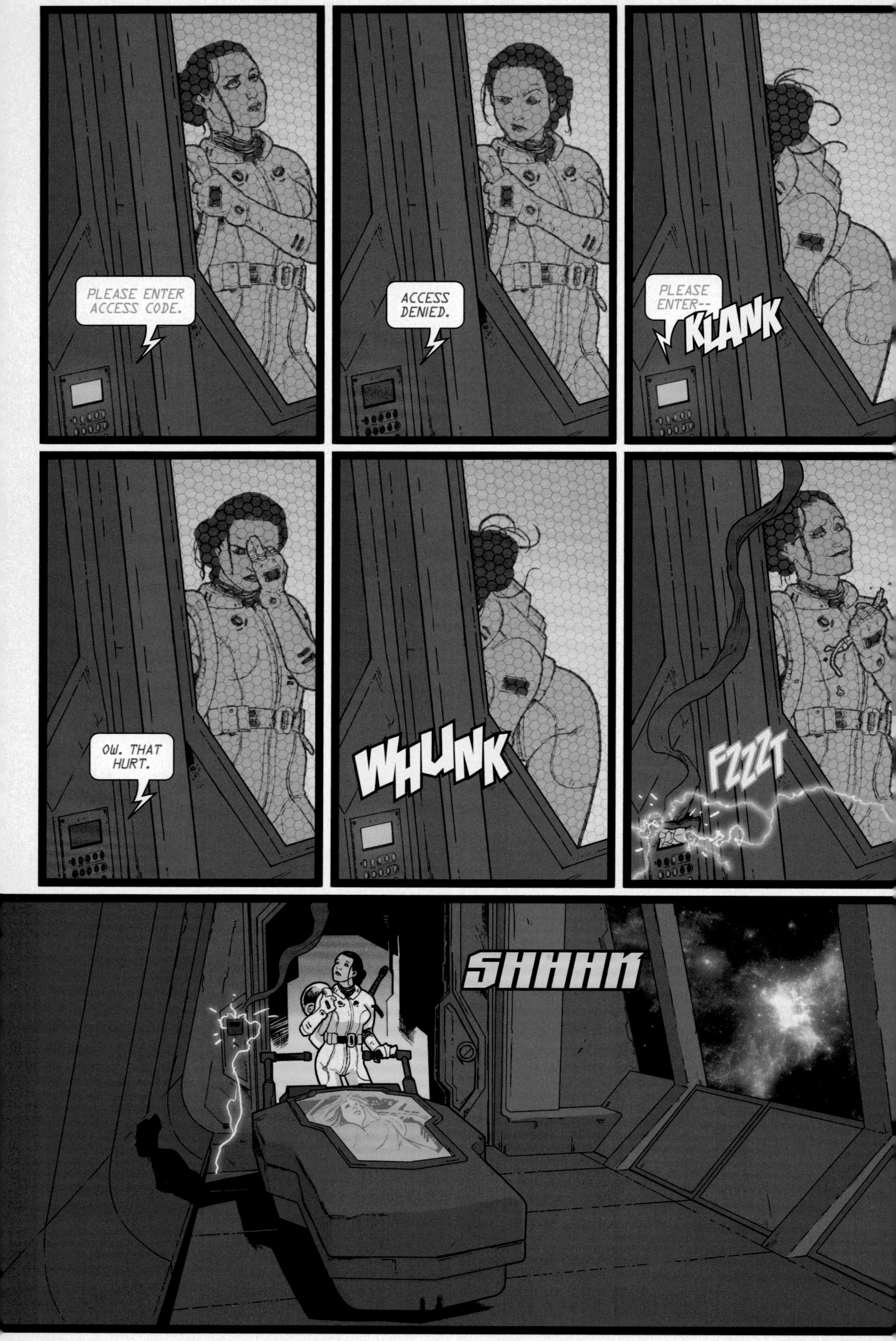
PLEASE ENTER ACCESS CODE.
ACCESS DENIED.
PLEASE ENTER--
KLANK
OW. THAT HURT.
WHUNK
FZZZT
SHHHK

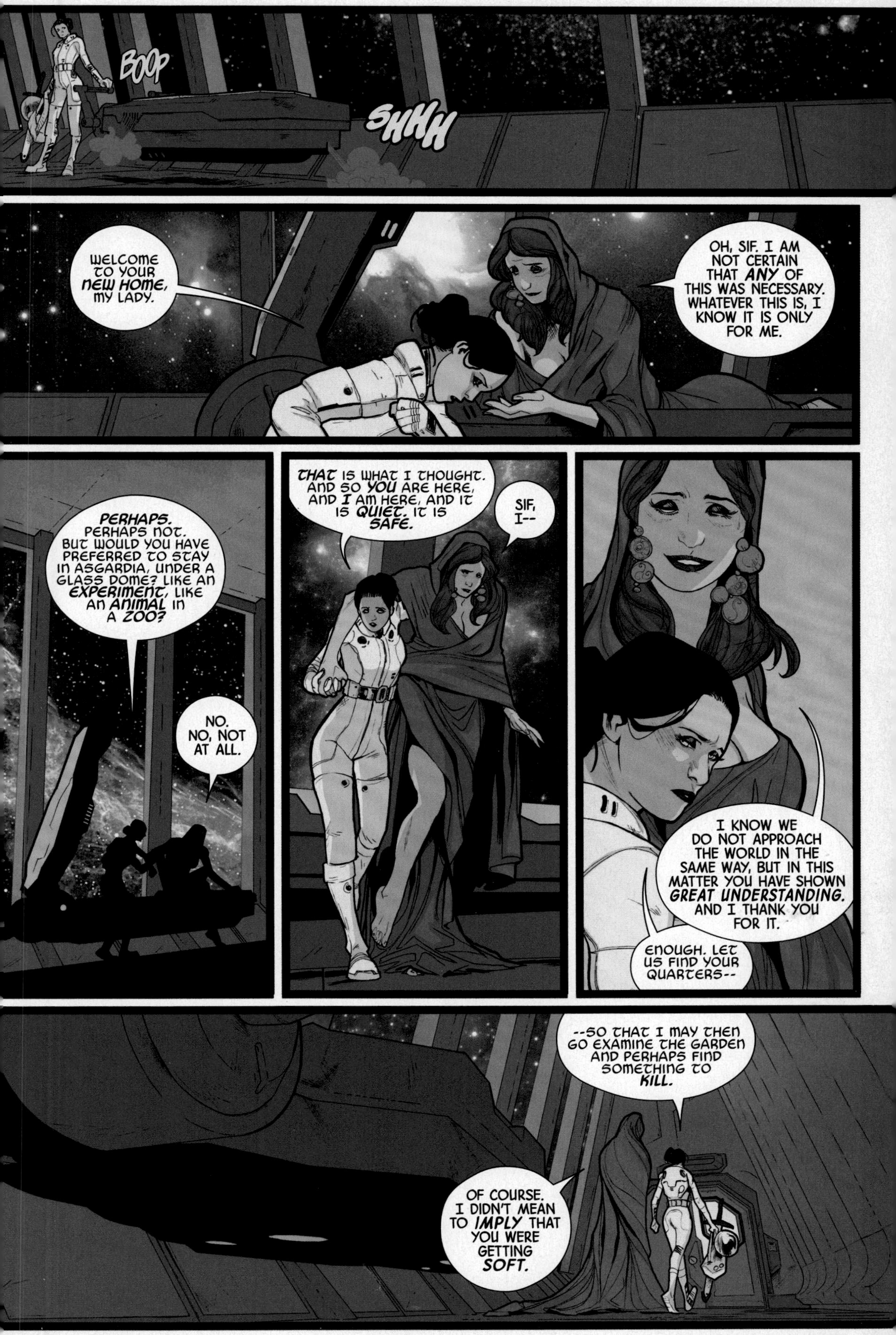
BOOP
SHHH
WELCOME TO YOUR NEW HOME, MY LADY.
OH, SIF. I AM NOT CERTAIN THAT ANY OF THIS WAS NECESSARY. WHATEVER THIS IS, I KNOW IT IS ONLY FOR ME.
PERHAPS. PERHAPS NOT. BUT WOULD YOU HAVE PREFERRED TO STAY IN ASGARDIA, UNDER A GLASS DOME? LIKE AN EXPERIMENT, LIKE AN ANIMAL IN A ZOO?
NO. NO, NOT AT ALL.
THAT IS WHAT I THOUGHT. AND SO YOU ARE HERE, AND I AM HERE, AND IT IS QUIET. IT IS SAFE.
SIF, I--
I KNOW WE DO NOT APPROACH THE WORLD IN THE SAME WAY, BUT IN THIS MATTER YOU HAVE SHOWN GREAT UNDERSTANDING. AND I THANK YOU FOR IT.
ENOUGH. LET US FIND YOUR QUARTERS--
--SO THAT I MAY THEN GO EXAMINE THE GARDEN AND PERHAPS FIND SOMETHING TO KILL.
OF COURSE. I DIDN'T MEAN TO IMPLY THAT YOU WERE GETTING SOFT.

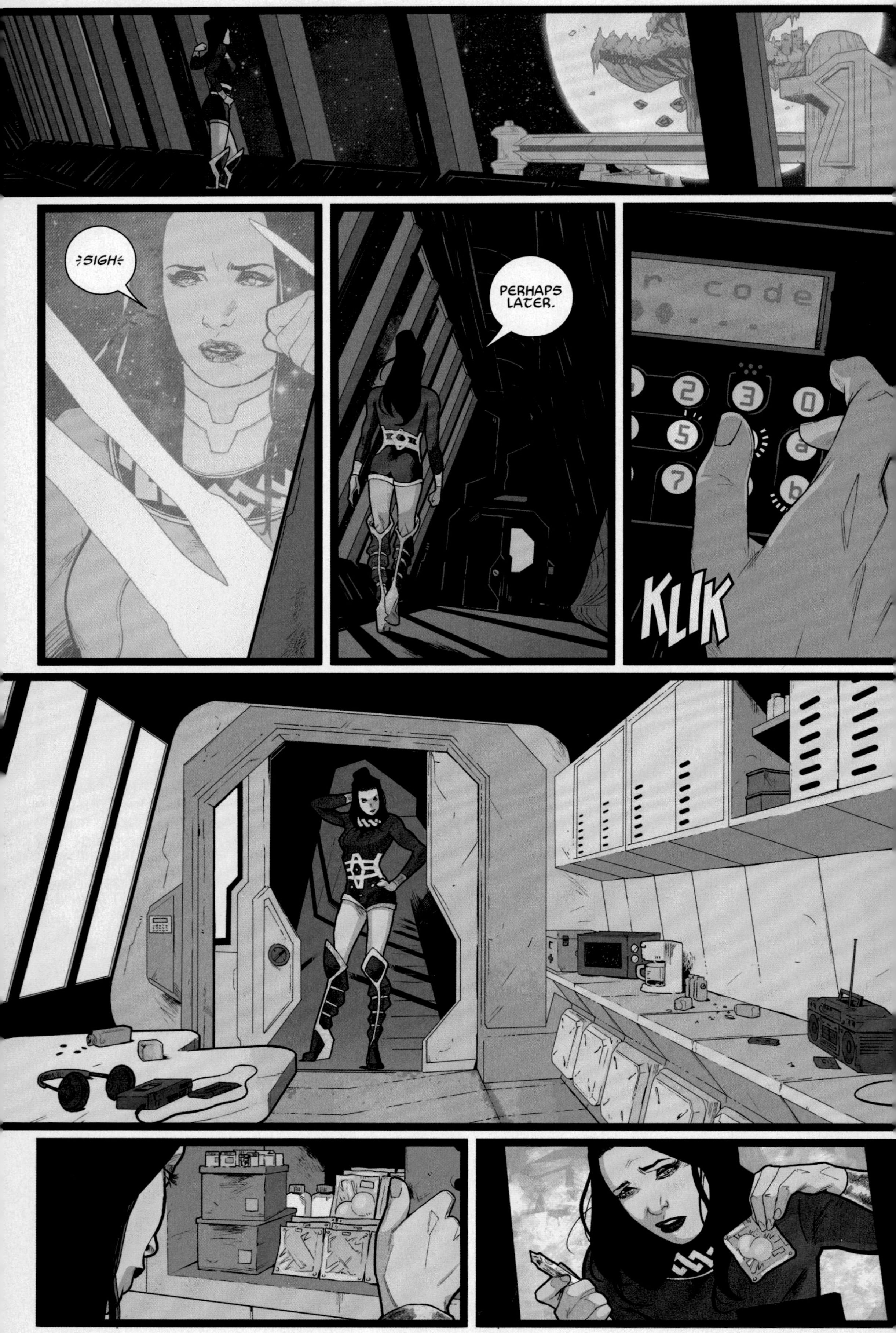

⸗SIGH⸗
PERHAPS LATER.
r code
KLIK

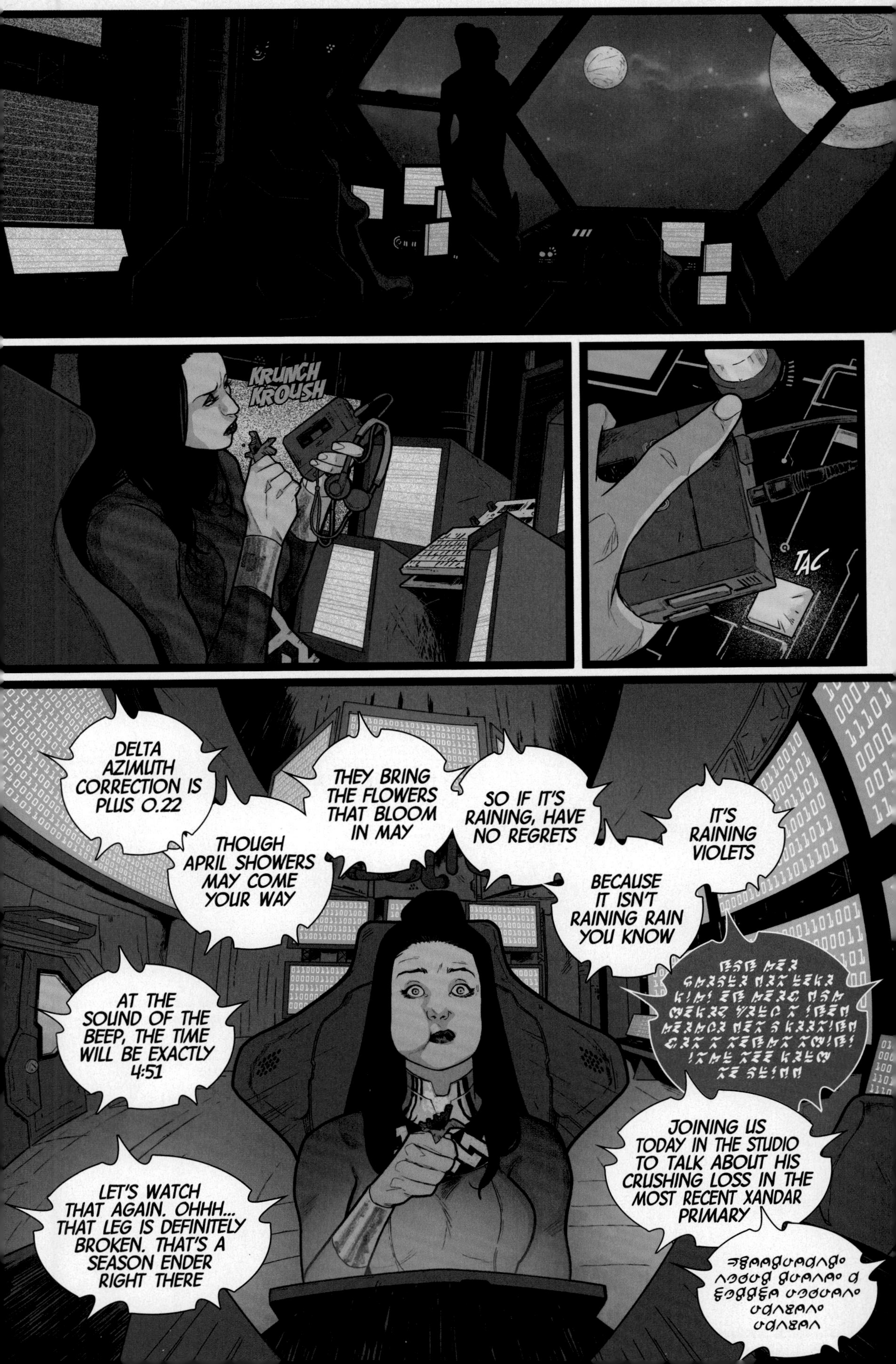
KRUNCH
KROUSH
TAC
DELTA AZIMUTH CORRECTION IS PLUS 0.22
THOUGH APRIL SHOWERS MAY COME YOUR WAY
THEY BRING THE FLOWERS THAT BLOOM IN MAY
SO IF IT'S RAINING, HAVE NO REGRETS
BECAUSE IT ISN'T RAINING RAIN YOU KNOW
IT'S RAINING VIOLETS
AT THE SOUND OF THE BEEP, THE TIME WILL BE EXACTLY 4:51
JOINING US TODAY IN THE STUDIO TO TALK ABOUT HIS CRUSHING LOSS IN THE MOST RECENT XANDAR PRIMARY
LET'S WATCH THAT AGAIN. OHHH... THAT LEG IS DEFINITELY BROKEN. THAT'S A SEASON ENDER RIGHT THERE

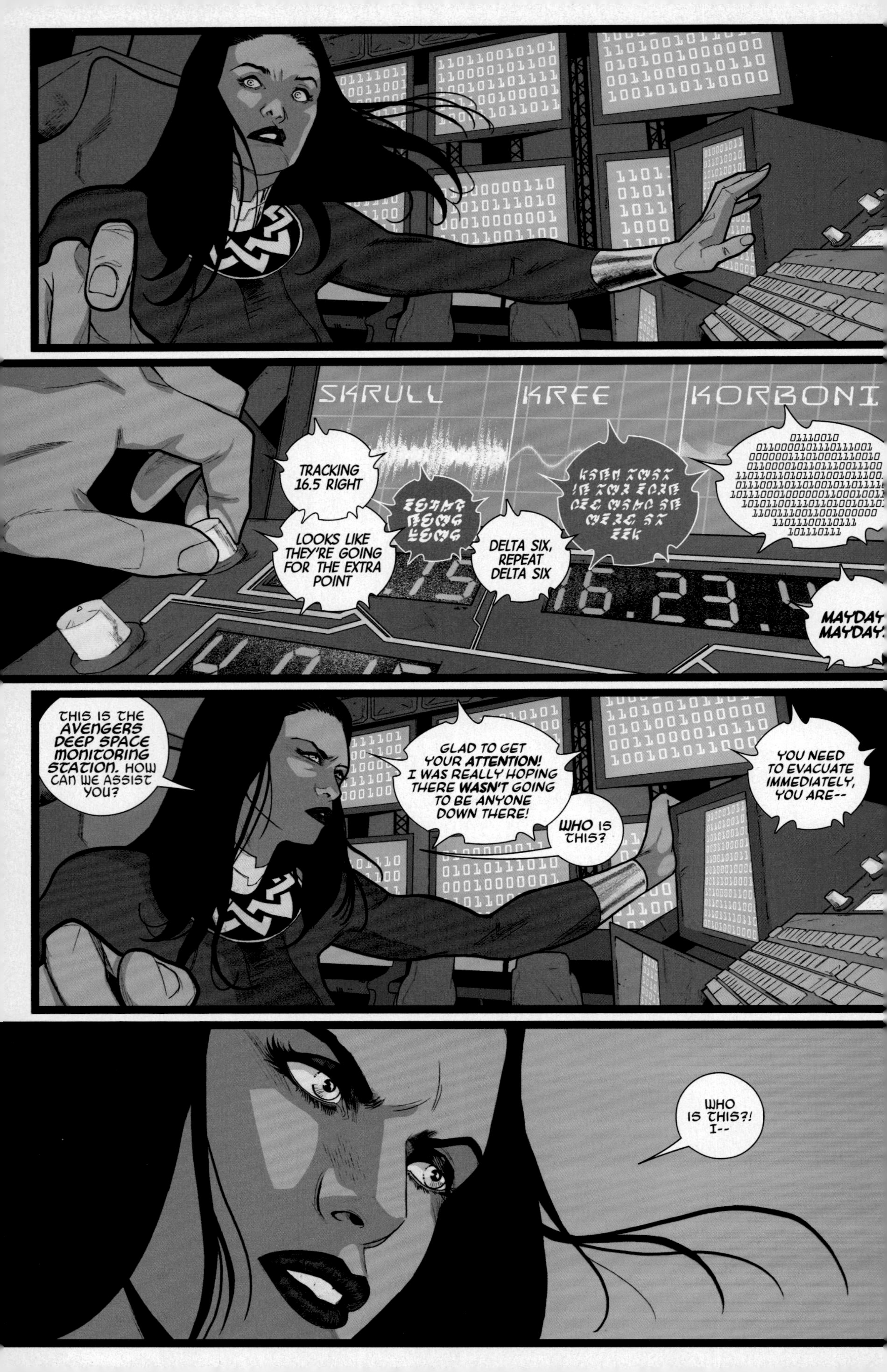
SKRULL
KREE
KORBONI
TRACKING 16.5 RIGHT
LOOKS LIKE THEY'RE GOING FOR THE EXTRA POINT
DELTA SIX, REPEAT DELTA SIX
MAYDAY MAYDAY
THIS IS THE AVENGERS DEEP SPACE MONITORING STATION. HOW CAN WE ASSIST YOU?
GLAD TO GET YOUR ATTENTION! I WAS REALLY HOPING THERE WASN'T GOING TO BE ANYONE DOWN THERE!
WHO IS THIS?
YOU NEED TO EVACUATE IMMEDIATELY, YOU ARE--
WHO IS THIS?! I--

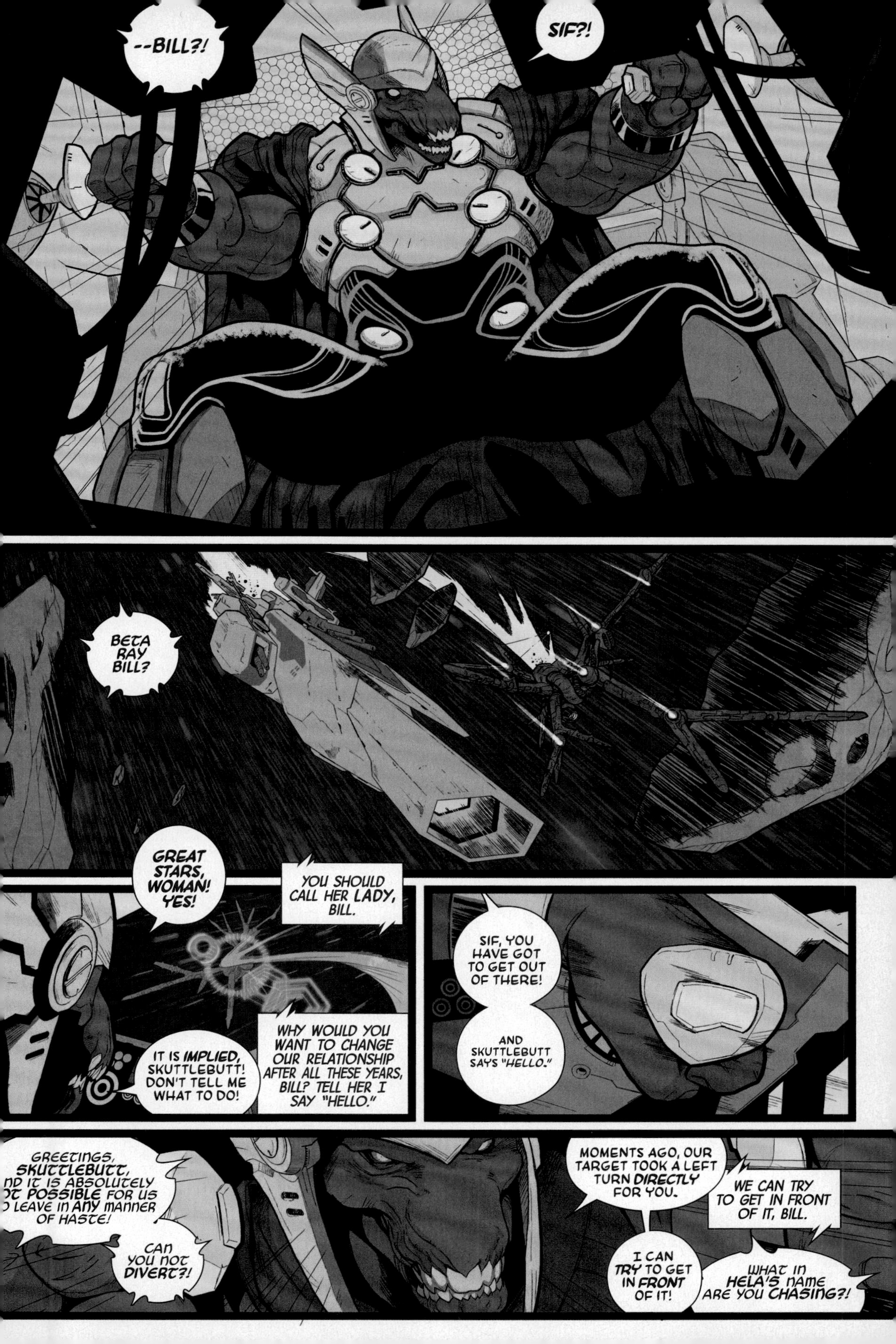
--BILL?!
SIF?!
BETA RAY BILL?
GREAT STARS, WOMAN! YES!
YOU SHOULD CALL HER LADY, BILL.
IT IS IMPLIED, SKUTTLEBUTT! DON'T TELL ME WHAT TO DO!
WHY WOULD YOU WANT TO CHANGE OUR RELATIONSHIP AFTER ALL THESE YEARS, BILL? TELL HER I SAY "HELLO."
SIF, YOU HAVE GOT TO GET OUT OF THERE!
AND SKUTTLEBUTT SAYS "HELLO."
GREETINGS, SKUTTLEBUTT, ND IT IS ABSOLUTELY OT POSSIBLE FOR US O LEAVE IN ANY MANNER OF HASTE!
CAN YOU NOT DIVERT?!
MOMENTS AGO, OUR TARGET TOOK A LEFT TURN DIRECTLY FOR YOU.
WE CAN TRY TO GET IN FRONT OF IT, BILL.
I CAN TRY TO GET IN FRONT OF IT!
WHAT IN HELA'S NAME ARE YOU CHASING?!

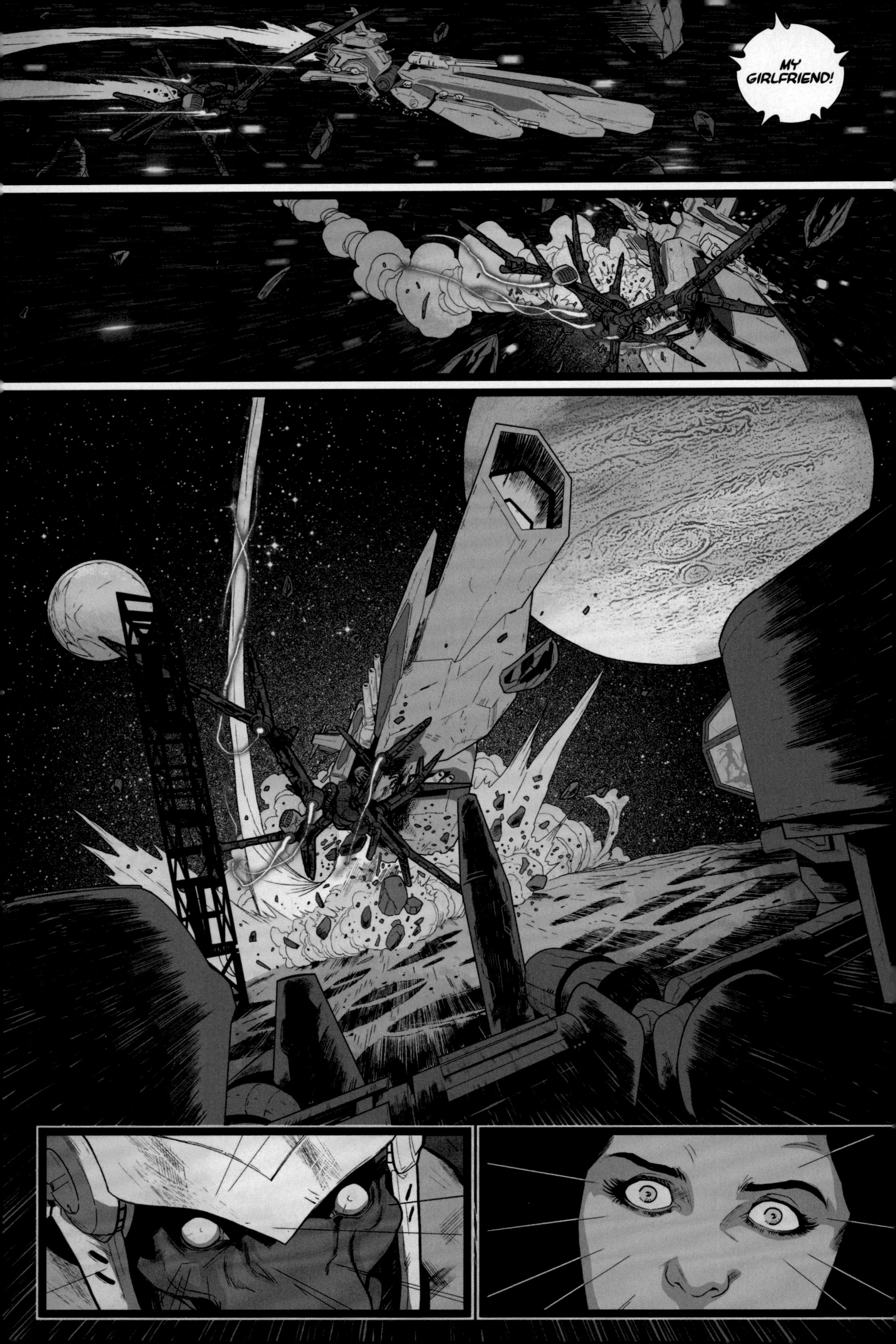
MY GIRLFRIEND!

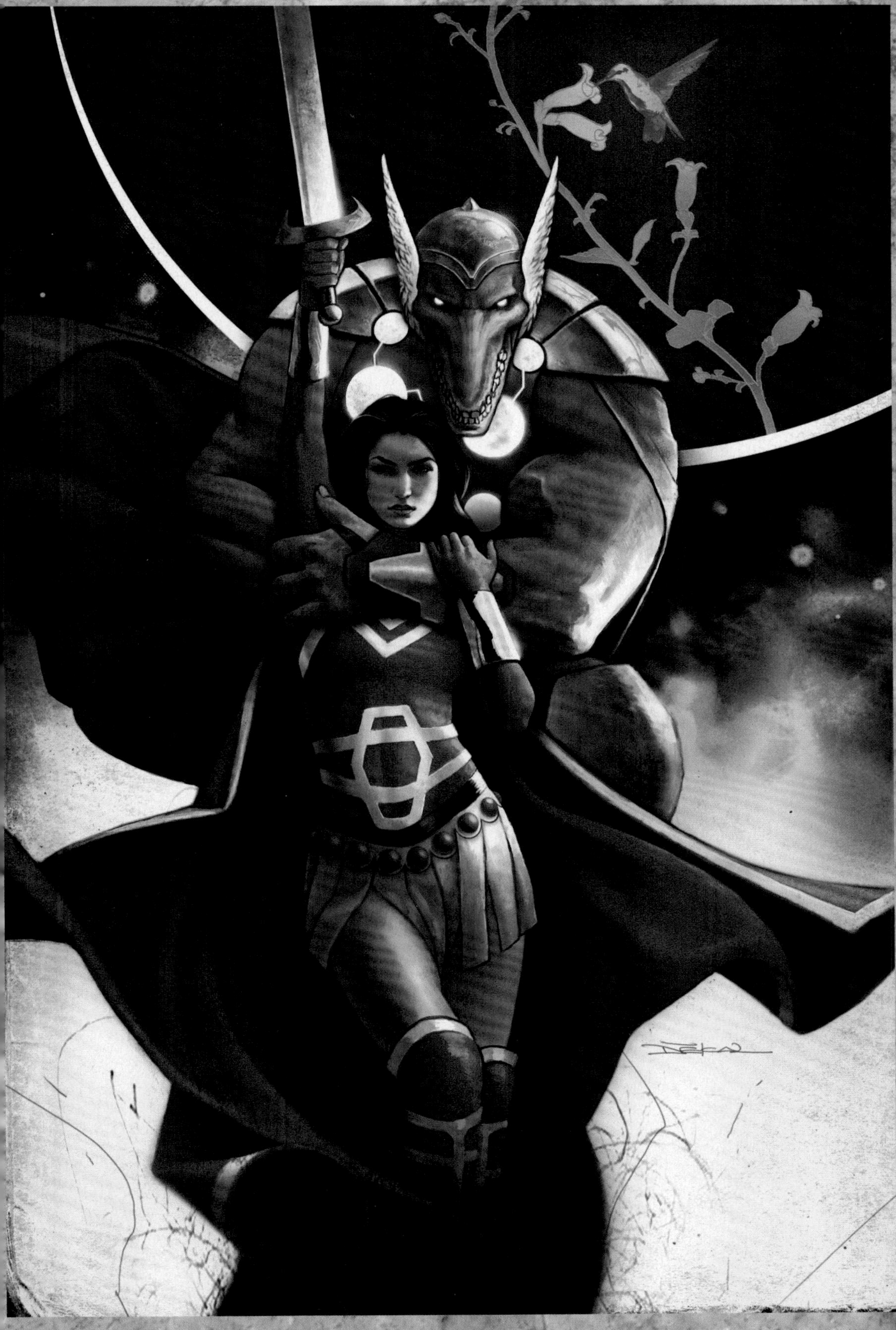

#653

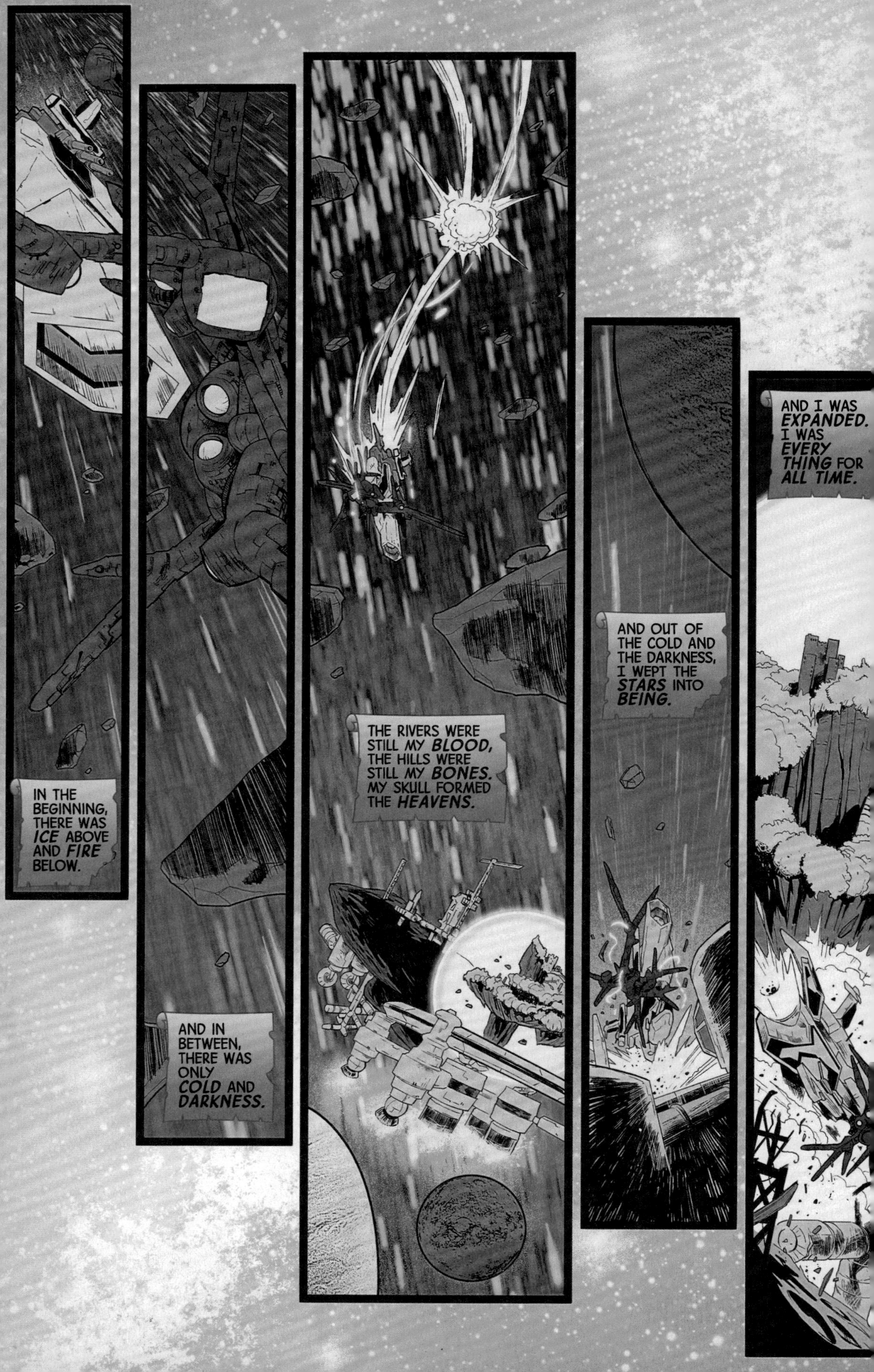
IN THE BEGINNING, THERE WAS ICE ABOVE AND FIRE BELOW.
AND IN BETWEEN, THERE WAS ONLY COLD AND DARKNESS.
THE RIVERS WERE STILL MY BLOOD, THE HILLS WERE STILL MY BONES. MY SKULL FORMED THE HEAVENS.
AND OUT OF THE COLD AND THE DARKNESS, I WEPT THE STARS INTO BEING.
AND I WAS EXPANDED. I WAS EVERY THING FOR ALL TIME.

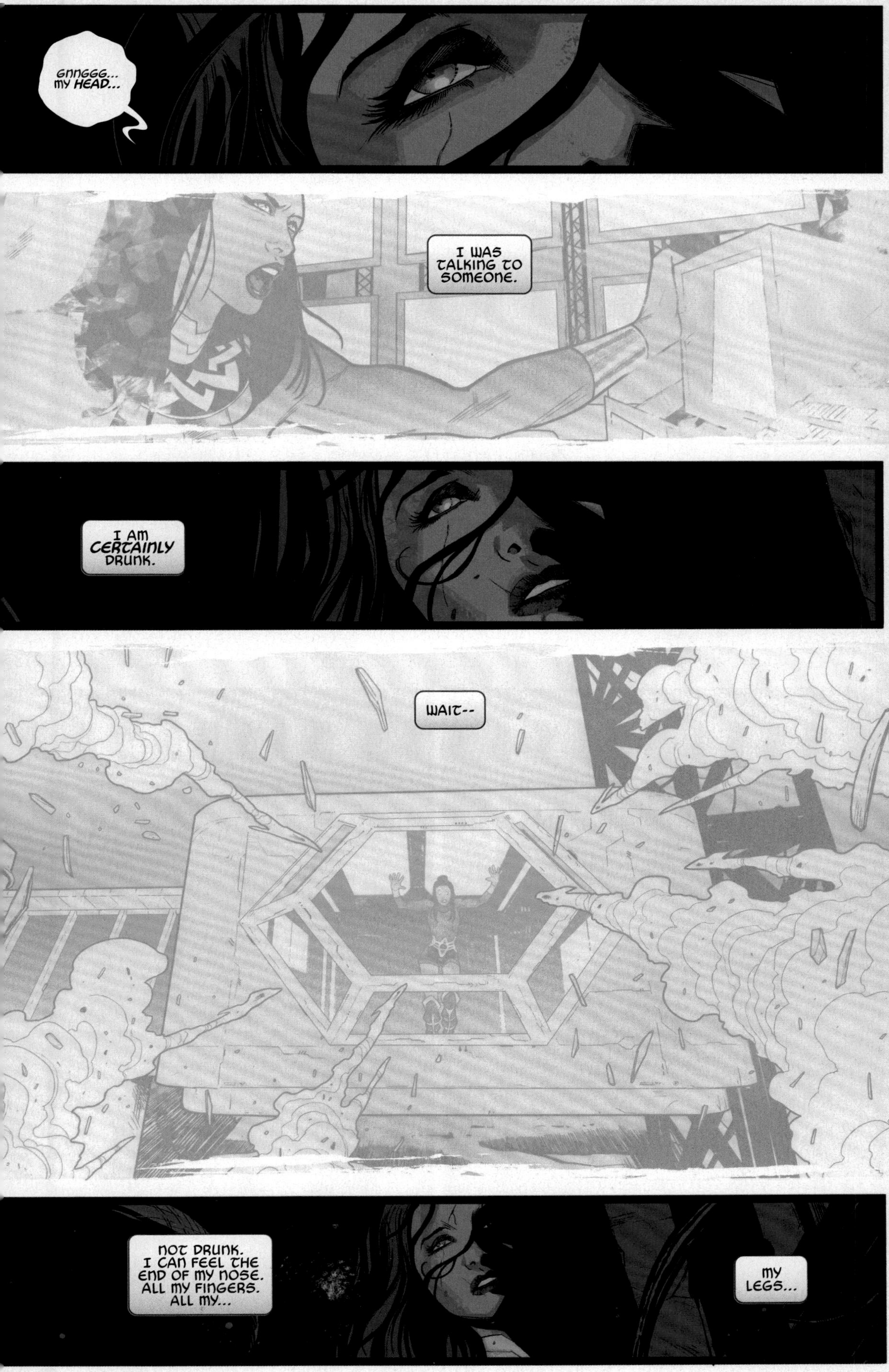
GNNGGG... MY HEAD...
I WAS TALKING TO SOMEONE.
I AM CERTAINLY DRUNK.
WAIT--
NOT DRUNK. I CAN FEEL THE END OF MY NOSE. ALL MY FINGERS. ALL MY...
MY LEGS...

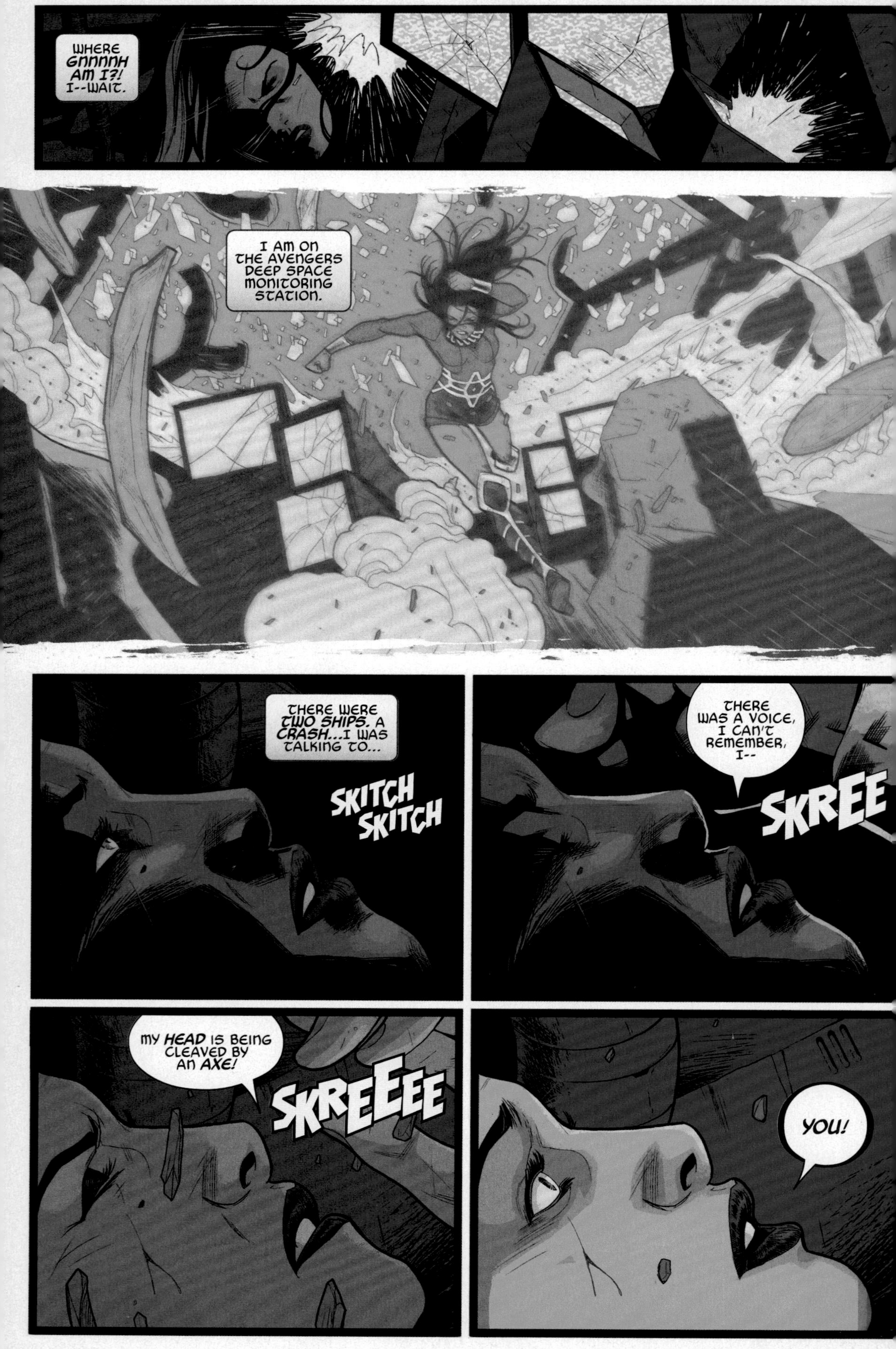
WHERE GNNNNH AM I?! I--WAIT.
I AM ON THE AVENGERS DEEP SPACE MONITORING STATION.
THERE WERE TWO SHIPS. A CRASH...I WAS TALKING TO...
SKITCH SKITCH
THERE WAS A VOICE, I CAN'T REMEMBER, I--
SKREE
MY HEAD IS BEING CLEAVED BY AN AXE!
SKREEEEE
YOU!

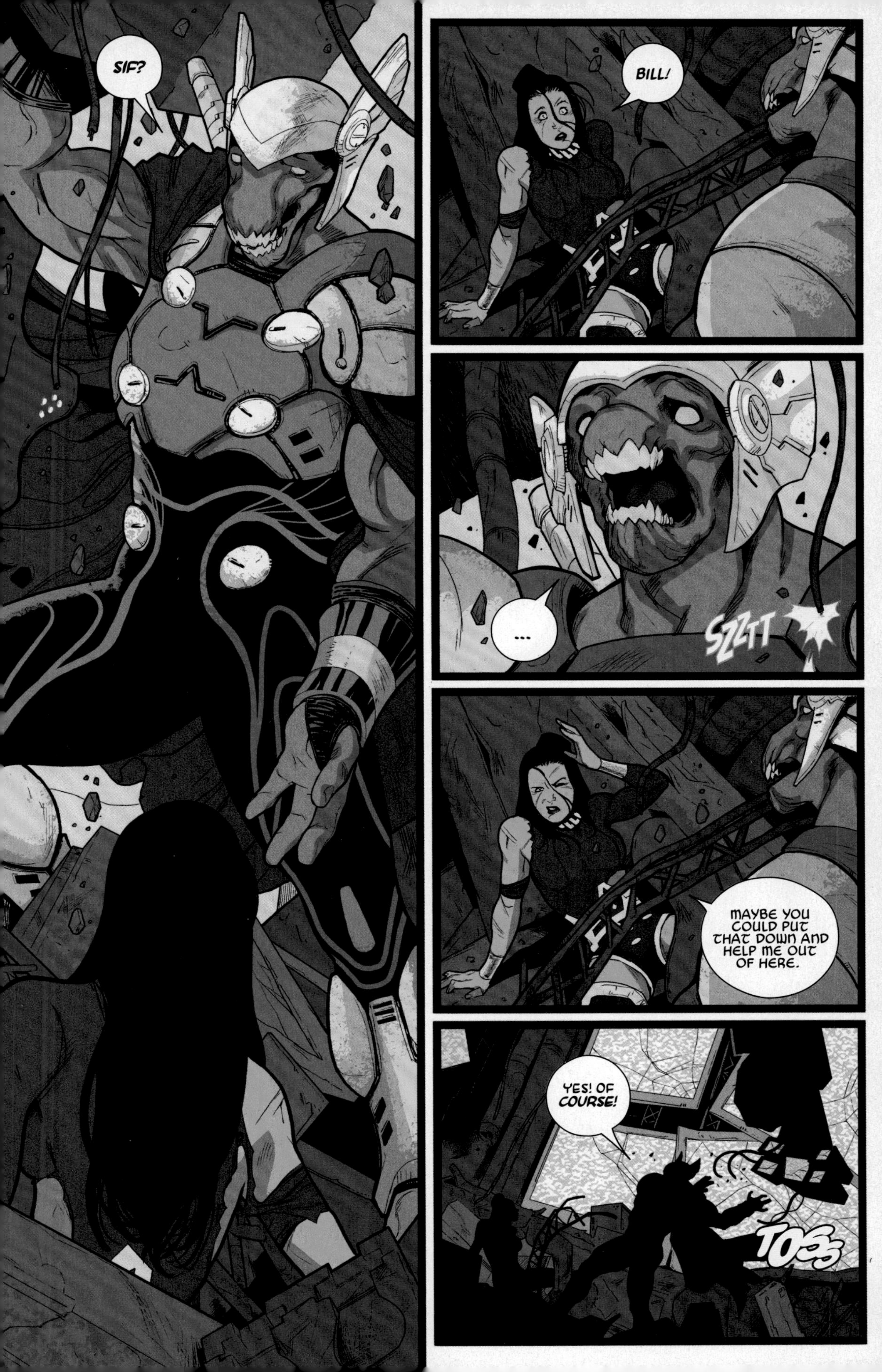
SIF?
BILL!
...
SZZTT
MAYBE YOU COULD PUT THAT DOWN AND HELP ME OUT OF HERE.
YES! OF COURSE!
TOSS

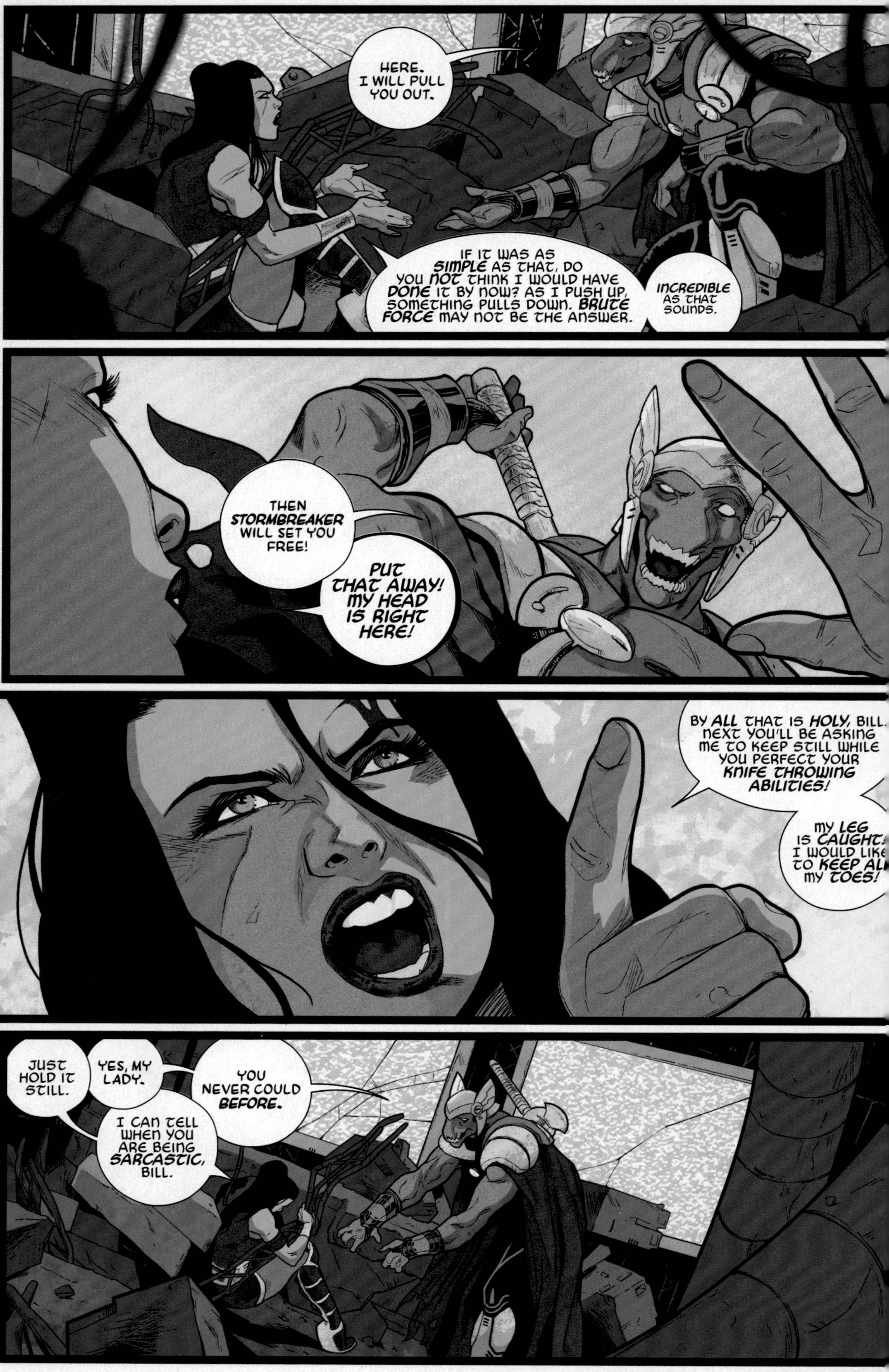
HERE. I WILL PULL YOU OUT.
IF IT WAS AS SIMPLE AS THAT, DO YOU NOT THINK I WOULD HAVE DONE IT BY NOW? AS I PUSH UP, SOMETHING PULLS DOWN. BRUTE FORCE MAY NOT BE THE ANSWER.
INCREDIBLE AS THAT SOUNDS.
THEN STORMBREAKER WILL SET YOU FREE!
PUT THAT AWAY! MY HEAD IS RIGHT HERE!
BY ALL THAT IS HOLY, BILL. NEXT YOU'LL BE ASKING ME TO KEEP STILL WHILE YOU PERFECT YOUR KNIFE THROWING ABILITIES!
MY LEG IS CAUGHT! I WOULD LIKE TO KEEP ALL MY TOES!
JUST HOLD IT STILL.
YES, MY LADY.
YOU NEVER COULD BEFORE.
I CAN TELL WHEN YOU ARE BEING SARCASTIC, BILL.

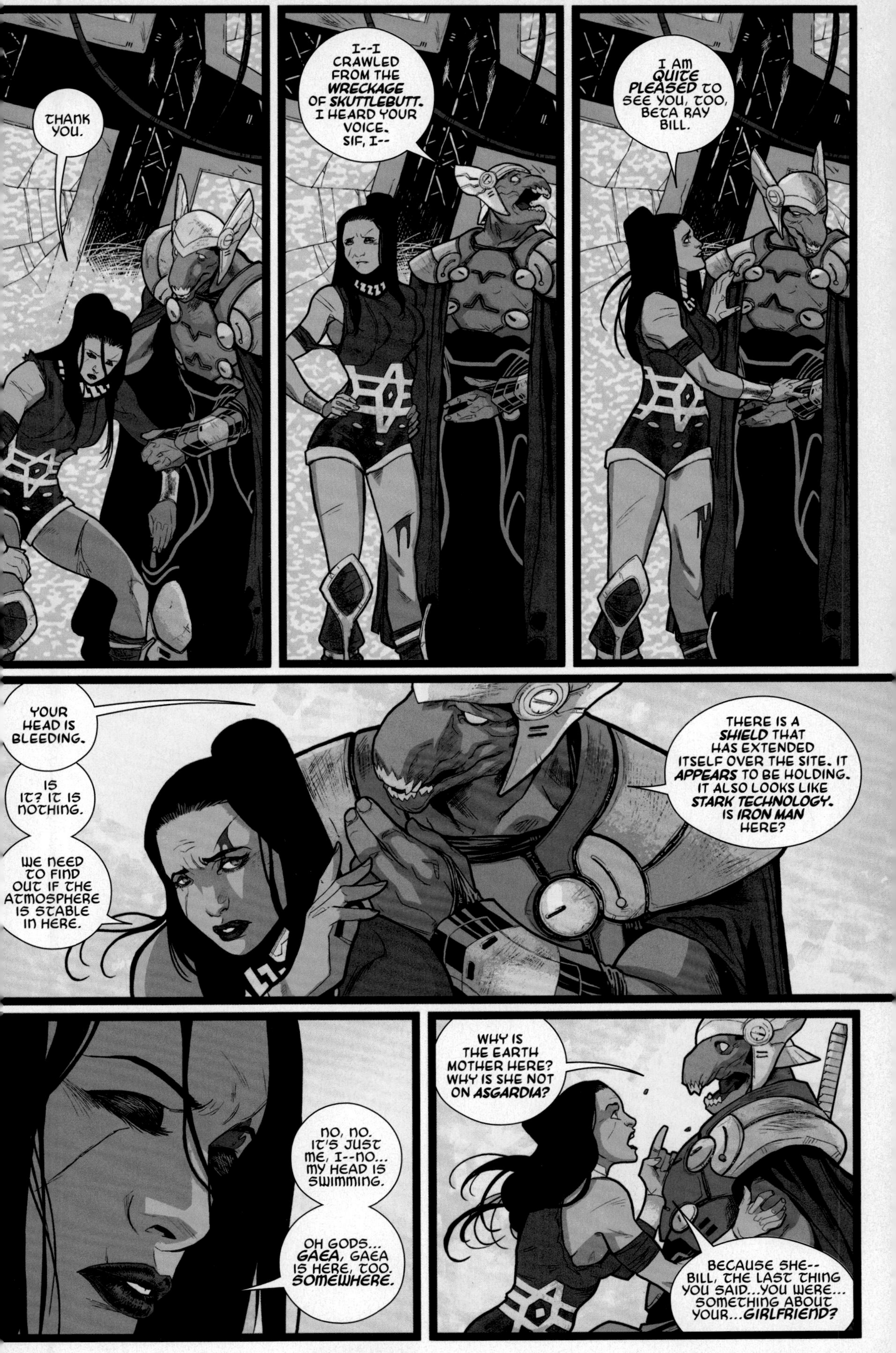
THANK YOU.
I--I CRAWLED FROM THE WRECKAGE OF SKUTTLEBUTT. I HEARD YOUR VOICE. SIF, I--
I AM QUITE PLEASED TO SEE YOU, TOO, BETA RAY BILL.
YOUR HEAD IS BLEEDING.
IS IT? IT IS NOTHING.
WE NEED TO FIND OUT IF THE ATMOSPHERE IS STABLE IN HERE.
THERE IS A SHIELD THAT HAS EXTENDED ITSELF OVER THE SITE. IT APPEARS TO BE HOLDING. IT ALSO LOOKS LIKE STARK TECHNOLOGY. IS IRON MAN HERE?
NO, NO. IT'S JUST ME, I--NO... MY HEAD IS SWIMMING.
OH GODS... GAEA, GAEA IS HERE, TOO. SOMEWHERE.
WHY IS THE EARTH MOTHER HERE? WHY IS SHE NOT ON ASGARDIA?
BECAUSE SHE-- BILL, THE LAST THING YOU SAID...YOU WERE... SOMETHING ABOUT YOUR...GIRLFRIEND?

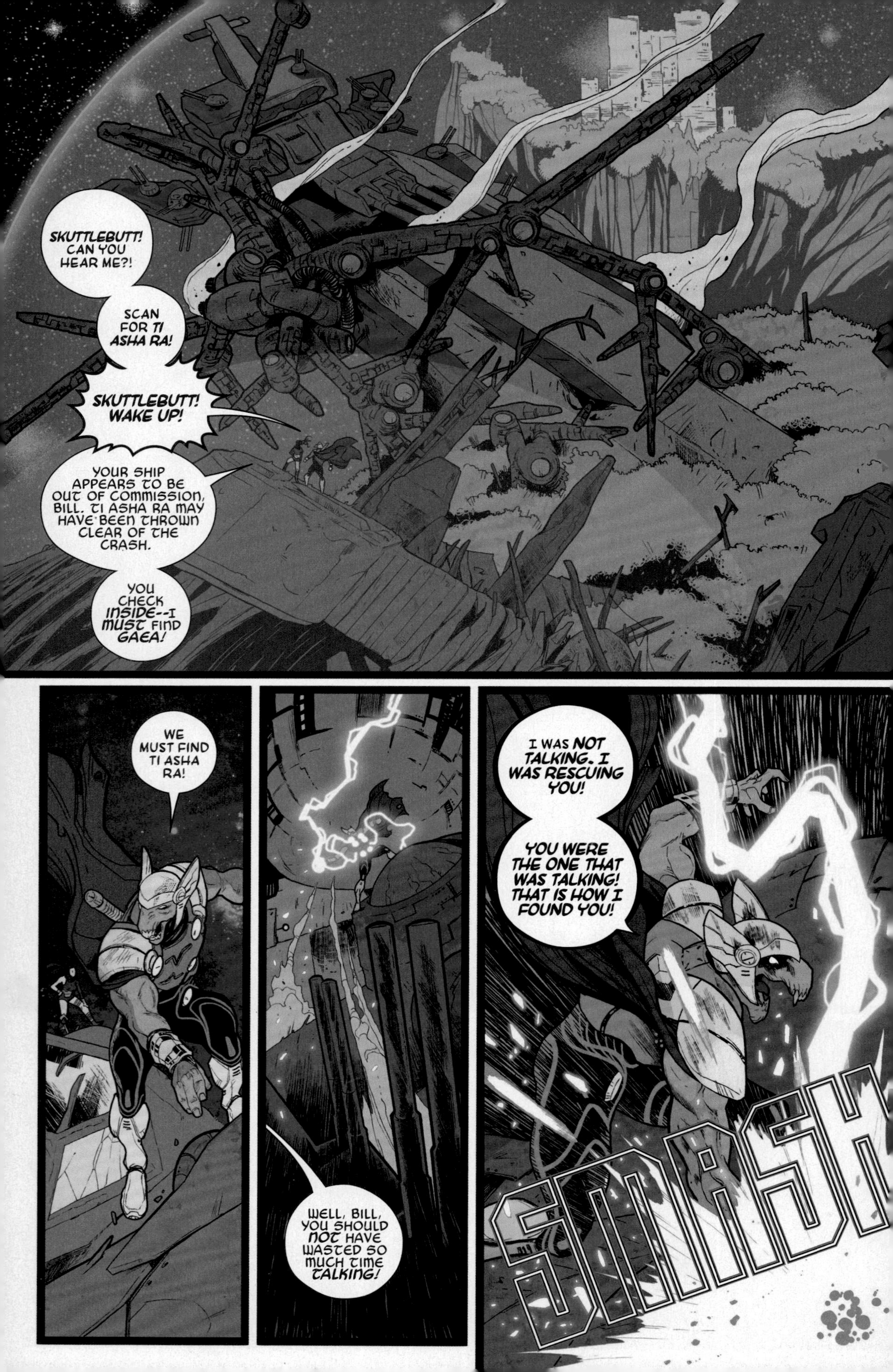

SKUTTLEBUTT! CAN YOU HEAR ME?!
SCAN FOR TI ASHA RA!
SKUTTLEBUTT! WAKE UP!
YOUR SHIP APPEARS TO BE OUT OF COMMISSION, BILL. TI ASHA RA MAY HAVE BEEN THROWN CLEAR OF THE CRASH.
YOU CHECK INSIDE--I MUST FIND GAEA!
WE MUST FIND TI ASHA RA!
WELL, BILL, YOU SHOULD NOT HAVE WASTED SO MUCH TIME TALKING!
I WAS NOT TALKING. I WAS RESCUING YOU!
YOU WERE THE ONE THAT WAS TALKING! THAT IS HOW I FOUND YOU!
SMASH

THAT WOMAN COULD *TALK* FOR *ASGARD.* IT'S ONLY SLIGHTLY LESS ANNOYING BECAUSE SHE CAN FIGHT AT THE *SAME TIME.*

TI ASHA RA! CAN YOU HEAR ME?

WHAT ON--?

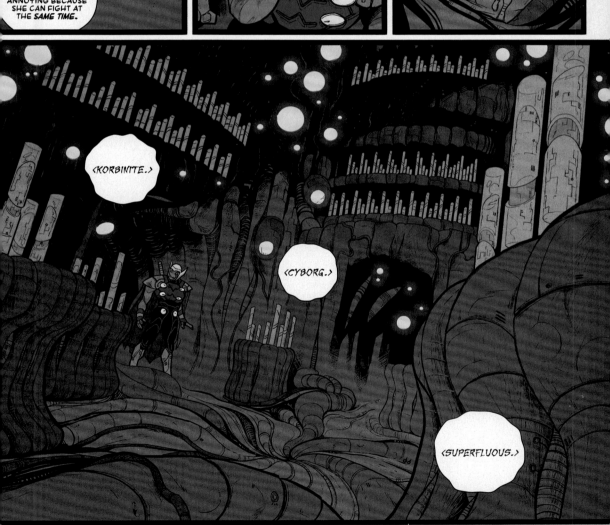

<KORBINITE.>

<CYBORG.>

<SUPERFLUOUS.>

ARRR!

<REJECTED.>

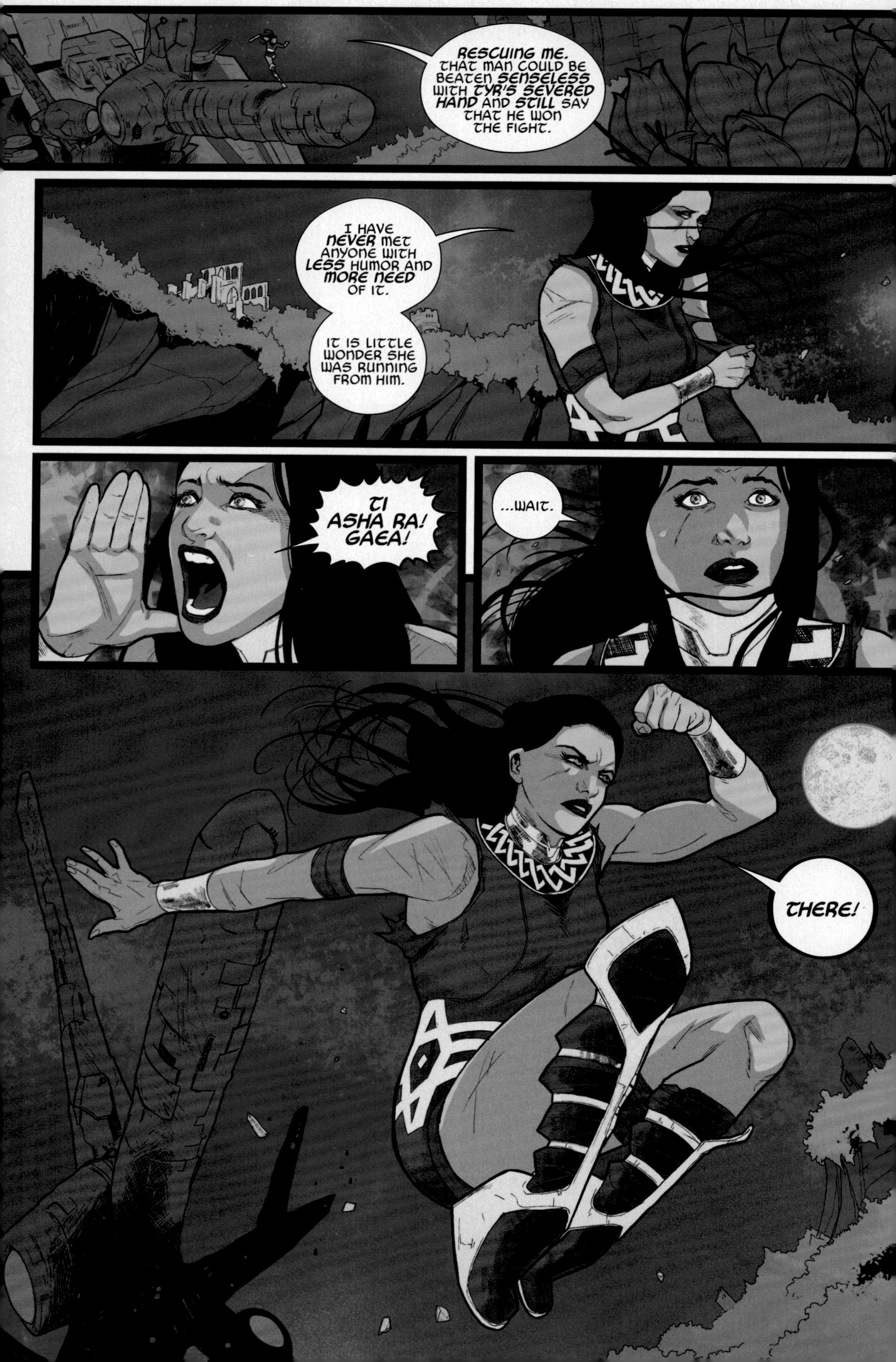
RESCUING ME. THAT MAN COULD BE BEATEN SENSELESS WITH TYR'S SEVERED HAND AND STILL SAY THAT HE WON THE FIGHT.
I HAVE NEVER MET ANYONE WITH LESS HUMOR AND MORE NEED OF IT.
IT IS LITTLE WONDER SHE WAS RUNNING FROM HIM.
TI ASHA RA! GAEA!
...WAIT.
THERE!

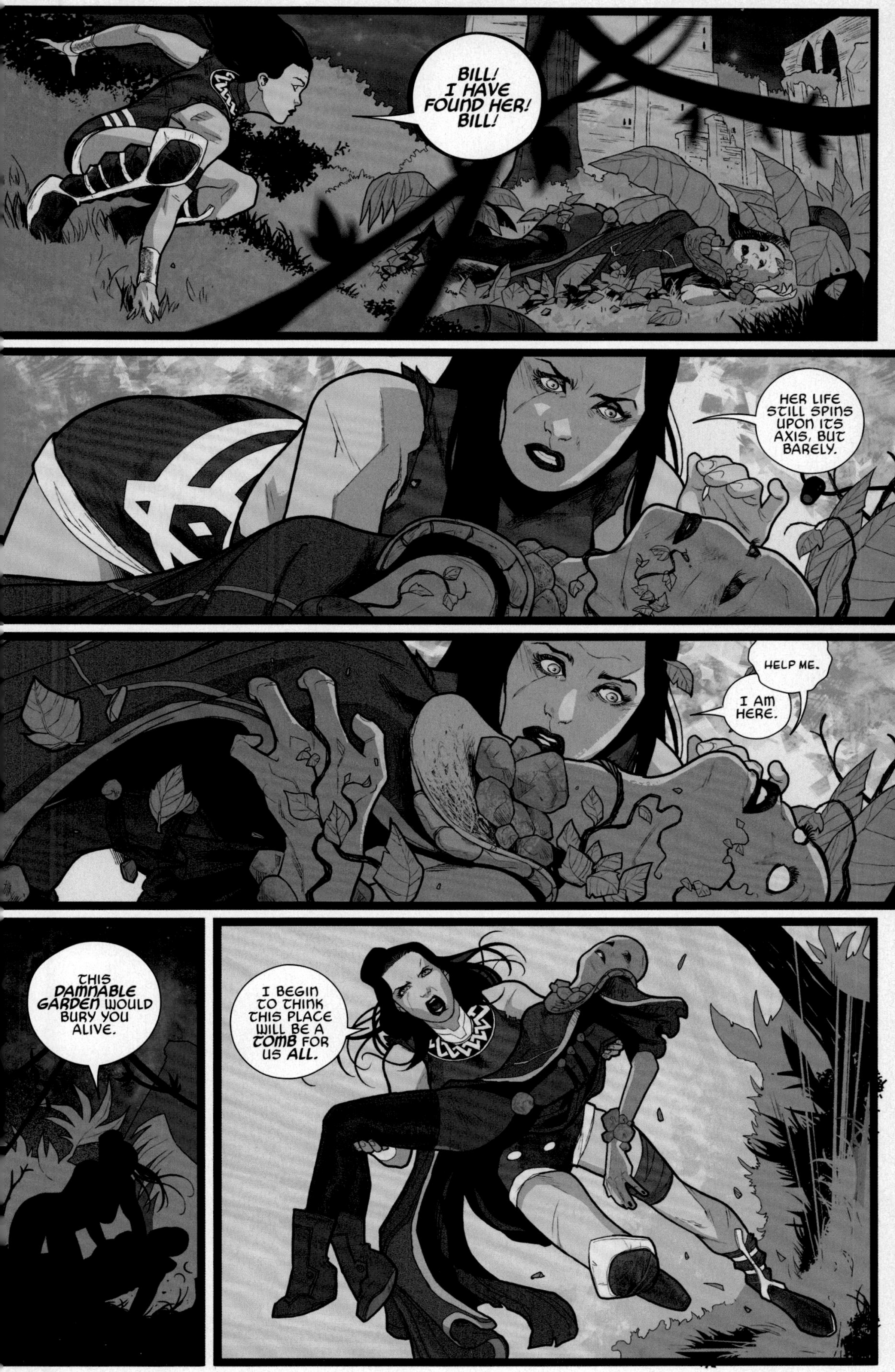
BILL! I HAVE FOUND HER! BILL!
HER LIFE STILL SPINS UPON ITS AXIS, BUT BARELY.
HELP ME.
I AM HERE.
THIS DAMNABLE GARDEN WOULD BURY YOU ALIVE.
I BEGIN TO THINK THIS PLACE WILL BE A TOMB FOR US ALL.

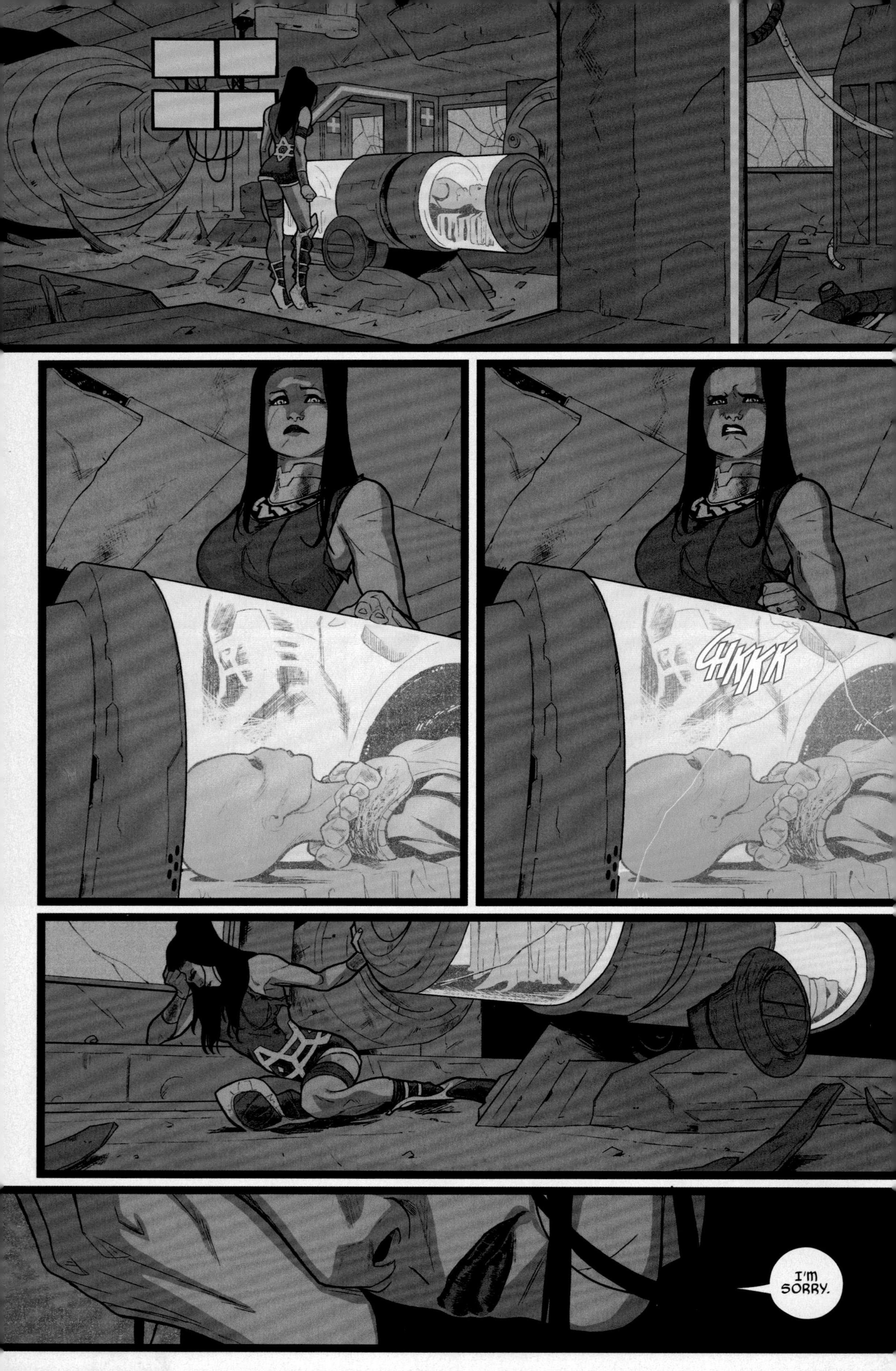
CHKKK
I'M SORRY.

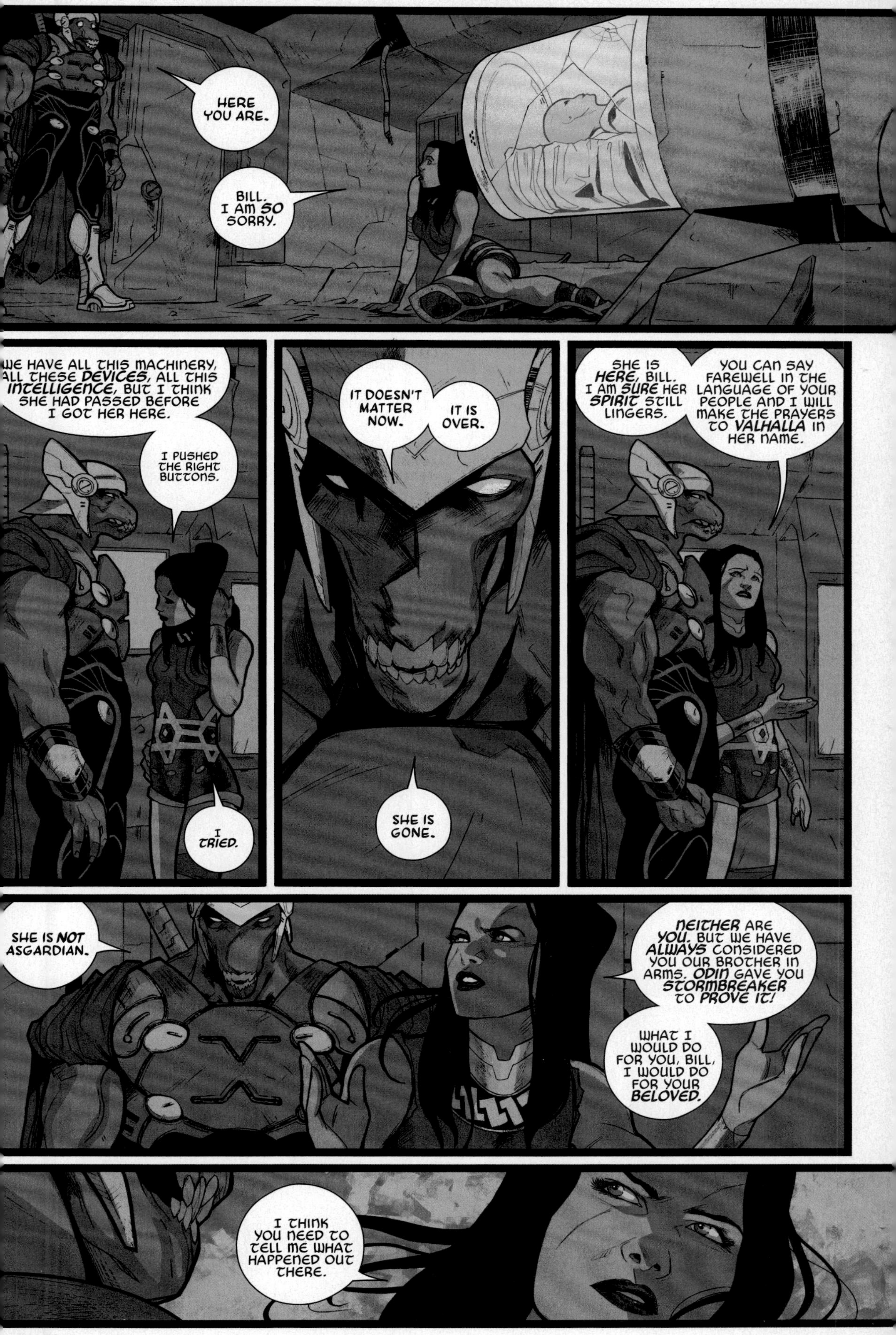
HERE YOU ARE.
BILL. I AM SO SORRY.
WE HAVE ALL THIS MACHINERY, ALL THESE DEVICES, ALL THIS INTELLIGENCE, BUT I THINK SHE HAD PASSED BEFORE I GOT HER HERE.
I PUSHED THE RIGHT BUTTONS.
I TRIED.
IT DOESN'T MATTER NOW.
IT IS OVER.
SHE IS GONE.
SHE IS HERE, BILL. I AM SURE HER SPIRIT STILL LINGERS.
YOU CAN SAY FAREWELL IN THE LANGUAGE OF YOUR PEOPLE AND I WILL MAKE THE PRAYERS TO VALHALLA IN HER NAME.
SHE IS NOT ASGARDIAN.
NEITHER ARE YOU. BUT WE HAVE ALWAYS CONSIDERED YOU OUR BROTHER IN ARMS. ODIN GAVE YOU STORMBREAKER TO PROVE IT!
WHAT I WOULD DO FOR YOU, BILL, I WOULD DO FOR YOUR BELOVED.
I THINK YOU NEED TO TELL ME WHAT HAPPENED OUT THERE.

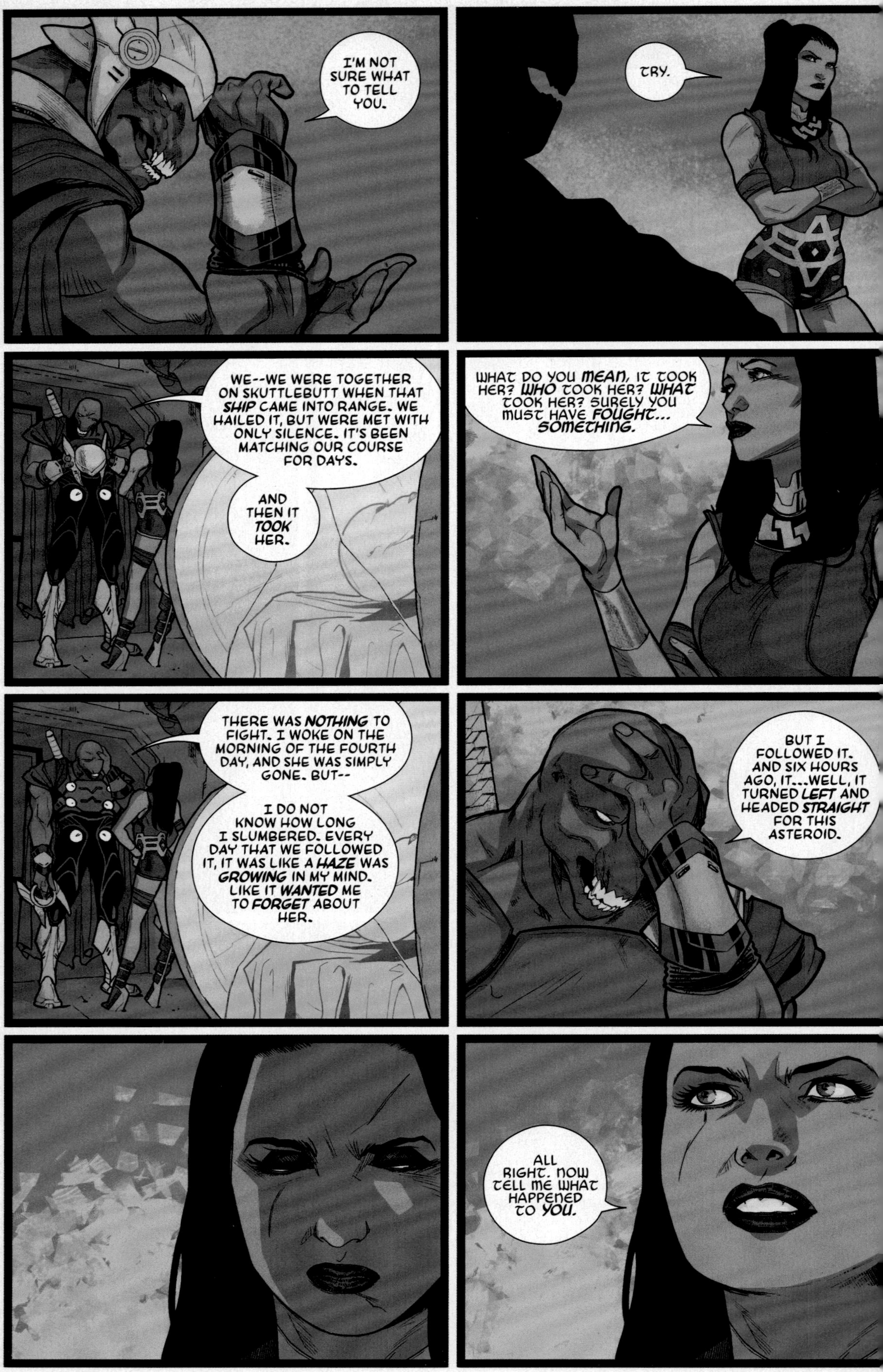
I'M NOT SURE WHAT TO TELL YOU.
TRY.
WE--WE WERE TOGETHER ON SKUTTLEBUTT WHEN THAT SHIP CAME INTO RANGE. WE HAILED IT, BUT WERE MET WITH ONLY SILENCE. IT'S BEEN MATCHING OUR COURSE FOR DAYS.
AND THEN IT TOOK HER.
WHAT DO YOU MEAN, IT TOOK HER? WHO TOOK HER? WHAT TOOK HER? SURELY YOU MUST HAVE FOUGHT... SOMETHING.
THERE WAS NOTHING TO FIGHT. I WOKE ON THE MORNING OF THE FOURTH DAY, AND SHE WAS SIMPLY GONE. BUT--
I DO NOT KNOW HOW LONG I SLUMBERED. EVERY DAY THAT WE FOLLOWED IT, IT WAS LIKE A HAZE WAS GROWING IN MY MIND. LIKE IT WANTED ME TO FORGET ABOUT HER.
BUT I FOLLOWED IT. AND SIX HOURS AGO, IT...WELL, IT TURNED LEFT AND HEADED STRAIGHT FOR THIS ASTEROID.
ALL RIGHT. NOW TELL ME WHAT HAPPENED TO YOU.

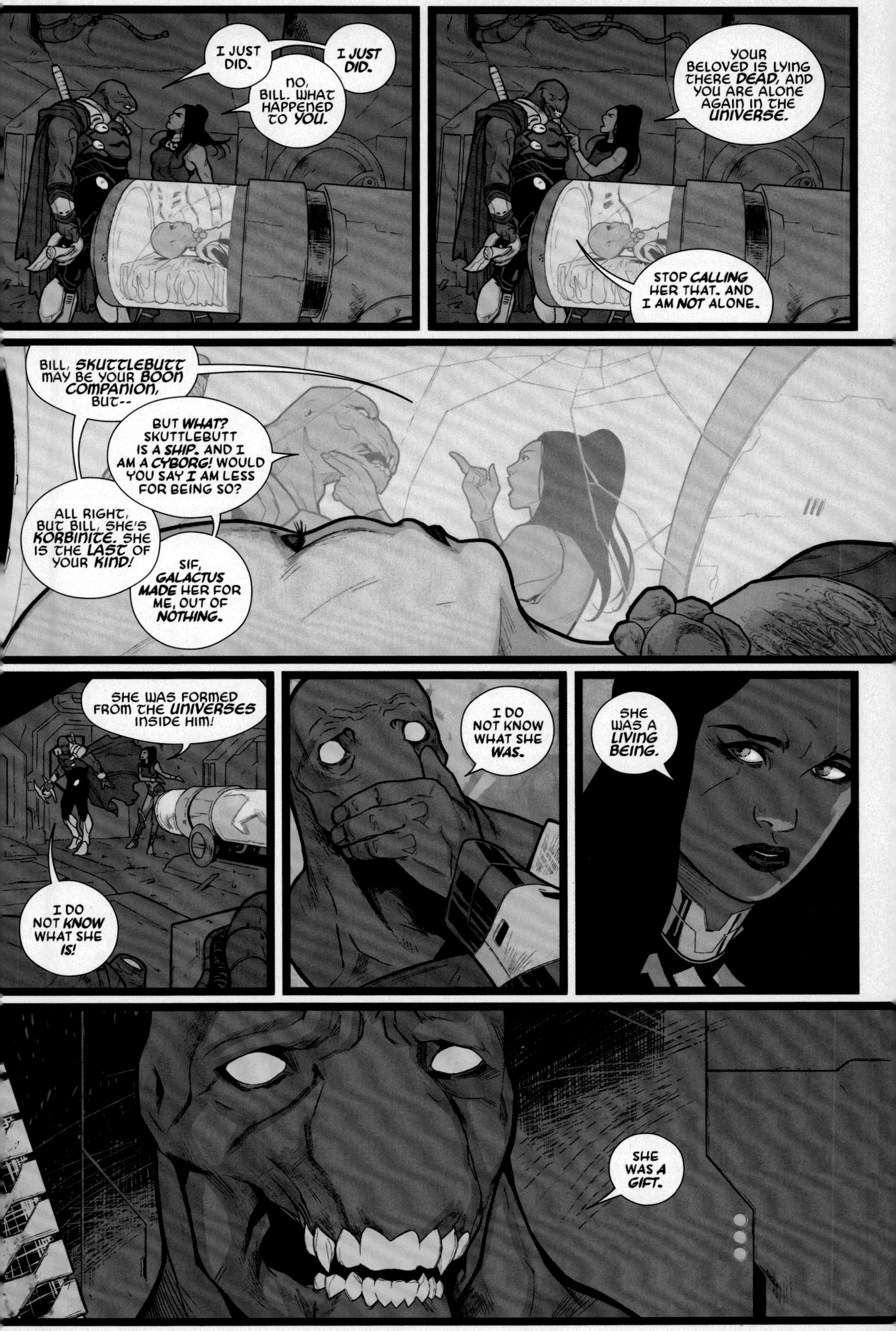
I JUST DID.
I JUST DID.
NO, BILL. WHAT HAPPENED TO YOU.
YOUR BELOVED IS LYING THERE DEAD, AND YOU ARE ALONE AGAIN IN THE UNIVERSE.
STOP CALLING HER THAT. AND I AM NOT ALONE.
BILL, SKUTTLEBUTT MAY BE YOUR BOON COMPANION, BUT--
BUT WHAT? SKUTTLEBUTT IS A SHIP. AND I AM A CYBORG! WOULD YOU SAY I AM LESS FOR BEING SO?
ALL RIGHT, BUT BILL, SHE'S KORBINITE. SHE IS THE LAST OF YOUR KIND!
SIF, GALACTUS MADE HER FOR ME, OUT OF NOTHING.
SHE WAS FORMED FROM THE UNIVERSES INSIDE HIM!
I DO NOT KNOW WHAT SHE IS!
I DO NOT KNOW WHAT SHE WAS.
SHE WAS A LIVING BEING.
SHE WAS A GIFT.

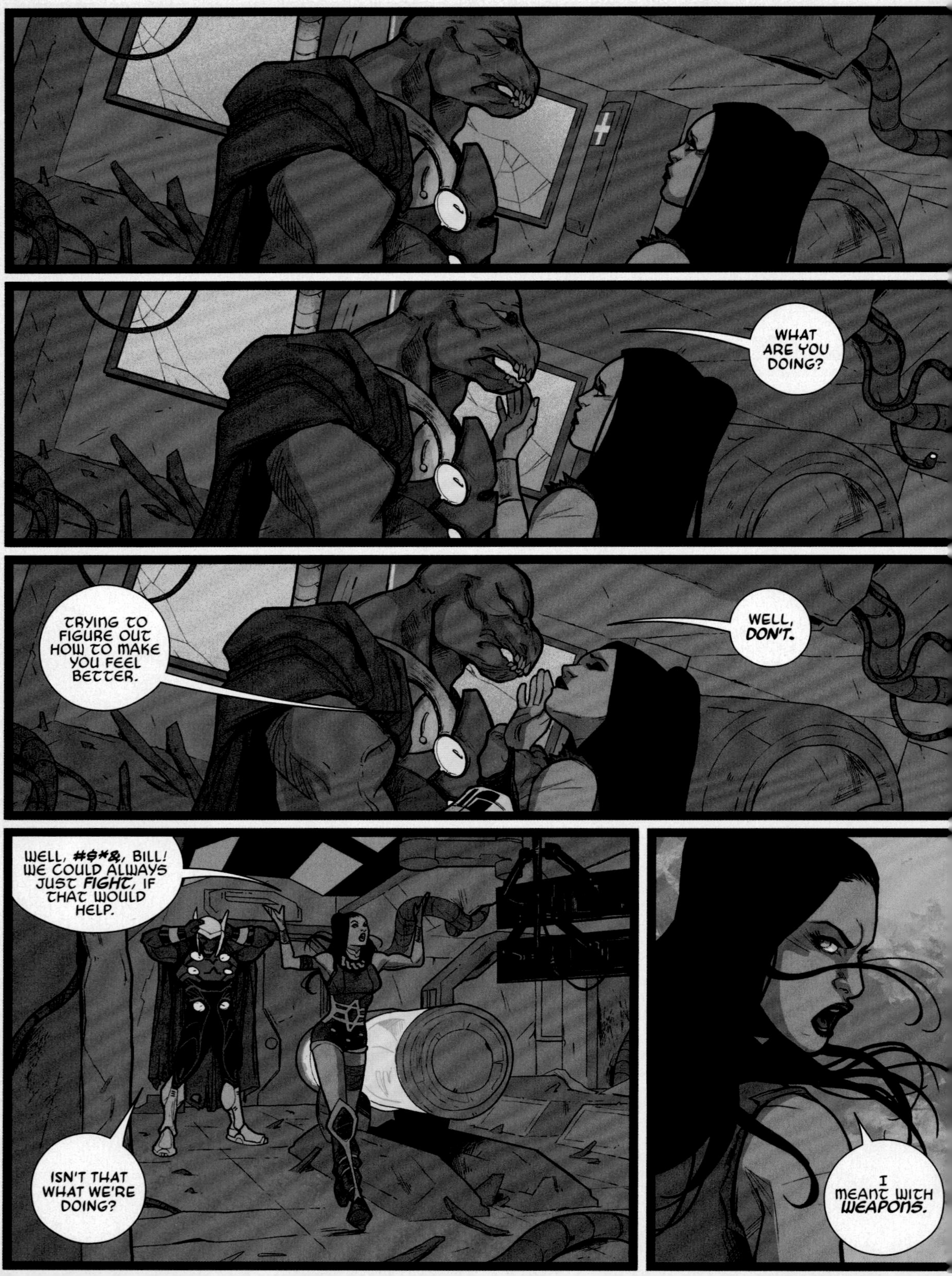
WHAT ARE YOU DOING?
TRYING TO FIGURE OUT HOW TO MAKE YOU FEEL BETTER.
WELL, DON'T.
WELL, #$*&, BILL! WE COULD ALWAYS JUST FIGHT, IF THAT WOULD HELP.
ISN'T THAT WHAT WE'RE DOING?
I MEANT WITH WEAPONS.

BILL--
I'M SO SORRY.
TI ASHA RA. I HAVE NEVER KNOWN SOMEONE WHO COULD CONTAIN SO MUCH SORROW. HE KNOWS NOT WHAT HE DOES.
CHKK
SHHHHHH
AND WHAT HE DOES, HE DOES NOT MEAN.
FOR YOU. FOR YOUR JOURNEY.
IN THE BEGINNING, THERE WAS ICE ABOVE AND FIRE BELOW.
AND IN BETWEEN, THERE WAS ONLY COLD AND DARKNESS.
ONLY COLD AND DARKNESS.

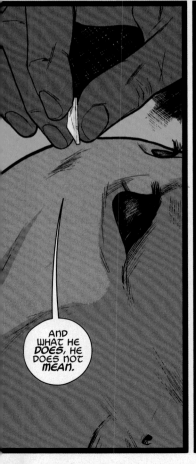

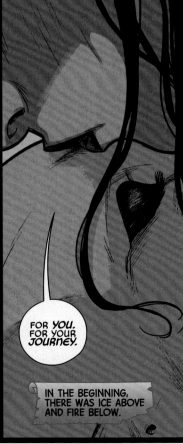

COME ON, OL' GAL. I NEED TO HEAR YOUR VOICE.
COME ON, SKUTTLEBUTT. WAKE UP!
KKK-UHN-UHHHZZZ
H-H-HELLO.
SKUTTLEBUTT! MY OLD FRIEND!
HELLO. THIS IS THE EMERGENCY AUDIO INTERFACE. P-PLEASE STATE THE NATURE OF YOUR PROBLEM.
SKUTTLEBUTT? WHERE ARE YOU?!
THERE EXIST NO RECORDS OR REFERENTS FOR SKUTTLEBUTT. PLEASE RESTATE.
CHECK AGAIN!
REPEAT. THERE IS NO EVIDENCE. EXTANT OR EXTINCT.
SKUTTLEBUTT DOES NOT EXIST.

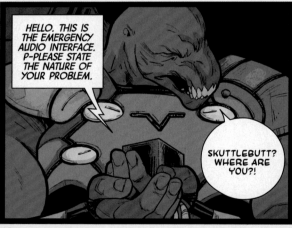

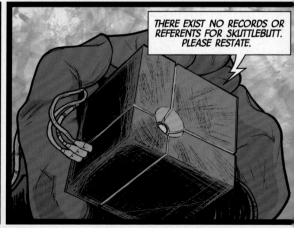

THE RIVERS WERE STILL MY BLOOD, THE HILLS WERE STILL MY BONES. MY SKULL FORMED THE HEAVENS.

WE LIVE IN THE COMPANY OF OUR BROTHERS AND SISTERS. AND WE *DIE* THERE ALSO.

BILL LOVED YOU, SOMEHOW. HE MUST HAVE. YOU AND HE ARE THE REMNANTS OF YOUR RACE.

I THINK HE HAS MADE A *NOBLE RELIGION* OF *LONELINESS.* BUT HIS LOVE WILL FOLLOW YOU.

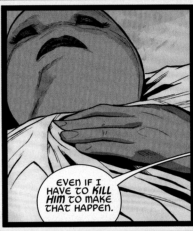

EVEN IF I HAVE TO *KILL HIM* TO MAKE THAT HAPPEN.

ND OUT F THE COLD ND THE ARKNESS, WEPT THE TARS INTO EING.

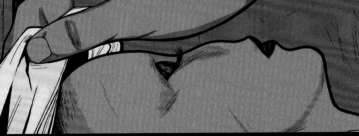

I WAS GLAD TO SEE HIM, TI ASHA RA, AND I KNOW HE IS *BETTER* FOR HAVING KNOWN YOU. PERHAPS THAT IS WHY--

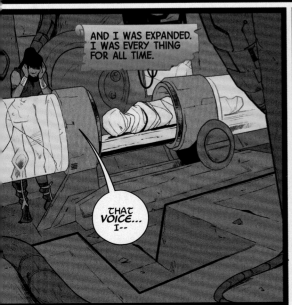

AND I WAS EXPANDED. I WAS EVERY THING FOR ALL TIME.

THAT *VOICE...* I--

⇒GASP!⇐

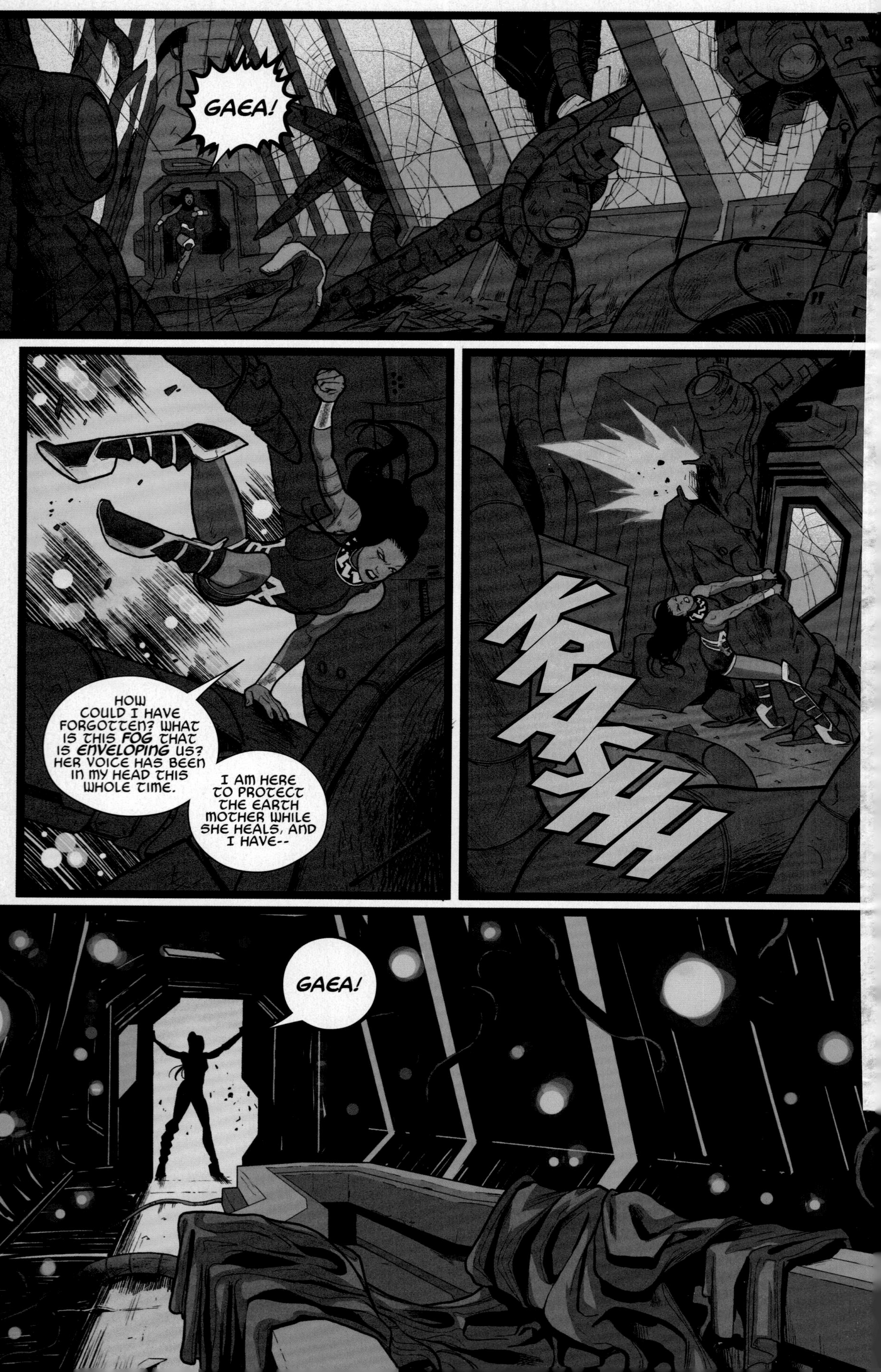
GAEA!
HOW COULD I HAVE FORGOTTEN? WHAT IS THIS FOG THAT IS ENVELOPING US? HER VOICE HAS BEEN IN MY HEAD THIS WHOLE TIME.
I AM HERE TO PROTECT THE EARTH MOTHER WHILE SHE HEALS, AND I HAVE--
KRASHH
GAEA!

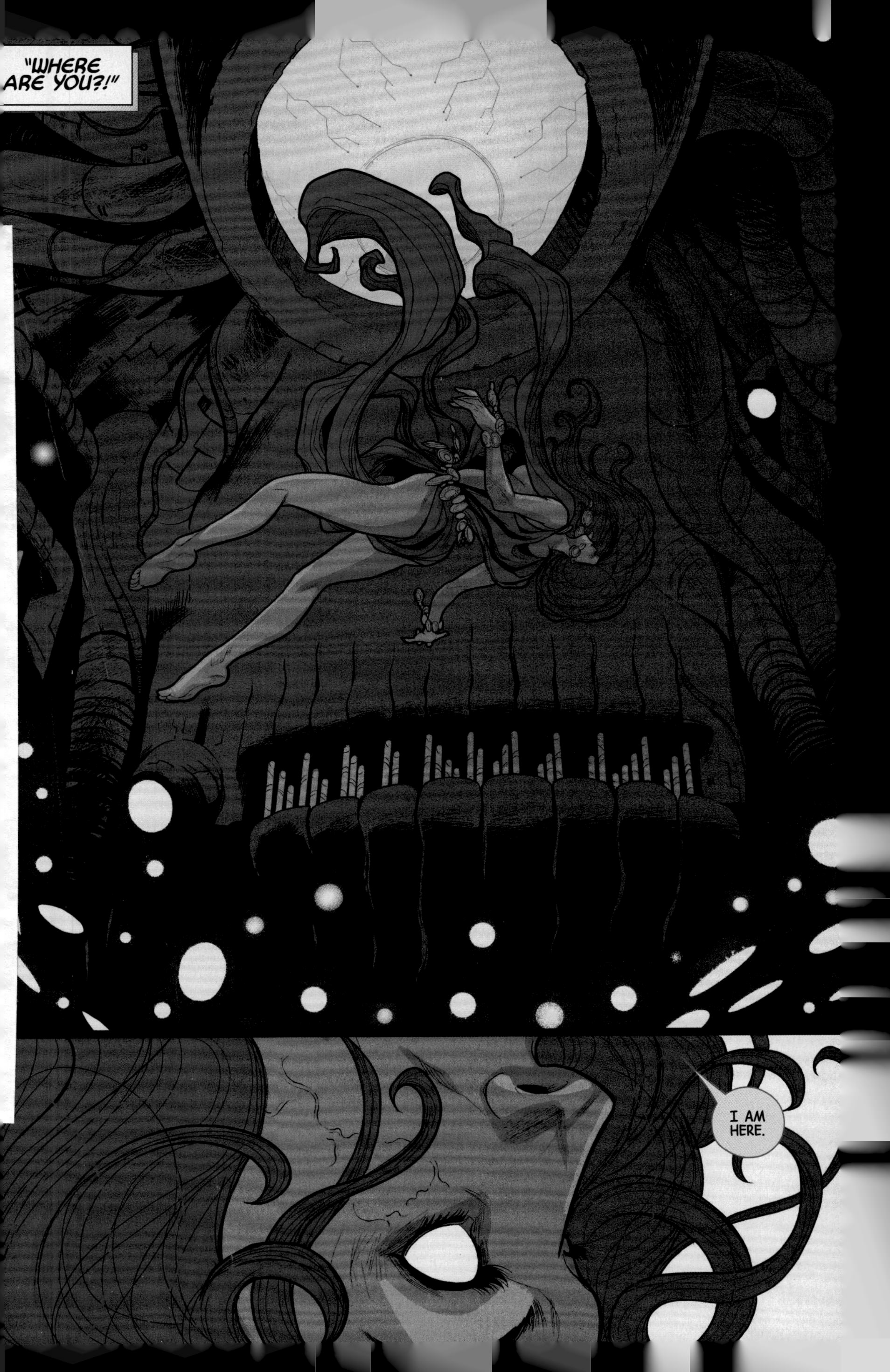
"WHERE ARE YOU?!"
I AM HERE.

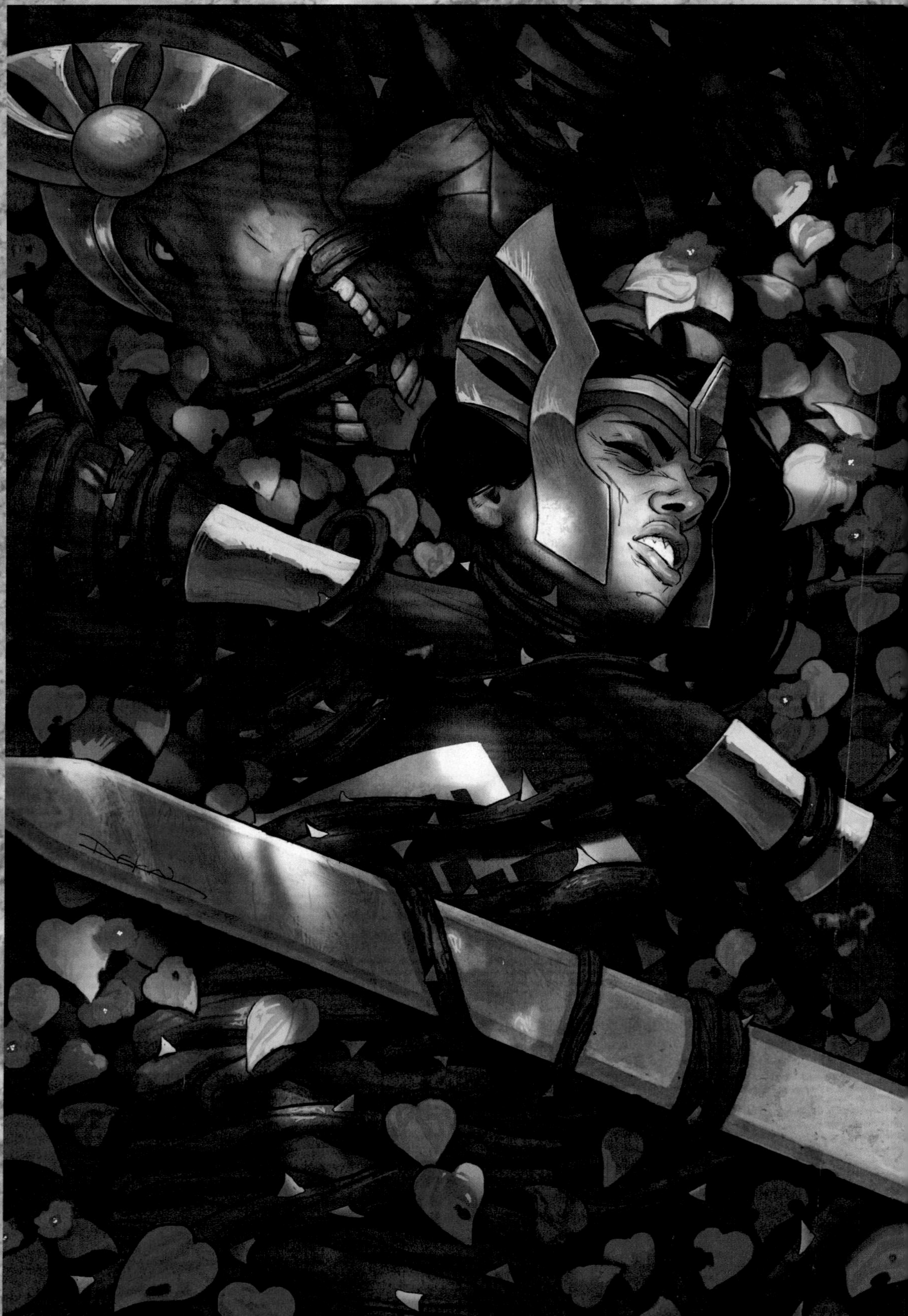

#654

WHAT IS A WARRIOR WITHOUT A WAR?

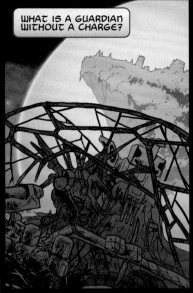

WHAT IS A GUARDIAN WITHOUT A CHARGE?

HOW COULD YOU LEAVE ME?

HOW COULD I LOSE YOU?

SKUTTLEBUTT, WE WERE MEANT TO TRAVEL THE STARS *TOGETHER.*

SMASH

I WAS MEANT TO *PROTECT* YOU, GAEA, WHILE YOU *HEALED!*

HACK

FOREVER.

AND NOW--

TI ASHA RA IS DEAD. SKUTTLEBUTT IS GONE AND I AM ALONE...AGAIN.

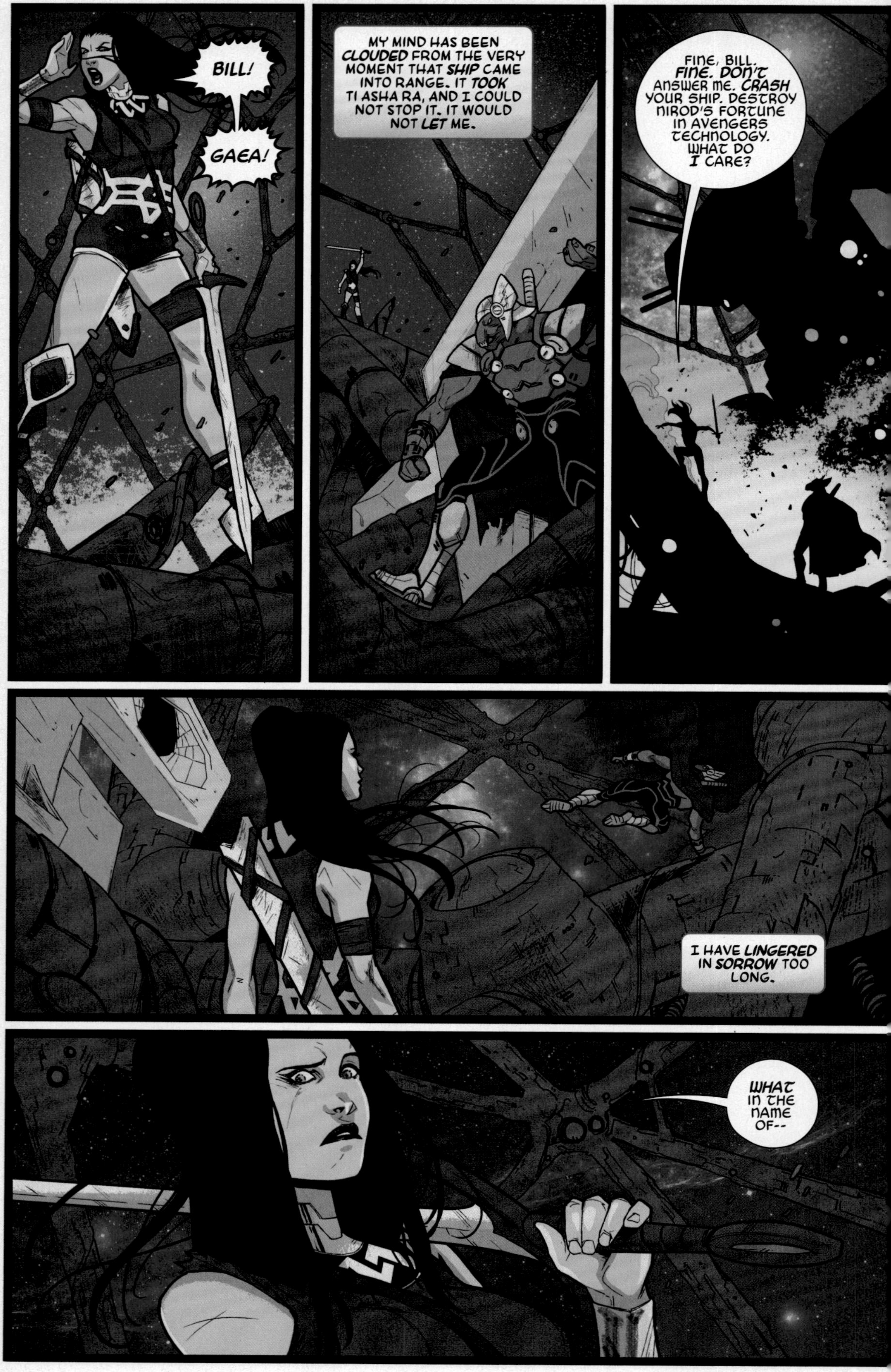
BILL!
GAEA!
MY MIND HAS BEEN CLOUDED FROM THE VERY MOMENT THAT SHIP CAME INTO RANGE. IT TOOK TI ASHA RA, AND I COULD NOT STOP IT. IT WOULD NOT LET ME.
FINE, BILL. FINE. DON'T ANSWER ME. CRASH YOUR SHIP. DESTROY NIROD'S FORTUNE IN AVENGERS TECHNOLOGY. WHAT DO I CARE?
I HAVE LINGERED IN SORROW TOO LONG.
WHAT IN THE NAME OF--

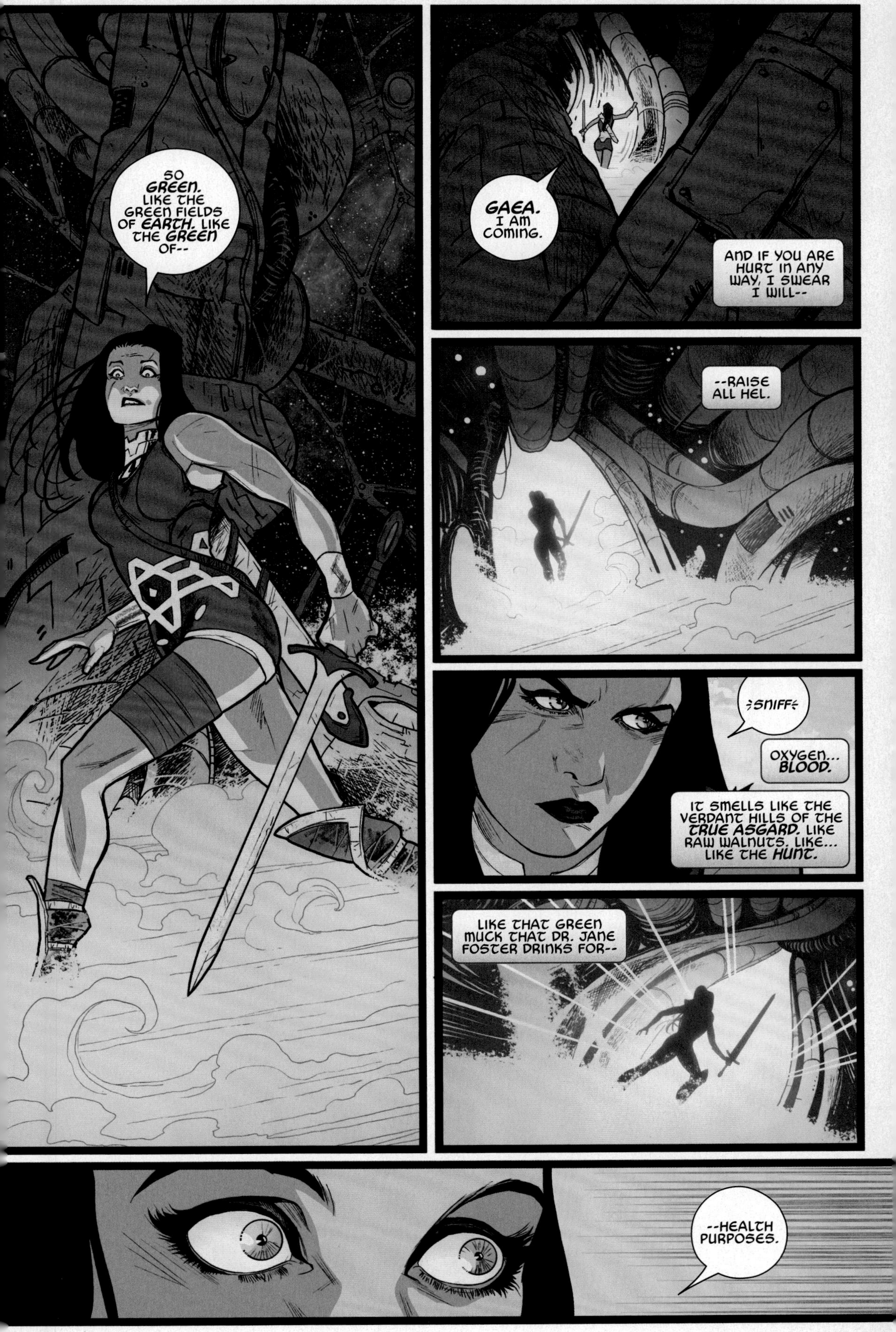

SO GREEN. LIKE THE GREEN FIELDS OF EARTH. LIKE THE GREEN OF--
GAEA. I AM COMING.
AND IF YOU ARE HURT IN ANY WAY, I SWEAR I WILL--
--RAISE ALL HEL.
SNIFF
OXYGEN... BLOOD.
IT SMELLS LIKE THE VERDANT HILLS OF THE TRUE ASGARD. LIKE RAW WALNUTS. LIKE... LIKE THE HUNT.
LIKE THAT GREEN MUCK THAT DR. JANE FOSTER DRINKS FOR--
--HEALTH PURPOSES.

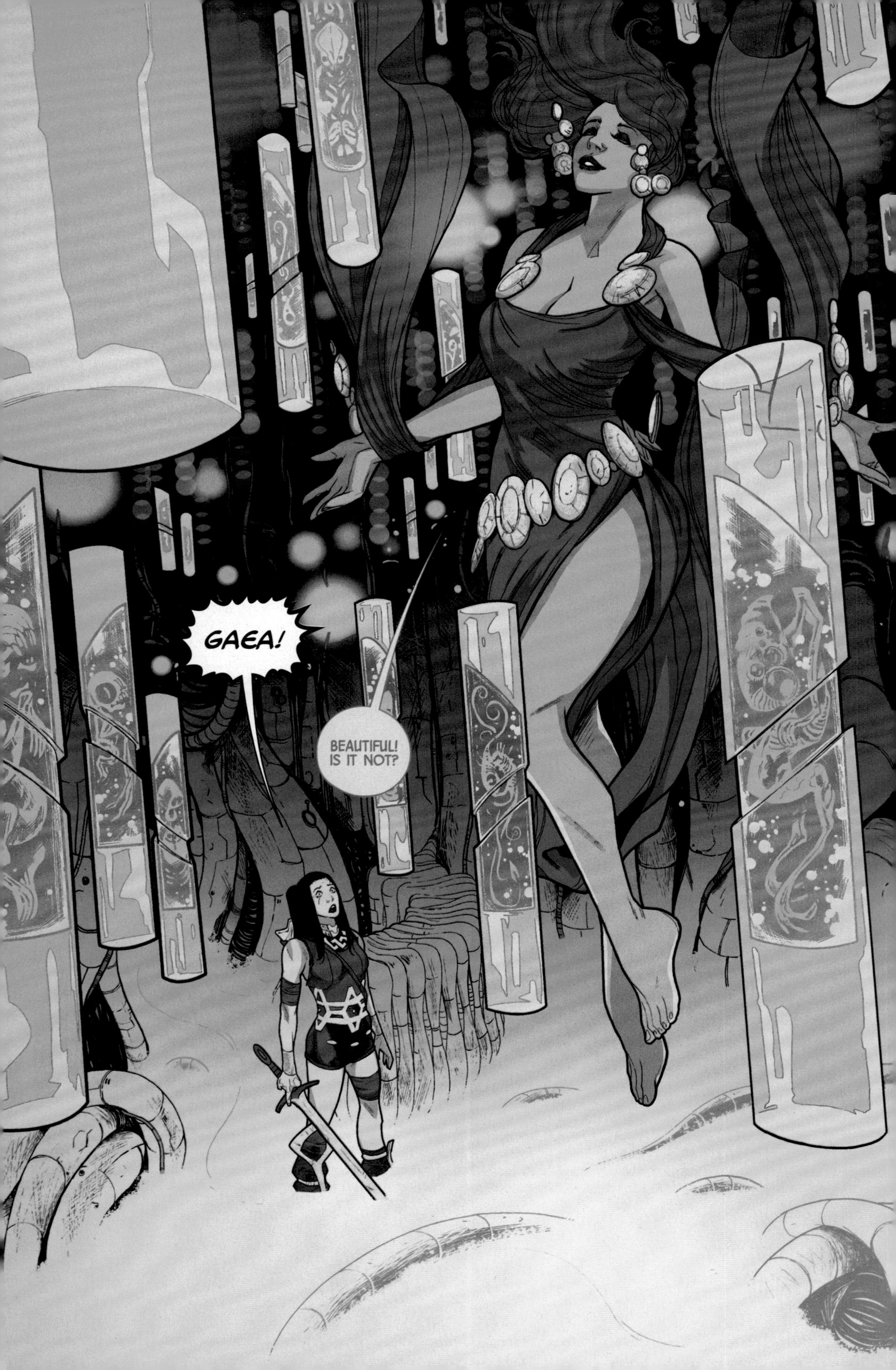
GAEA!
BEAUTIFUL! IS IT NOT?

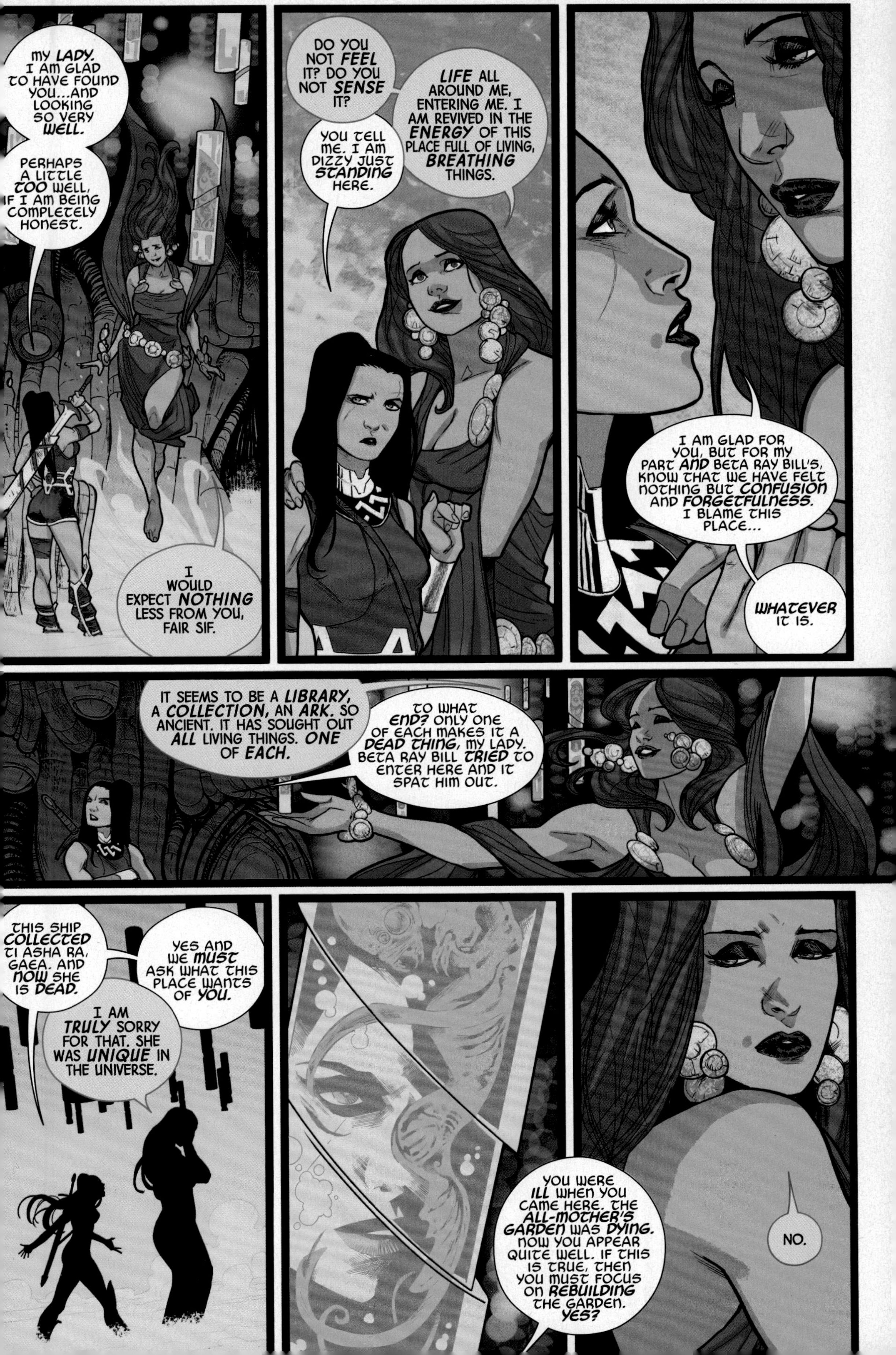
my LADY. I AM GLAD TO HAVE FOUND YOU...AND LOOKING SO VERY WELL.
PERHAPS A LITTLE TOO WELL, IF I AM BEING COMPLETELY HONEST.
I WOULD EXPECT NOTHING LESS FROM YOU, FAIR SIF.
DO YOU NOT FEEL IT? DO YOU NOT SENSE IT?
LIFE ALL AROUND ME, ENTERING ME. I AM REVIVED IN THE ENERGY OF THIS PLACE FULL OF LIVING, BREATHING THINGS.
YOU TELL ME. I AM DIZZY JUST STANDING HERE.
I AM GLAD FOR YOU, BUT FOR MY PART AND BETA RAY BILL'S, KNOW THAT WE HAVE FELT NOTHING BUT CONFUSION AND FORGETFULNESS. I BLAME THIS PLACE...
WHATEVER IT IS.
IT SEEMS TO BE A LIBRARY, A COLLECTION, AN ARK. SO ANCIENT. IT HAS SOUGHT OUT ALL LIVING THINGS. ONE OF EACH.
TO WHAT END? ONLY ONE OF EACH MAKES IT A DEAD THING, MY LADY. BETA RAY BILL TRIED TO ENTER HERE AND IT SPAT HIM OUT.
THIS SHIP COLLECTED TI ASHA RA, GAEA. AND NOW SHE IS DEAD.
YES AND WE MUST ASK WHAT THIS PLACE WANTS OF YOU.
I AM TRULY SORRY FOR THAT. SHE WAS UNIQUE IN THE UNIVERSE.
YOU WERE ILL WHEN YOU CAME HERE. THE ALL-MOTHER'S GARDEN WAS DYING. NOW YOU APPEAR QUITE WELL. IF THIS IS TRUE, THEN YOU MUST FOCUS ON REBUILDING THE GARDEN. YES?
NO.

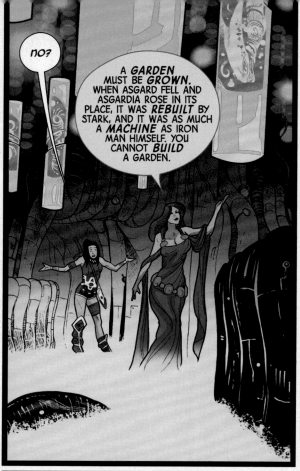

NO?

A GARDEN MUST BE GROWN. WHEN ASGARD FELL AND ASGARDIA ROSE IN ITS PLACE, IT WAS REBUILT BY STARK, AND IT WAS AS MUCH A MACHINE AS IRON MAN HIMSELF. YOU CANNOT BUILD A GARDEN.

I THINK THAT HE DID, MY LADY.

IT WAS NOT COMPLETE. SOME MICROBE IN THE LARGER ORGANISM, FORGOTTEN. WE DO NOT ALWAYS UNDERSTAND HOW INTIMATELY ALL THINGS ARE CONNECTED.

AND YOU THINK YOU WILL FIND IT HERE?

I FEEL IT.

I SEE NOTHING HERE THAT ASGARDIA IS MISSING.

HURK!

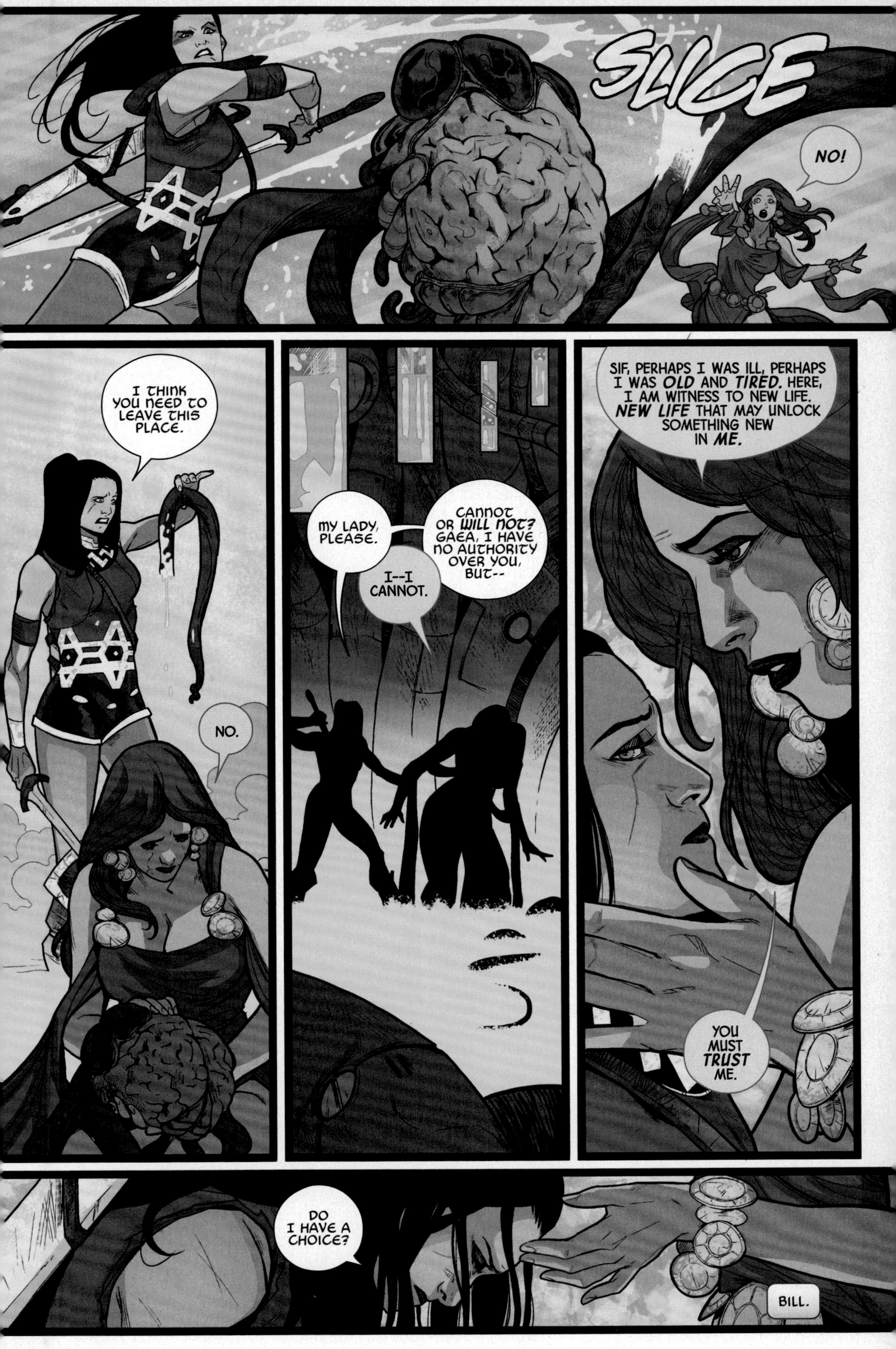
SLICE
NO!
I THINK YOU NEED TO LEAVE THIS PLACE.
NO.
MY LADY, PLEASE.
I--I CANNOT.
CANNOT OR WILL NOT? GAEA, I HAVE NO AUTHORITY OVER YOU, BUT--
SIF, PERHAPS I WAS ILL, PERHAPS I WAS OLD AND TIRED. HERE, I AM WITNESS TO NEW LIFE. NEW LIFE THAT MAY UNLOCK SOMETHING NEW IN ME.
YOU MUST TRUST ME.
DO I HAVE A CHOICE?
BILL.

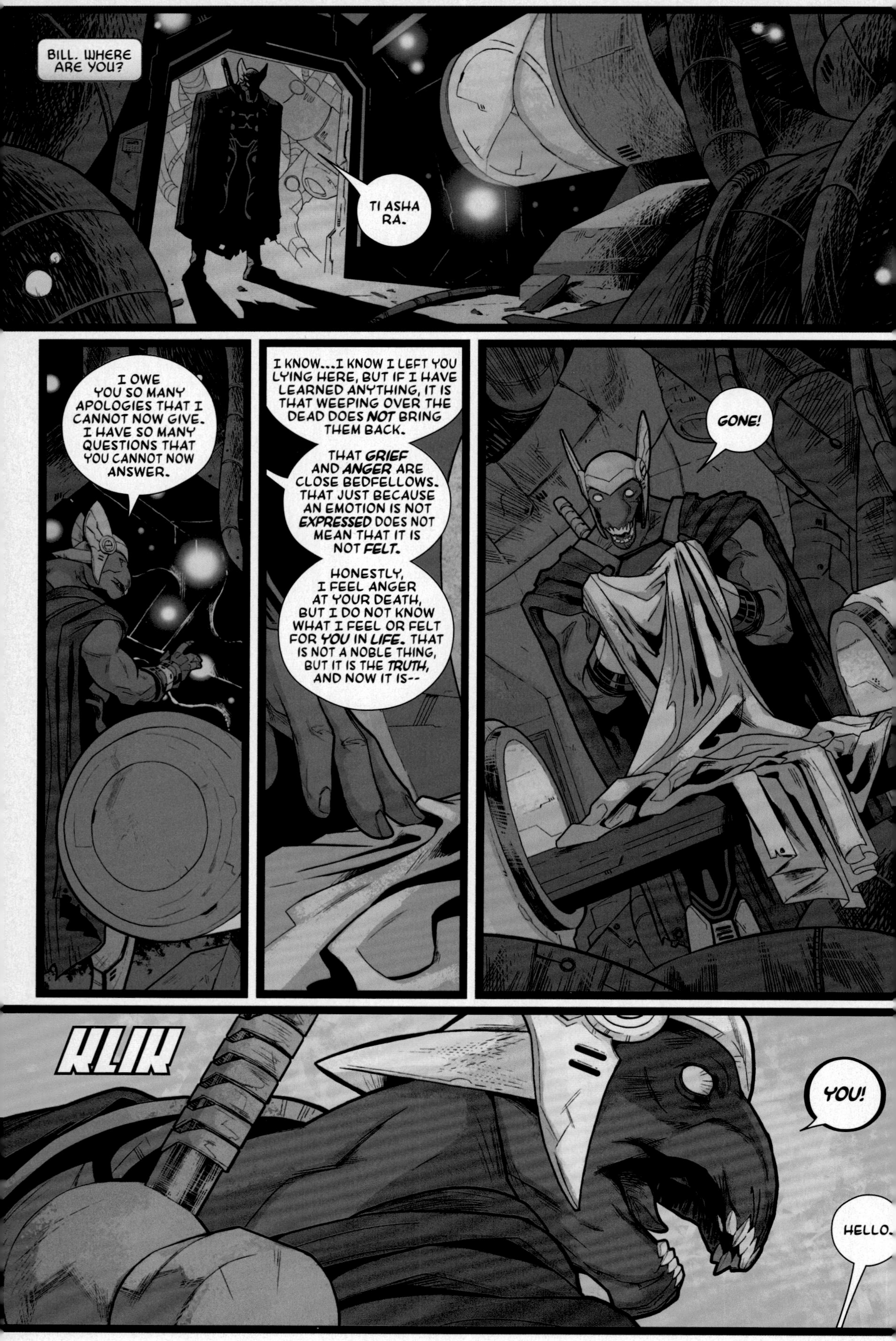
BILL. WHERE ARE YOU?
TI ASHA RA.
I OWE YOU SO MANY APOLOGIES THAT I CANNOT NOW GIVE. I HAVE SO MANY QUESTIONS THAT YOU CANNOT NOW ANSWER.
I KNOW...I KNOW I LEFT YOU LYING HERE, BUT IF I HAVE LEARNED ANYTHING, IT IS THAT WEEPING OVER THE DEAD DOES NOT BRING THEM BACK.
THAT GRIEF AND ANGER ARE CLOSE BEDFELLOWS. THAT JUST BECAUSE AN EMOTION IS NOT EXPRESSED DOES NOT MEAN THAT IT IS NOT FELT.
HONESTLY, I FEEL ANGER AT YOUR DEATH, BUT I DO NOT KNOW WHAT I FEEL OR FELT FOR YOU IN LIFE. THAT IS NOT A NOBLE THING, BUT IT IS THE TRUTH, AND NOW IT IS--
GONE!
KLIK
YOU!
HELLO.

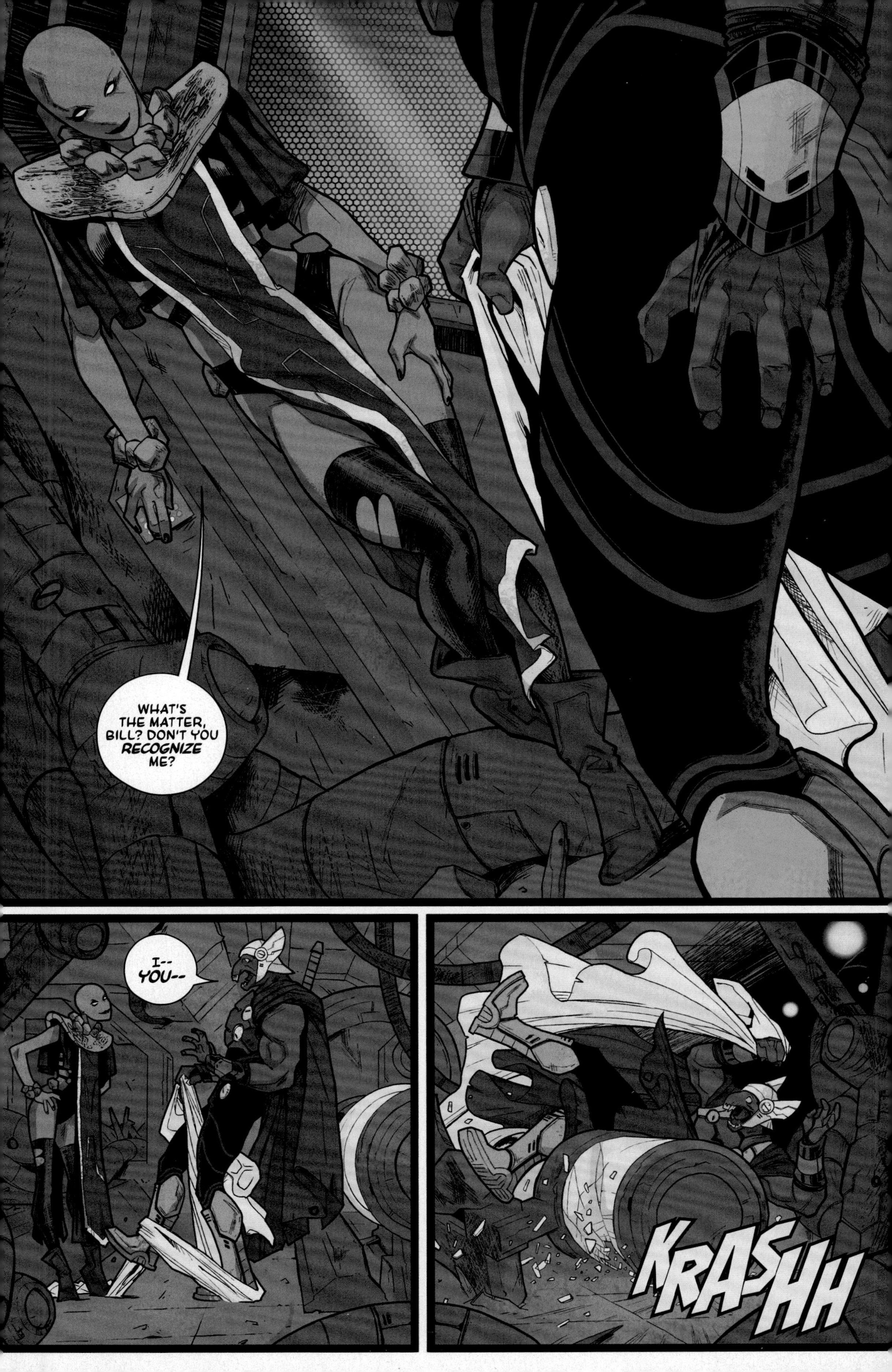
WHAT'S THE MATTER, BILL? DON'T YOU RECOGNIZE ME?
I-- YOU--
KRASHH

DO *NOT* TOUCH ME, WHATEVER YOU ARE.

YOU ALWAYS WERE A *STUBBORN LONER*, BILL. IT'S A MIRACLE WE'VE BEEN FRIENDS THIS LONG. IS THAT WHY YOU TRIED TO KILL ME?

WHAT?! I NEVER--

I KNOW WHY YOU LOOK SO *GUILTY*. YOU NEVER DID SAY *HELLO* TO *SIF*, LIKE I *ASKED* YOU TO, DID YOU?

SKUTTLEBUTT?

TA DAA.

HOW CAN YOU FIND THIS *AMUSING?*

FOR THE MOMENT, WHAT *ELSE* CAN I *DO?!*

ALL RIGHT, BIG FELLA. ALL RIGHT.

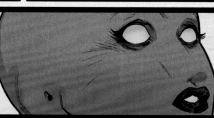

DO *NOT* MOVE.

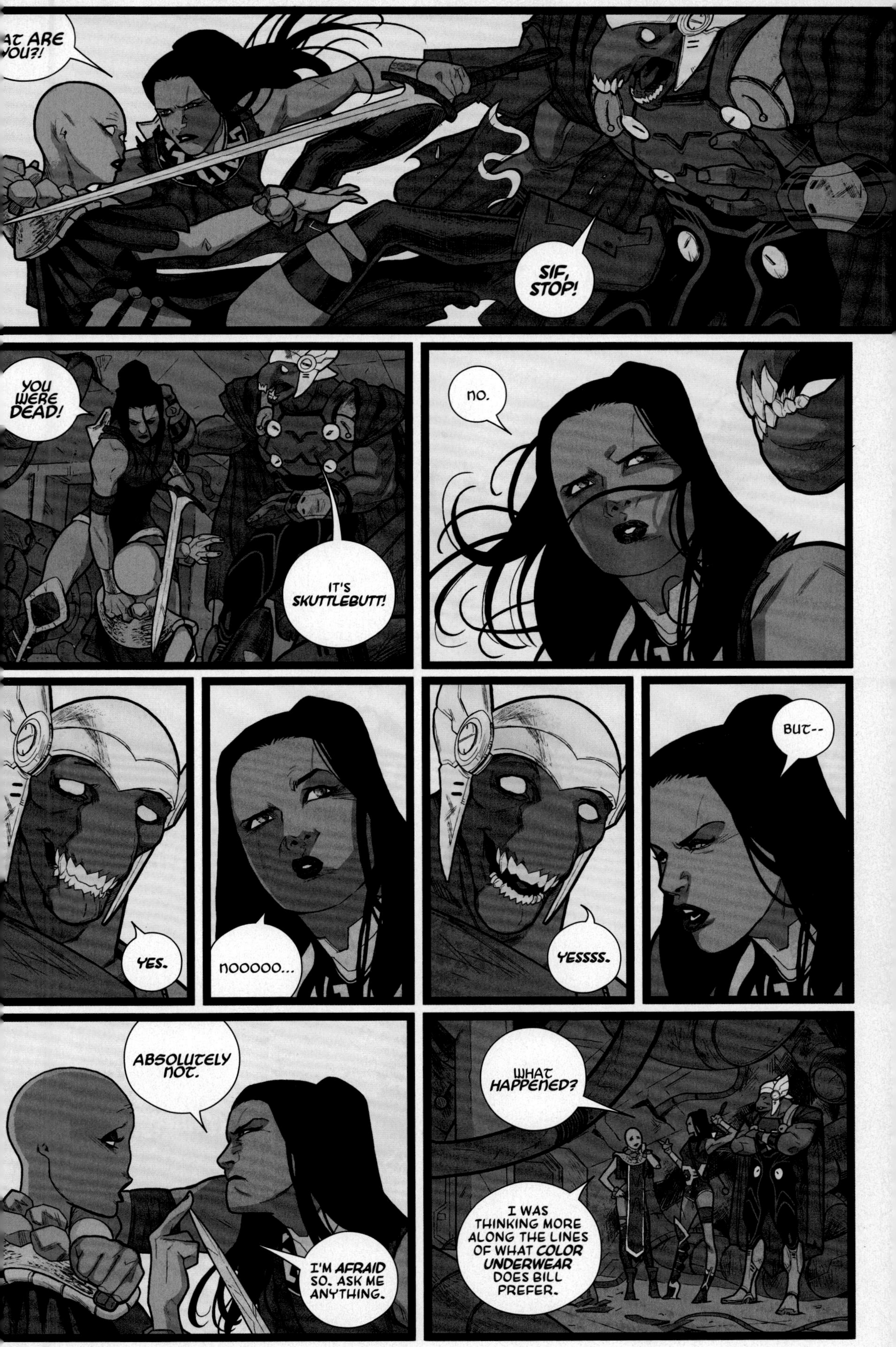
AT ARE YOU?!
SIF, STOP!
YOU WERE DEAD!
IT'S SKUTTLEBUTT!
no.
YES.
nooooo...
YESSSS.
BUT--
ABSOLUTELY NOT.
I'M AFRAID SO. ASK ME ANYTHING.
WHAT HAPPENED?
I WAS THINKING MORE ALONG THE LINES OF WHAT COLOR UNDERWEAR DOES BILL PREFER.

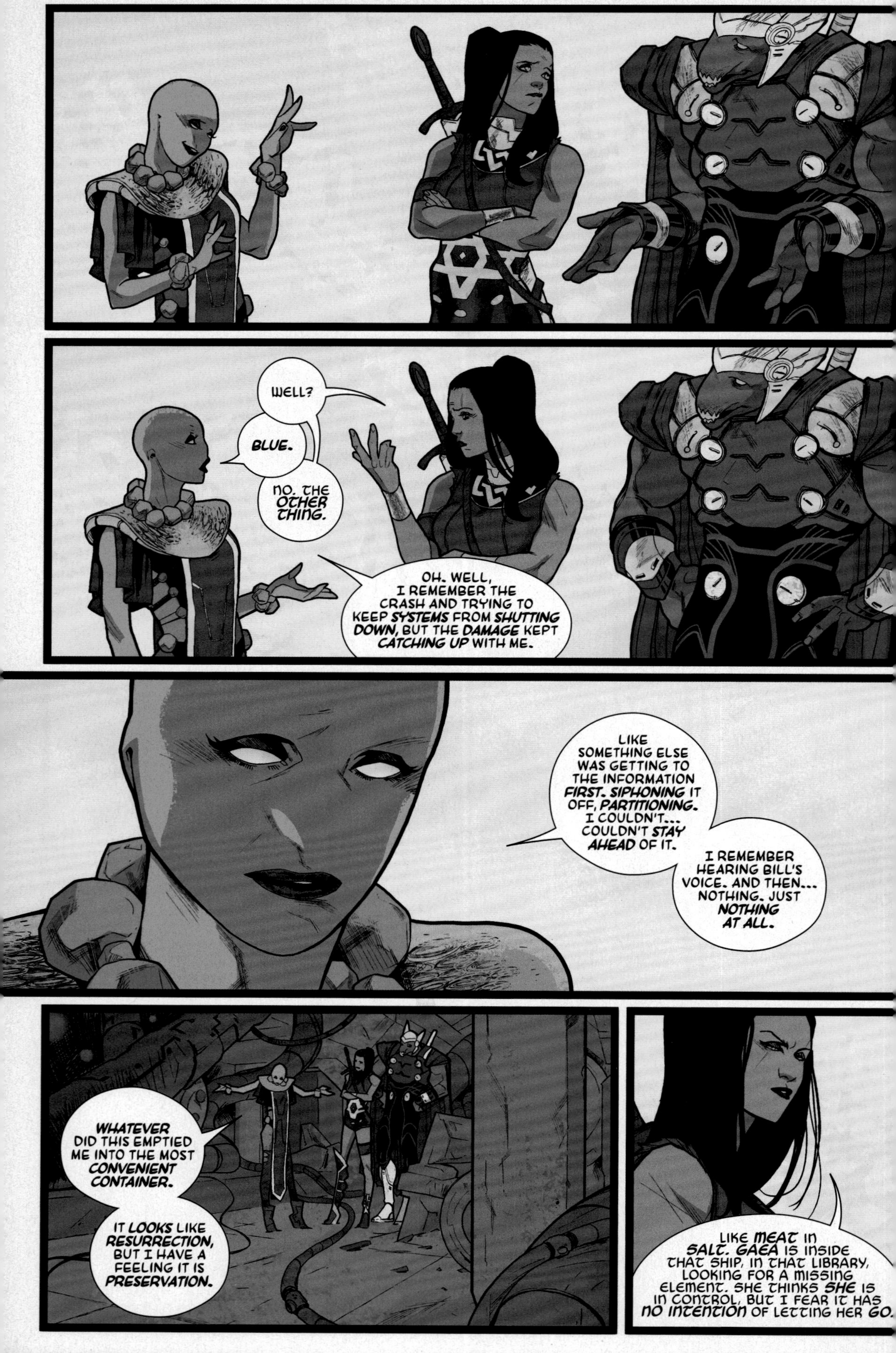

WELL?
BLUE.
NO. THE OTHER THING.
OH. WELL, I REMEMBER THE CRASH AND TRYING TO KEEP SYSTEMS FROM SHUTTING DOWN, BUT THE DAMAGE KEPT CATCHING UP WITH ME.
LIKE SOMETHING ELSE WAS GETTING TO THE INFORMATION FIRST. SIPHONING IT OFF, PARTITIONING. I COULDN'T... COULDN'T STAY AHEAD OF IT.
I REMEMBER HEARING BILL'S VOICE. AND THEN... NOTHING. JUST NOTHING AT ALL.
WHATEVER DID THIS EMPTIED ME INTO THE MOST CONVENIENT CONTAINER.
IT LOOKS LIKE RESURRECTION, BUT I HAVE A FEELING IT IS PRESERVATION.
LIKE MEAT IN SALT. GAEA IS INSIDE THAT SHIP, IN THAT LIBRARY, LOOKING FOR A MISSING ELEMENT. SHE THINKS SHE IS IN CONTROL, BUT I FEAR IT HAS NO INTENTION OF LETTING HER GO.

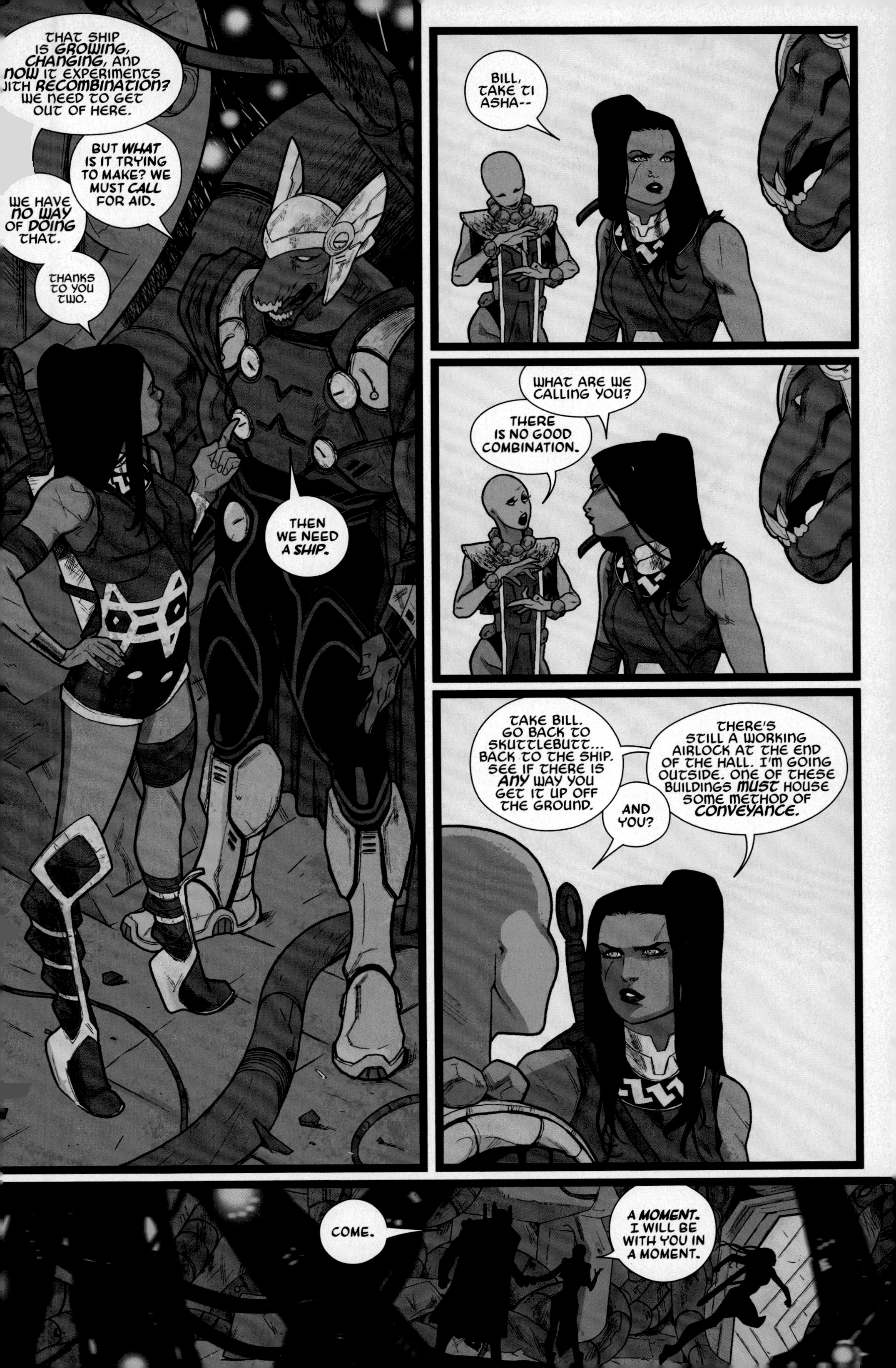
THAT SHIP IS GROWING, CHANGING, AND NOW IT EXPERIMENTS WITH RECOMBINATION? WE NEED TO GET OUT OF HERE.
BUT WHAT IS IT TRYING TO MAKE? WE MUST CALL FOR AID.
WE HAVE NO WAY OF DOING THAT.
THANKS TO YOU TWO.
THEN WE NEED A SHIP.
BILL, TAKE TI ASHA--
WHAT ARE WE CALLING YOU?
THERE IS NO GOOD COMBINATION.
TAKE BILL. GO BACK TO SKUTTLEBUTT... BACK TO THE SHIP. SEE IF THERE IS ANY WAY YOU GET IT UP OFF THE GROUND.
AND YOU?
THERE'S STILL A WORKING AIRLOCK AT THE END OF THE HALL. I'M GOING OUTSIDE. ONE OF THESE BUILDINGS MUST HOUSE SOME METHOD OF CONVEYANCE.
COME.
A MOMENT. I WILL BE WITH YOU IN A MOMENT.

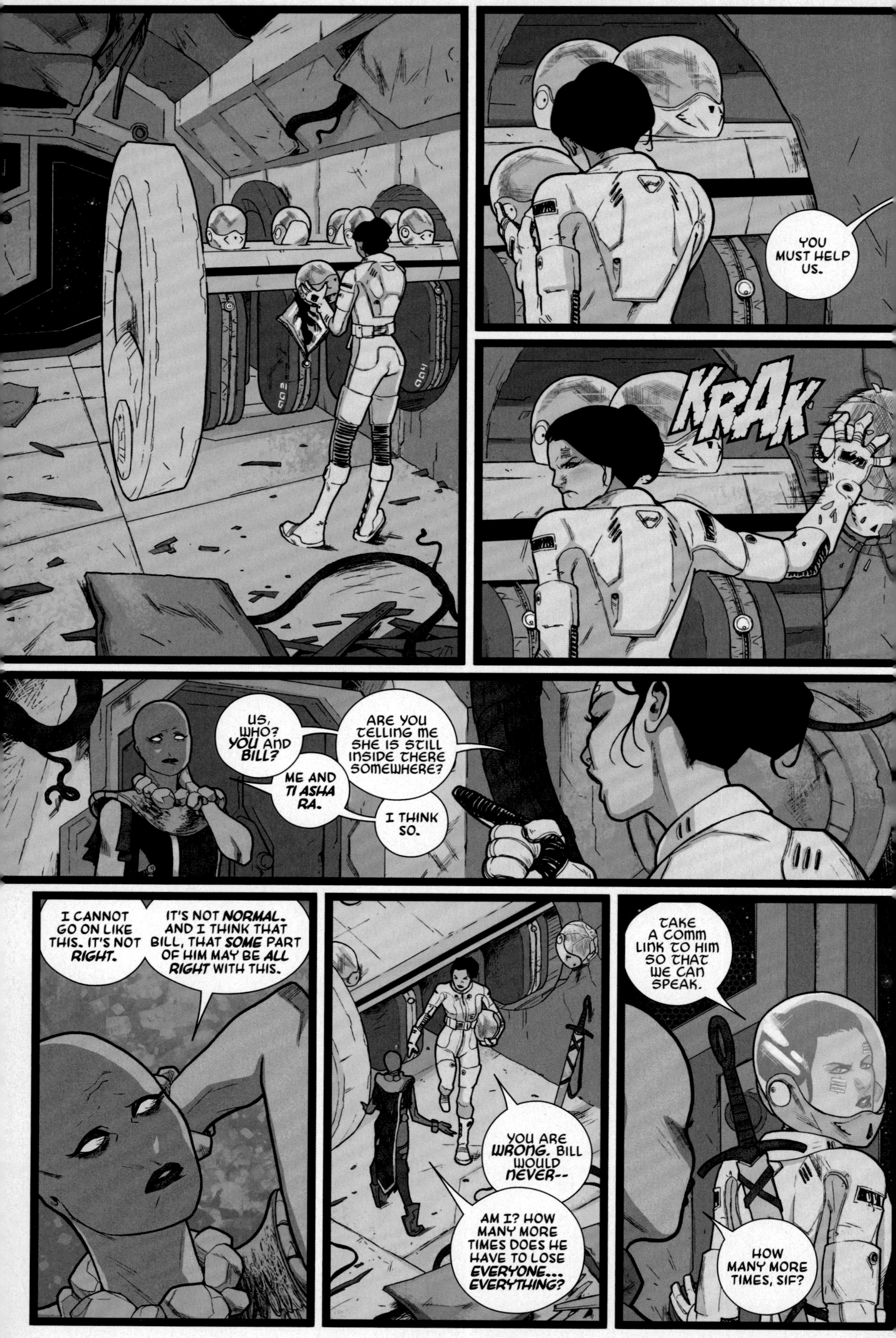
YOU MUST HELP US.
KRAK
US, WHO? YOU AND BILL?
ARE YOU TELLING ME SHE IS STILL INSIDE THERE SOMEWHERE?
ME AND TI ASHA RA.
I THINK SO.
I CANNOT GO ON LIKE THIS. IT'S NOT RIGHT.
IT'S NOT NORMAL. AND I THINK THAT BILL, THAT SOME PART OF HIM MAY BE ALL RIGHT WITH THIS.
YOU ARE WRONG. BILL WOULD NEVER--
AM I? HOW MANY MORE TIMES DOES HE HAVE TO LOSE EVERYONE... EVERYTHING?
TAKE A COMM LINK TO HIM SO THAT WE CAN SPEAK.
HOW MANY MORE TIMES, SIF?

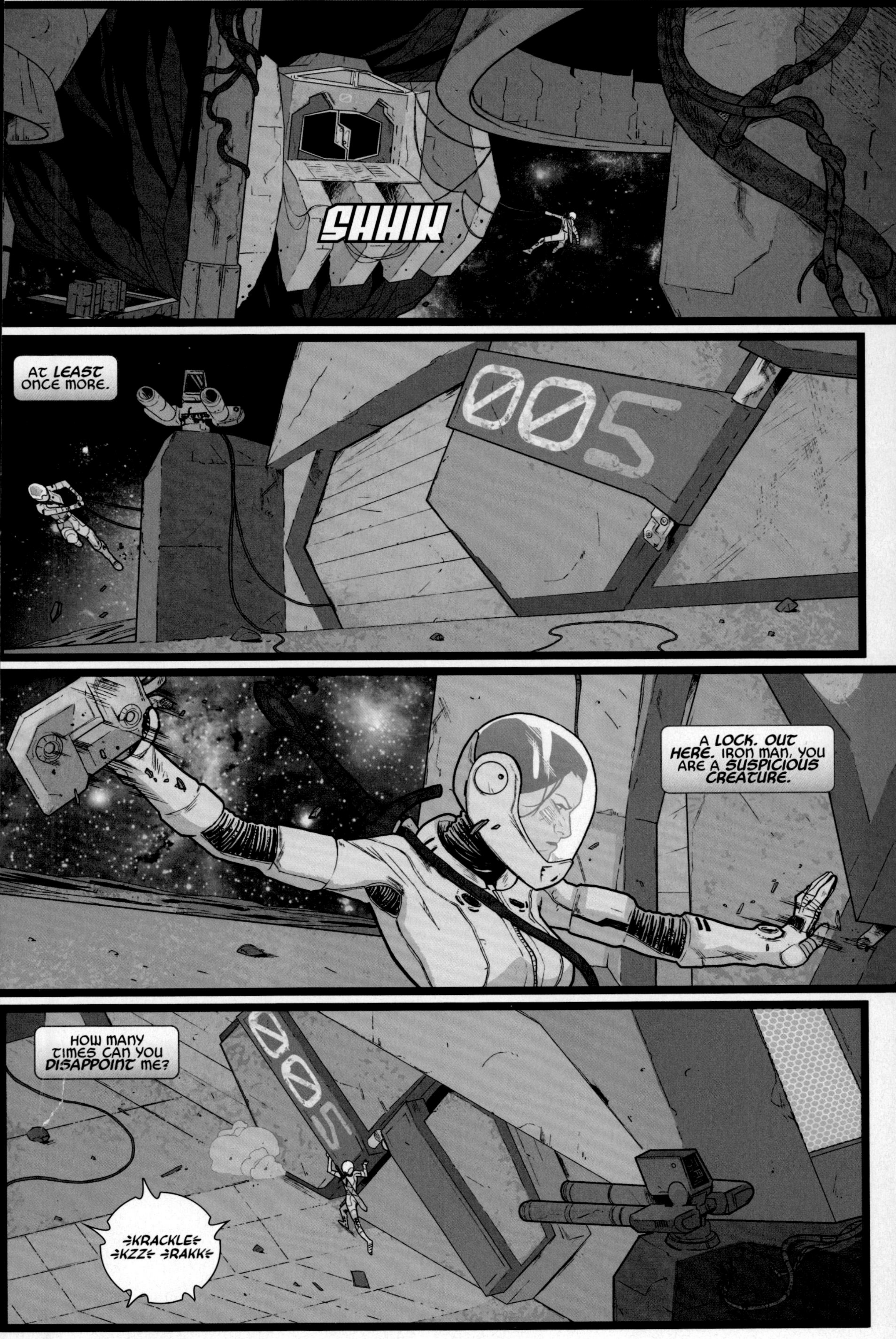
SHHIK
AT LEAST ONCE MORE.
A LOCK. OUT HERE. IRON MAN, YOU ARE A SUSPICIOUS CREATURE.
HOW MANY TIMES CAN YOU DISAPPOINT ME?
KRACKLE KZZ RAKK

AT LEAST ONCE MORE.

BILL? IS THAT YOU?

I HOPE YOU ARE HAVING BETTER FORTUNE THAN I.

N...

TELL ME AGAIN WHAT HAPPENED JUST BEFORE THE ALIEN SHIP TURNED FOR THE ASTEROID!

IT WAS APPROXIMATELY THIRTY MINUTES BEFORE YOU RECEIVED OUR HNNNHHH DISTRESS CALL!

GET OFF ME!

LIKE IT WA... LOOKING F... SOMETHING...

BUT WHAT, EXACTLY? WHAT IS THERE, HERE? ME... GAEA...WHAT ELSE?

THE GARDEN. BUT IT IS JUST A GARDEN. PLANTS. GROWING THINGS.

NO. NOT JUST A GARDEN...

ORGANIC TECHNOLOGY. OH, GODS...STA... TECHNOLOGY... BILL!

WHAT IF IT WAS LOOKING FOR A WAY TO GROW? TO USE ITS LIBRARY?

STARK

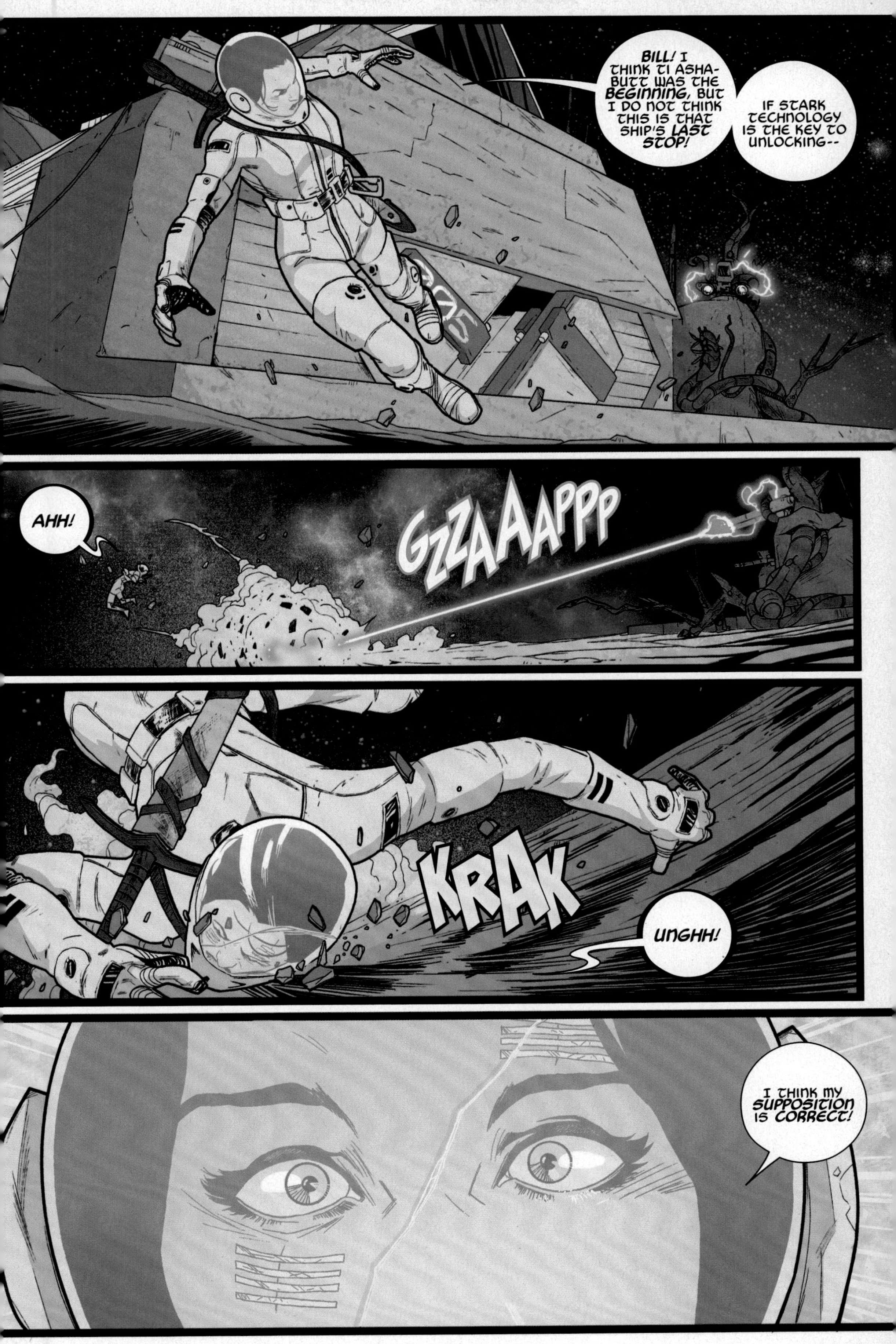

BILL! I THINK TI ASHA-BUTT WAS THE BEGINNING, BUT I DO NOT THINK THIS IS THAT SHIP'S LAST STOP!
IF STARK TECHNOLOGY IS THE KEY TO UNLOCKING--
AHH!
GZZAAAPPP
KRAK
UNGHH!
I THINK MY SUPPOSITION IS CORRECT!

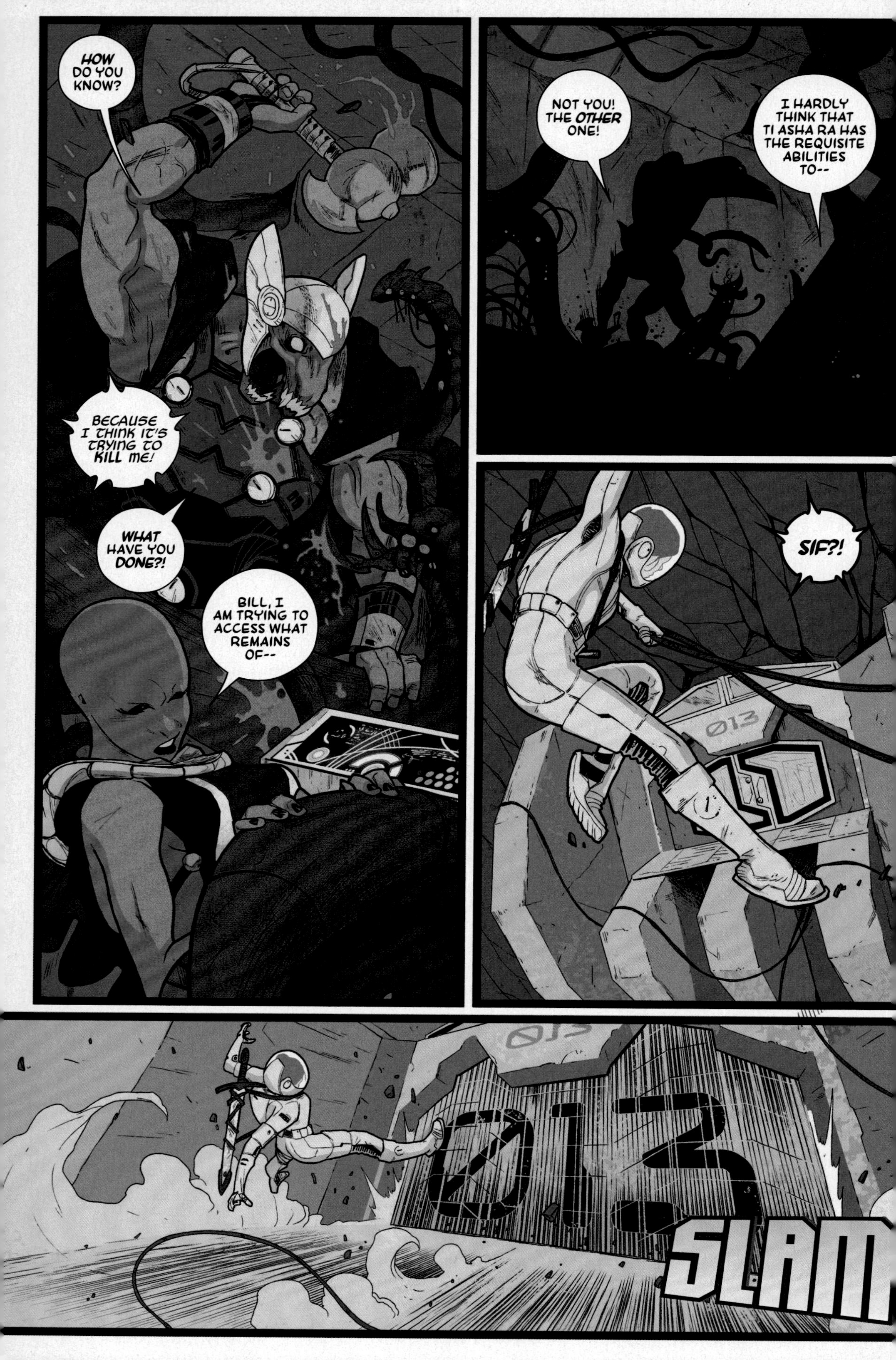
HOW DO YOU KNOW?
BECAUSE I THINK IT'S TRYING TO KILL ME!
WHAT HAVE YOU DONE?!
BILL, I AM TRYING TO ACCESS WHAT REMAINS OF--
NOT YOU! THE OTHER ONE!
I HARDLY THINK THAT TI ASHA RA HAS THE REQUISITE ABILITIES TO--
SIF?!
Ø13
Ø13
SLAM

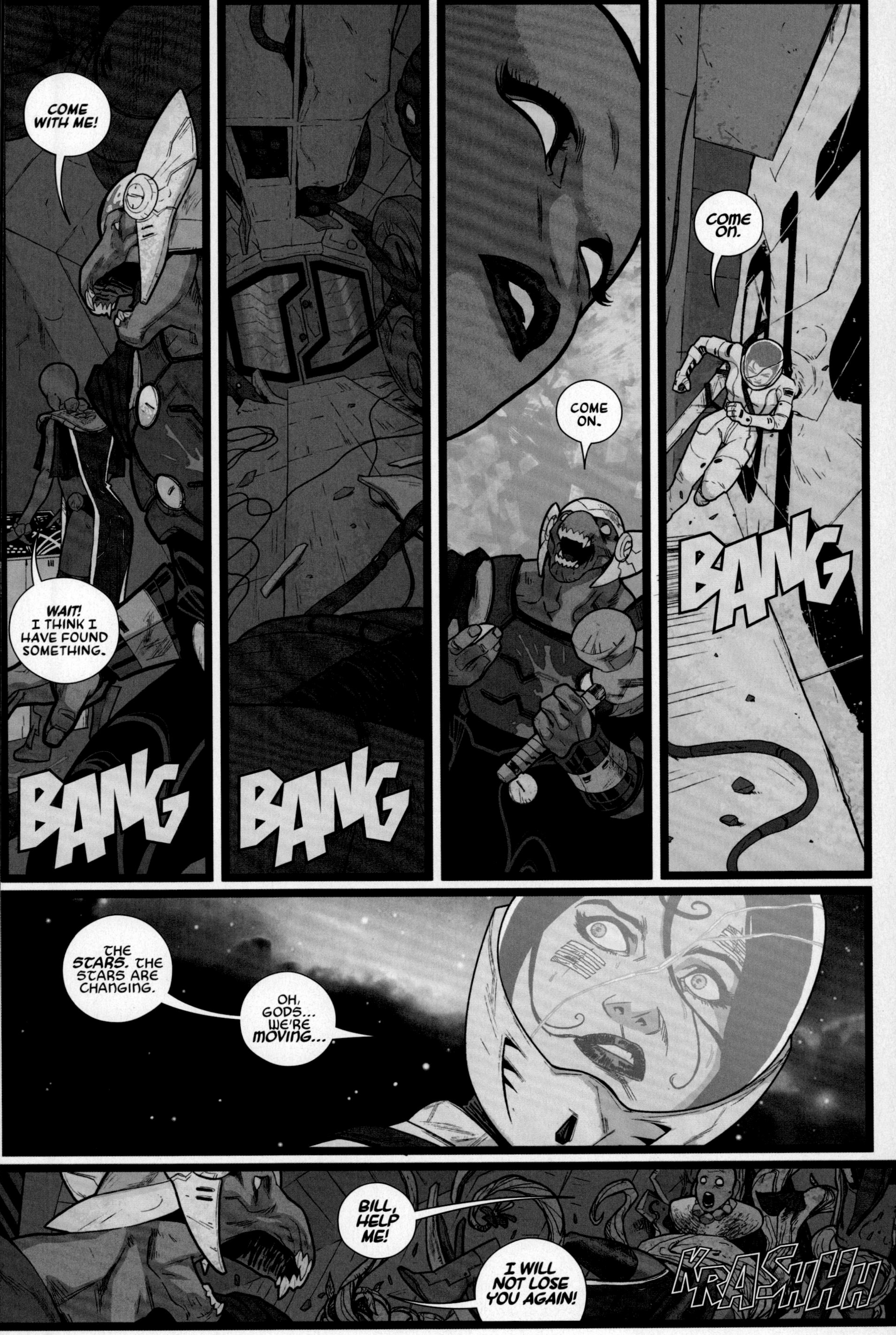
COME WITH ME!
WAIT! I THINK I HAVE FOUND SOMETHING.
BANG
BANG
COME ON.
COME ON.
BANG
THE STARS. THE STARS ARE CHANGING.
OH, GODS... WE'RE MOVING...
BILL, HELP ME!
I WILL NOT LOSE YOU AGAIN!
KRASHHH

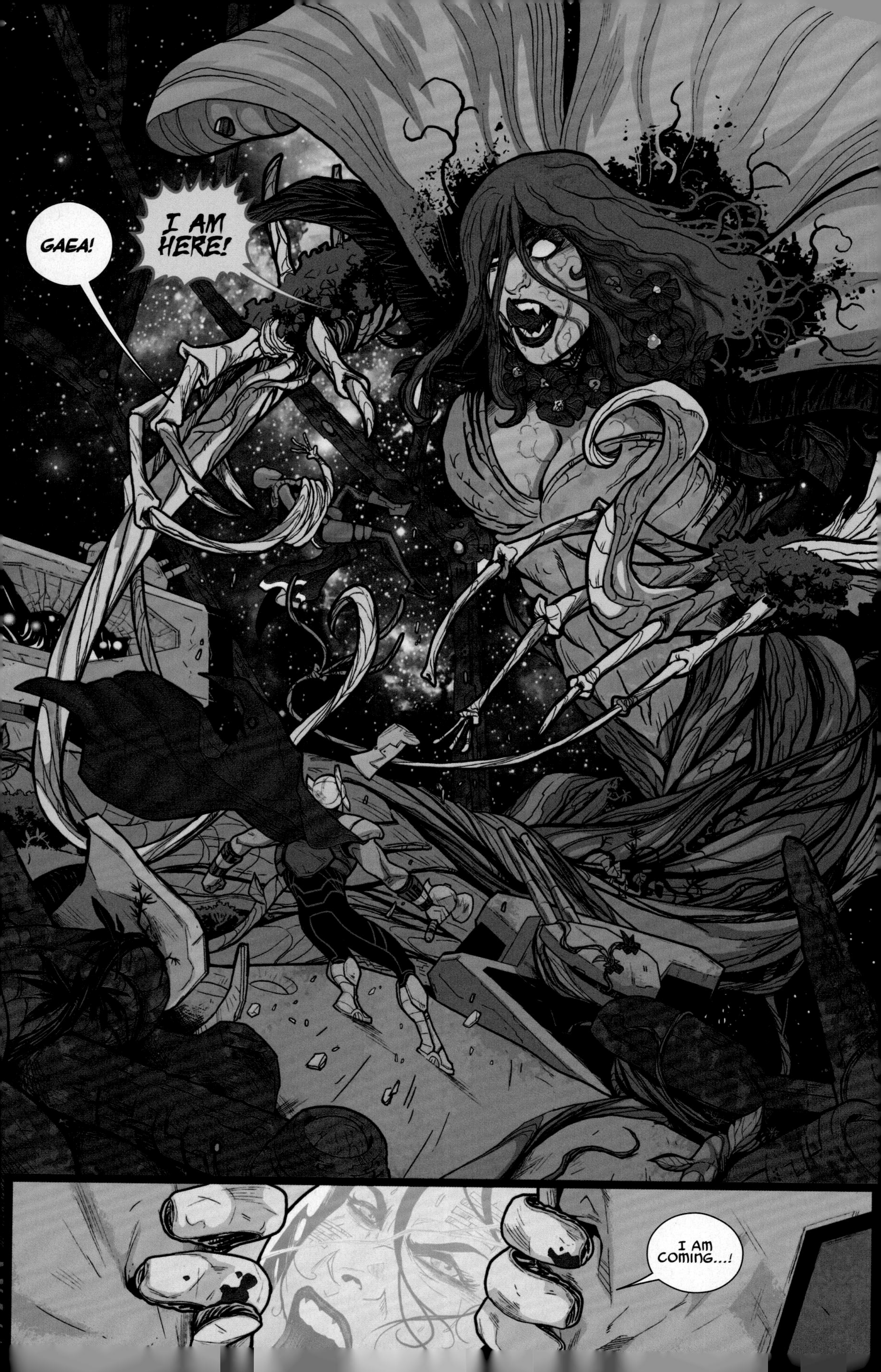
GAEA!
I AM HERE!
I AM COMING...!

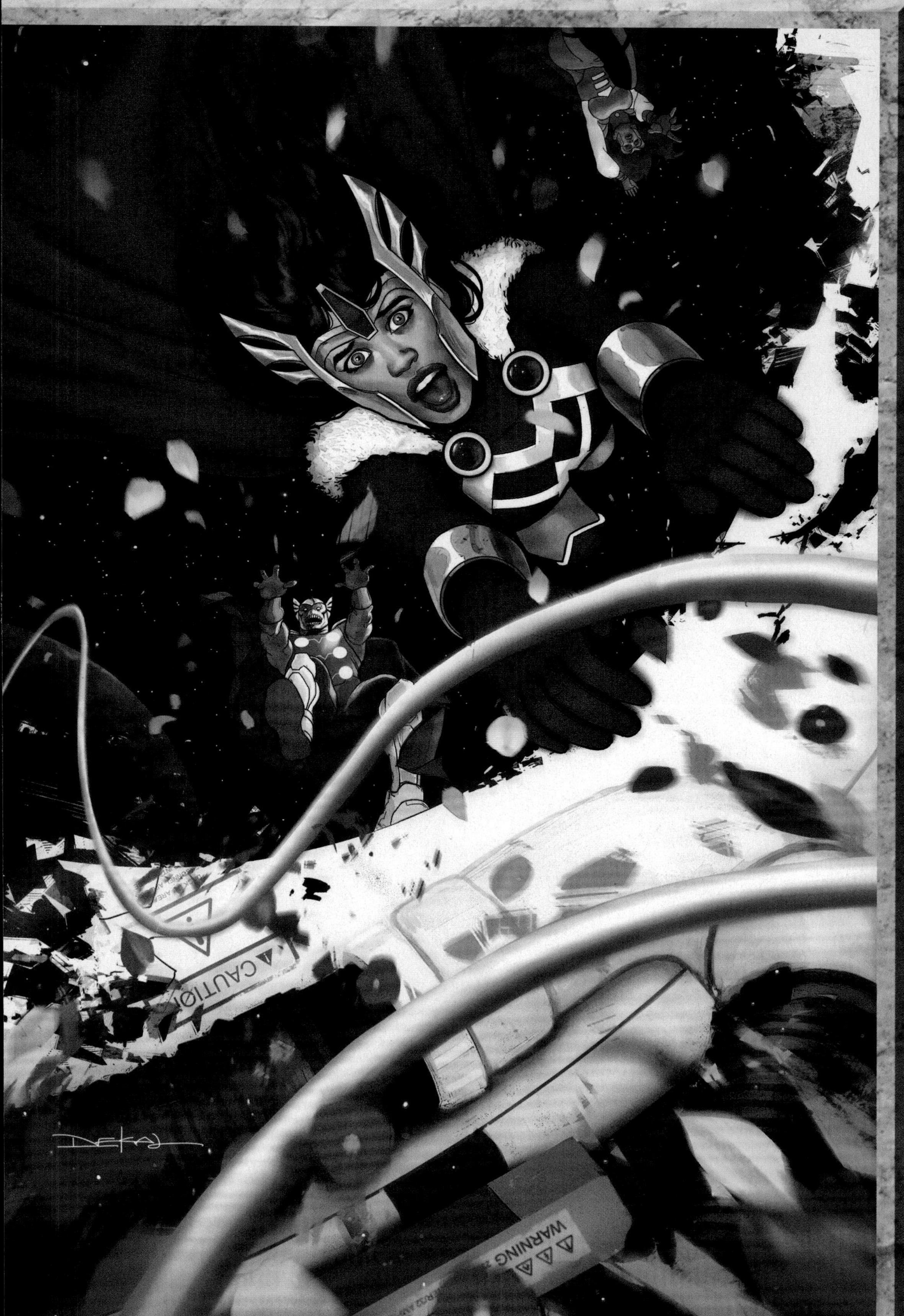
CAUTION
WARNING

#655

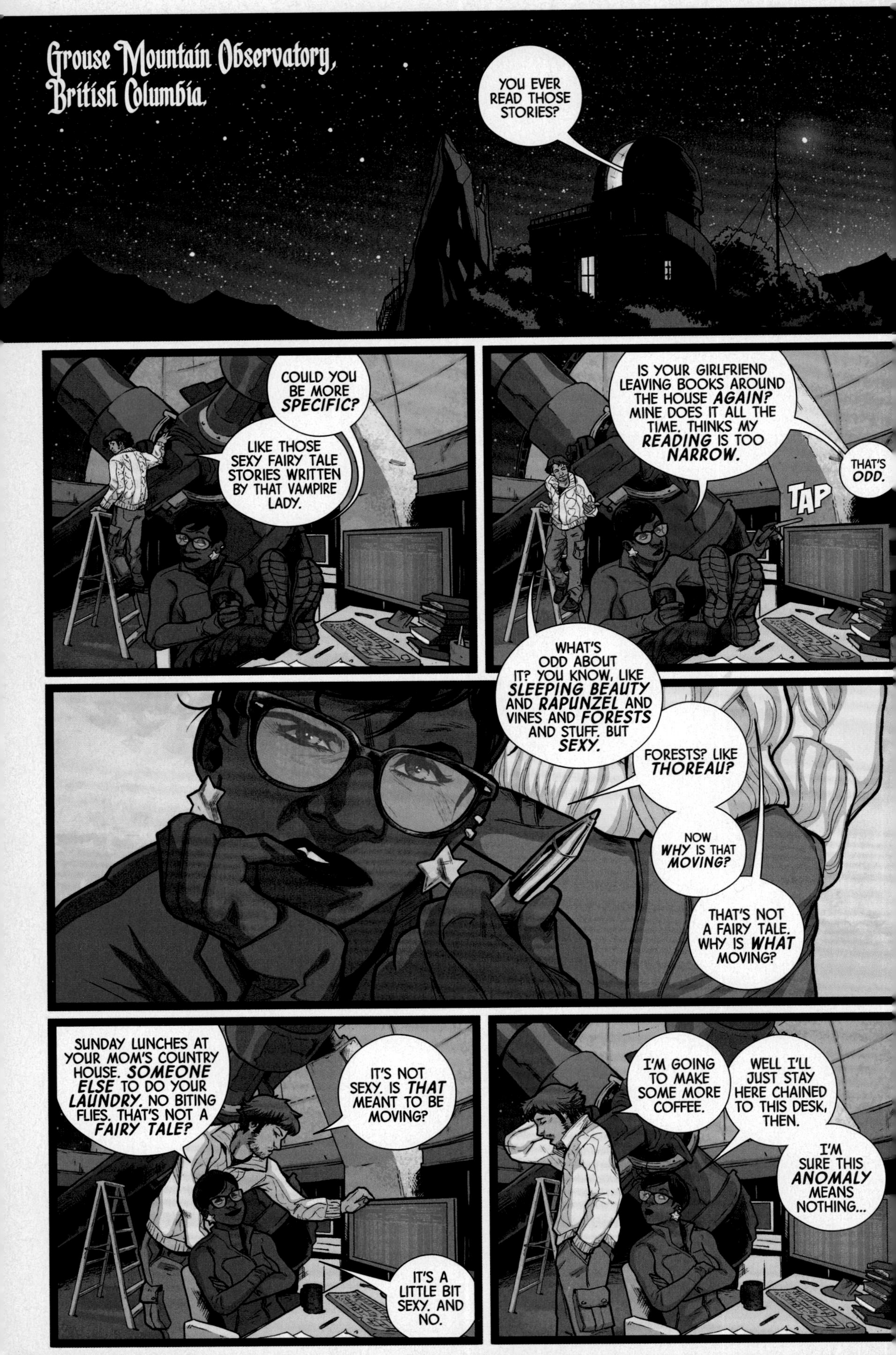
Grouse Mountain Observatory, British Columbia.
YOU EVER READ THOSE STORIES?
COULD YOU BE MORE SPECIFIC?
LIKE THOSE SEXY FAIRY TALE STORIES WRITTEN BY THAT VAMPIRE LADY.
IS YOUR GIRLFRIEND LEAVING BOOKS AROUND THE HOUSE AGAIN? MINE DOES IT ALL THE TIME. THINKS MY READING IS TOO NARROW.
TAP
THAT'S ODD.
WHAT'S ODD ABOUT IT? YOU KNOW, LIKE SLEEPING BEAUTY AND RAPUNZEL AND VINES AND FORESTS AND STUFF. BUT SEXY.
FORESTS? LIKE THOREAU?
NOW WHY IS THAT MOVING?
THAT'S NOT A FAIRY TALE. WHY IS WHAT MOVING?
SUNDAY LUNCHES AT YOUR MOM'S COUNTRY HOUSE. SOMEONE ELSE TO DO YOUR LAUNDRY. NO BITING FLIES. THAT'S NOT A FAIRY TALE?
IT'S NOT SEXY. IS THAT MEANT TO BE MOVING?
IT'S A LITTLE BIT SEXY. AND NO.
I'M GOING TO MAKE SOME MORE COFFEE.
WELL I'LL JUST STAY HERE CHAINED TO THIS DESK, THEN.
I'M SURE THIS ANOMALY MEANS NOTHING...

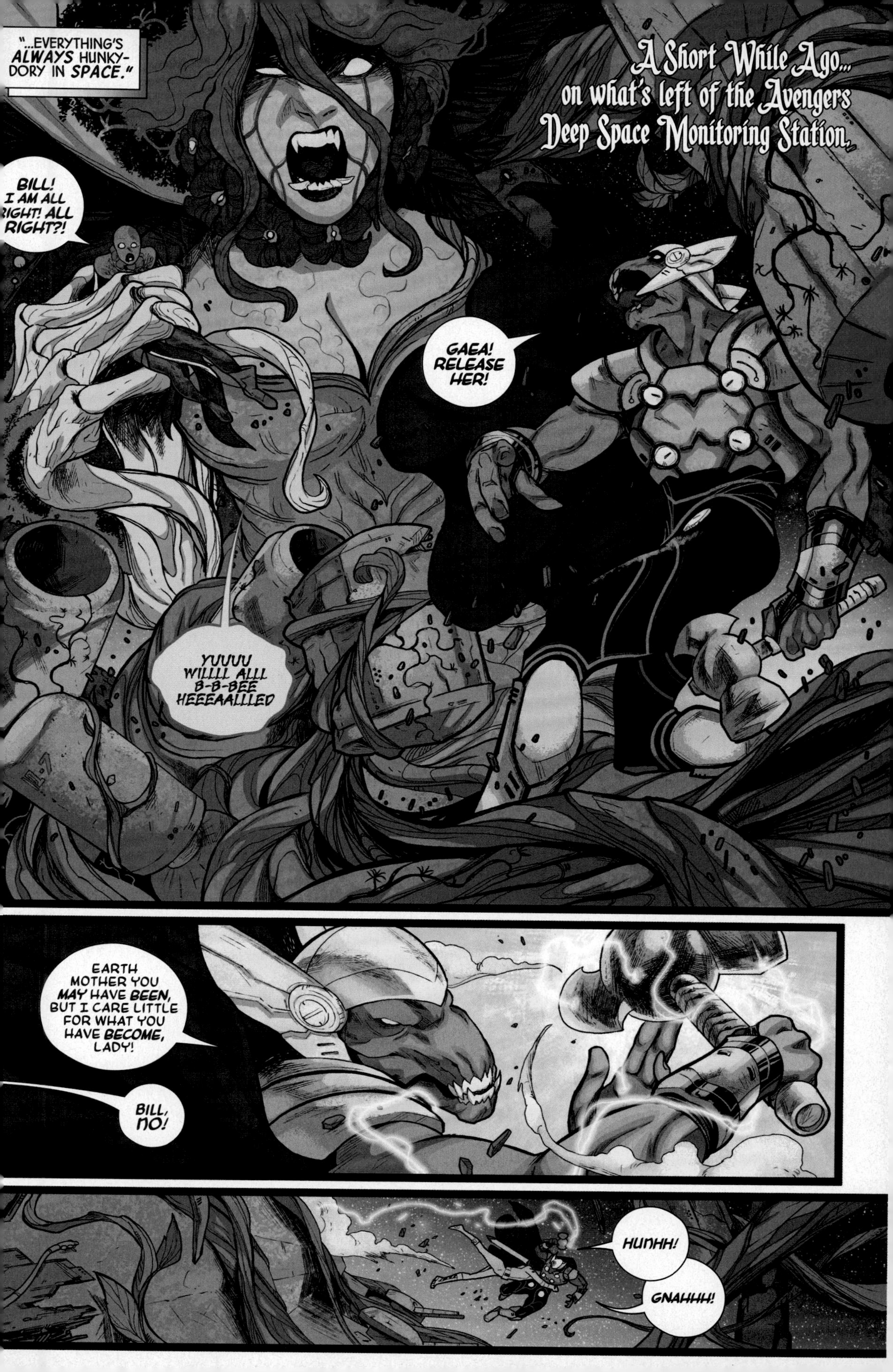
"...EVERYTHING'S ALWAYS HUNKY-DORY IN SPACE."
A Short While Ago... on what's left of the Avengers Deep Space Monitoring Station,
BILL! I AM ALL RIGHT! ALL RIGHT?!
GAEA! RELEASE HER!
YUUUU WILLLL ALLL B-B-BEE HEEEAALLLED
EARTH MOTHER YOU MAY HAVE BEEN, BUT I CARE LITTLE FOR WHAT YOU HAVE BECOME, LADY!
BILL, NO!
HUNHH!
GNAHHH!

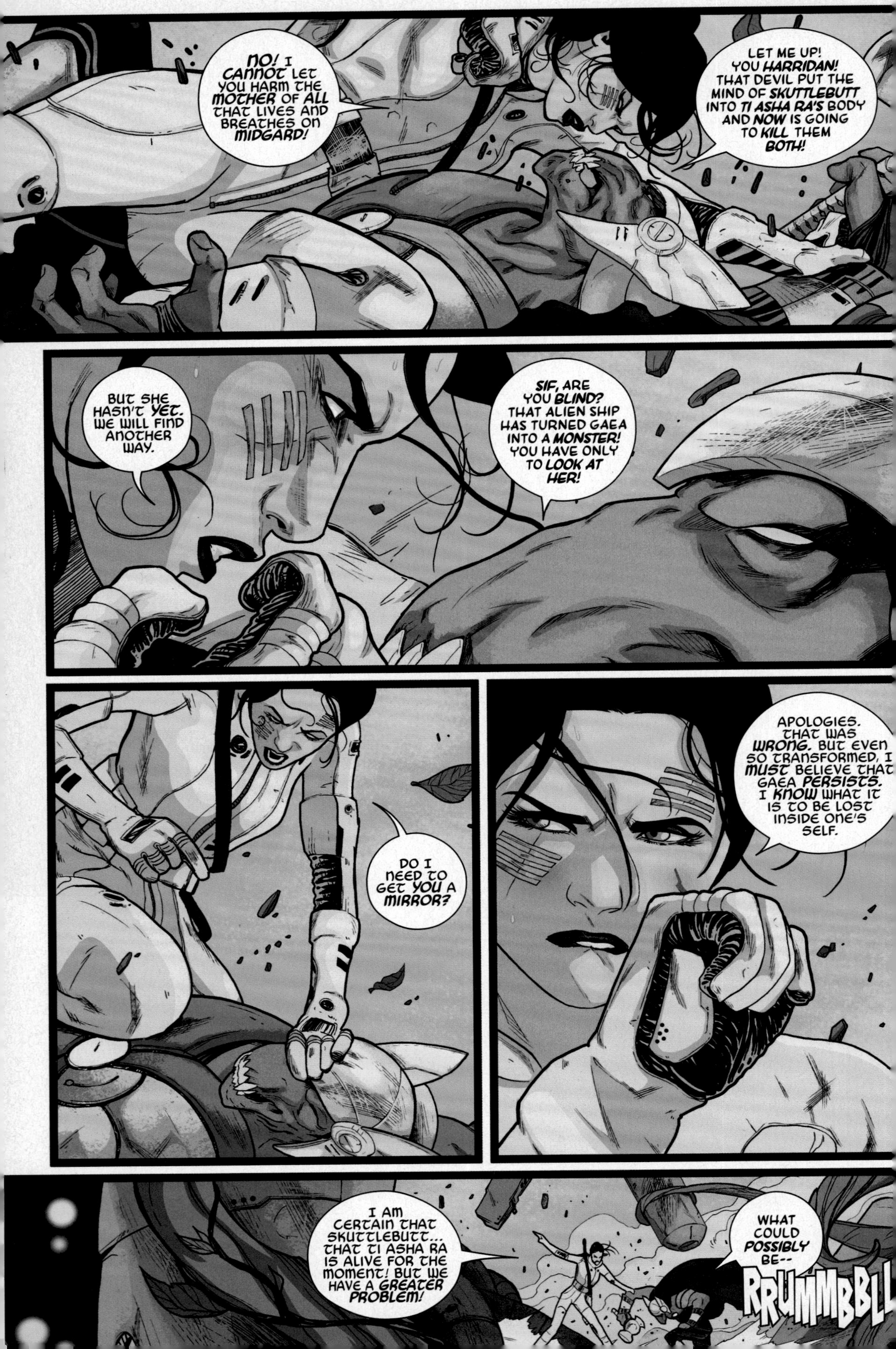
NO! I CANNOT LET YOU HARM THE MOTHER OF ALL THAT LIVES AND BREATHES ON MIDGARD!
LET ME UP! YOU HARRIDAN! THAT DEVIL PUT THE MIND OF SKUTTLEBUTT INTO TI ASHA RA'S BODY AND NOW IS GOING TO KILL THEM BOTH!
BUT SHE HASN'T YET. WE WILL FIND ANOTHER WAY.
SIF, ARE YOU BLIND? THAT ALIEN SHIP HAS TURNED GAEA INTO A MONSTER! YOU HAVE ONLY TO LOOK AT HER!
DO I NEED TO GET YOU A MIRROR?
APOLOGIES. THAT WAS WRONG. BUT EVEN SO TRANSFORMED, I MUST BELIEVE THAT GAEA PERSISTS. I KNOW WHAT IT IS TO BE LOST INSIDE ONE'S SELF.
I AM CERTAIN THAT SKUTTLEBUTT... THAT TI ASHA RA IS ALIVE FOR THE MOMENT! BUT WE HAVE A GREATER PROBLEM!
WHAT COULD POSSIBLY BE--
RRUMMBBLL

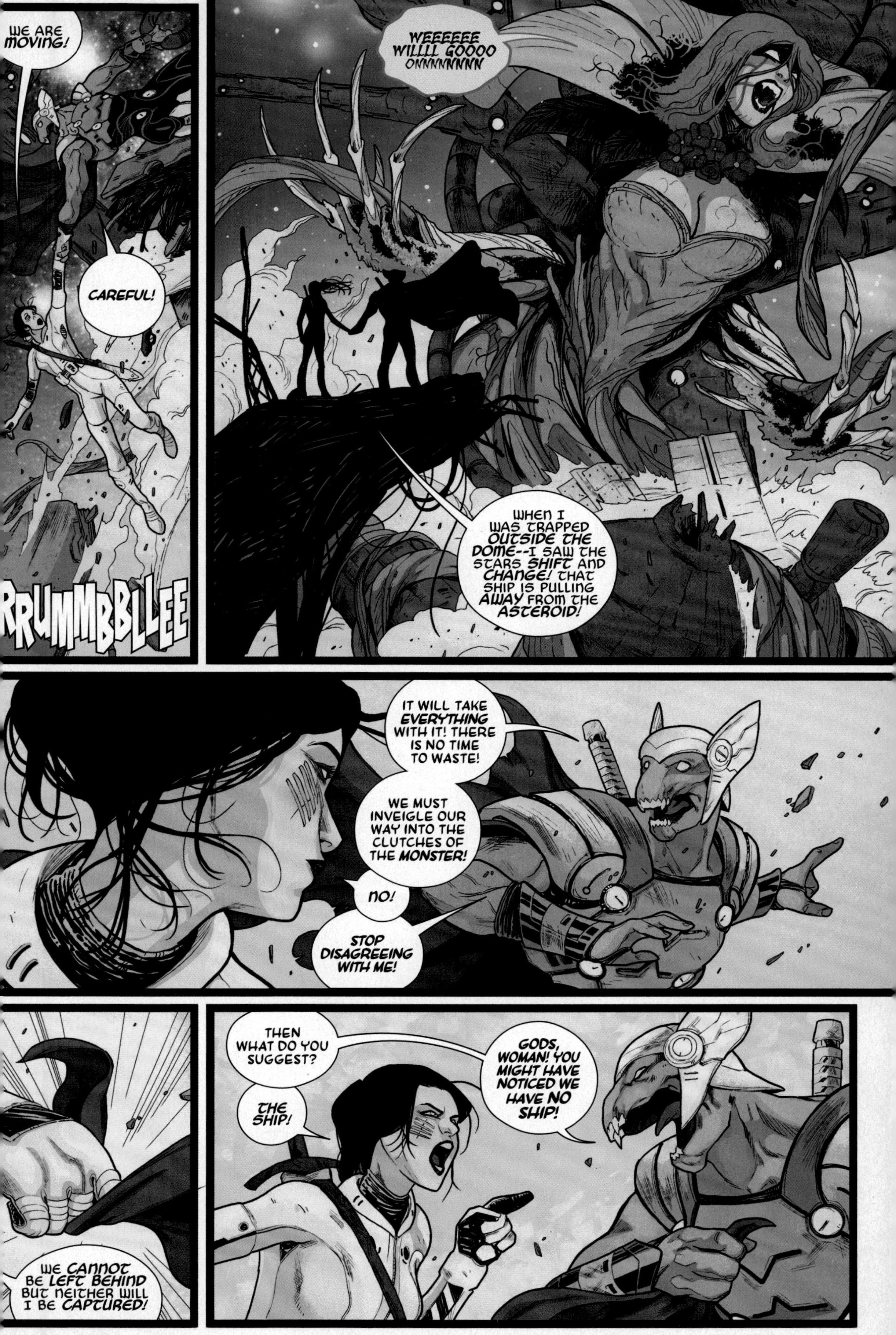

WE ARE MOVING!
CAREFUL!
RRUMMBBLLEE
WEEEEEE WILLLL GOOOO ONNNNNNN
WHEN I WAS TRAPPED OUTSIDE THE DOME--I SAW THE STARS SHIFT AND CHANGE! THAT SHIP IS PULLING AWAY FROM THE ASTEROID!
IT WILL TAKE EVERYTHING WITH IT! THERE IS NO TIME TO WASTE!
WE MUST INVEIGLE OUR WAY INTO THE CLUTCHES OF THE MONSTER!
NO!
STOP DISAGREEING WITH ME!
WE CANNOT BE LEFT BEHIND BUT NEITHER WILL I BE CAPTURED!
THEN WHAT DO YOU SUGGEST?
THE SHIP!
GODS, WOMAN! YOU MIGHT HAVE NOTICED WE HAVE NO SHIP!

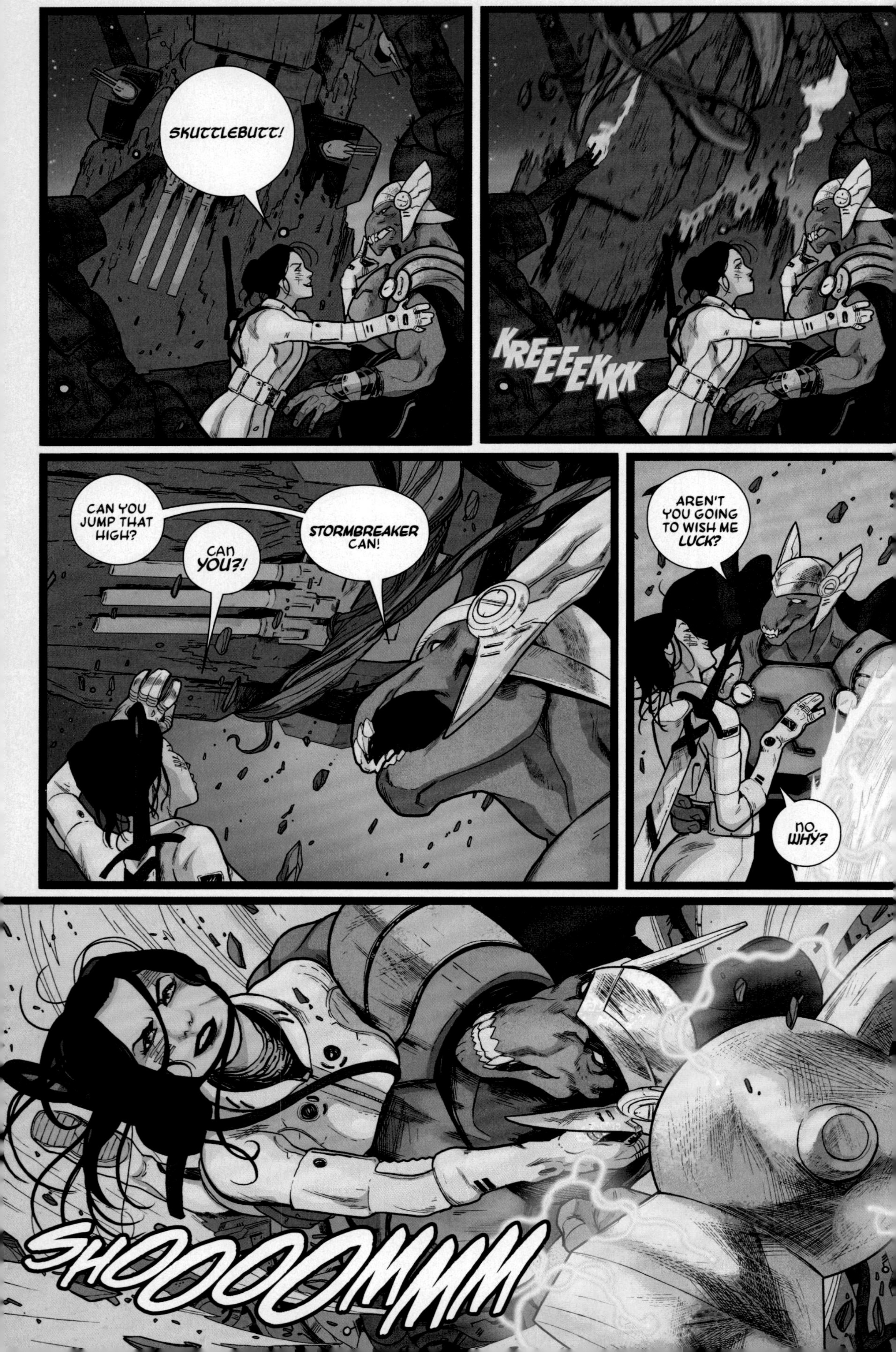
SKUTTLEBUTT!
KREEEEKKK
CAN YOU JUMP THAT HIGH?
STORMBREAKER CAN!
CAN YOU?!
AREN'T YOU GOING TO WISH ME LUCK?
NO. WHY?
SHOOOOMMM

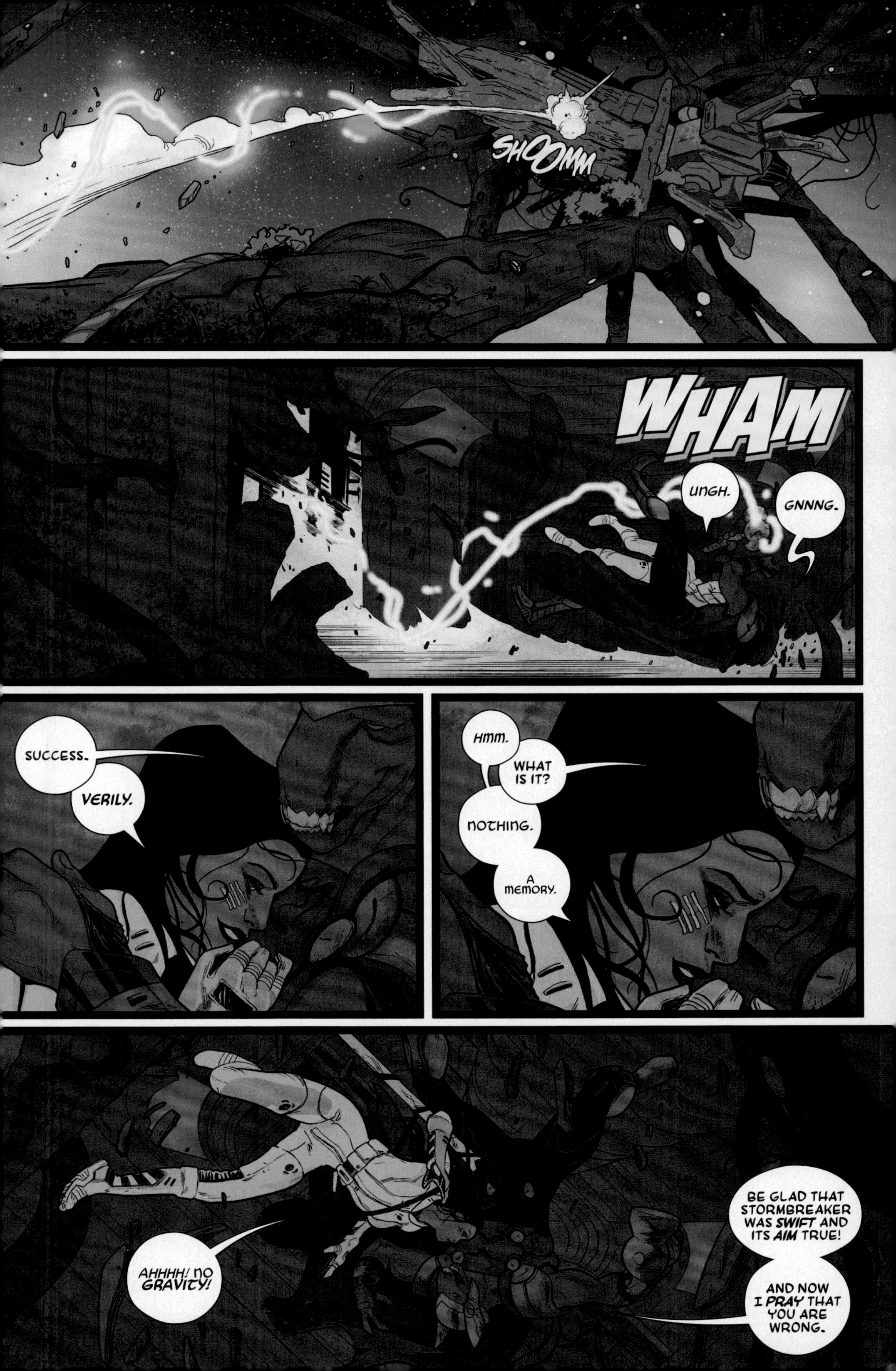
SHOOMM
WHAM
UNGH.
GNNNG.
SUCCESS.
VERILY.
HMM.
WHAT IS IT?
NOTHING.
A MEMORY.
BE GLAD THAT STORMBREAKER WAS SWIFT AND ITS AIM TRUE!
AHHHH! NO GRAVITY!
AND NOW I PRAY THAT YOU ARE WRONG.

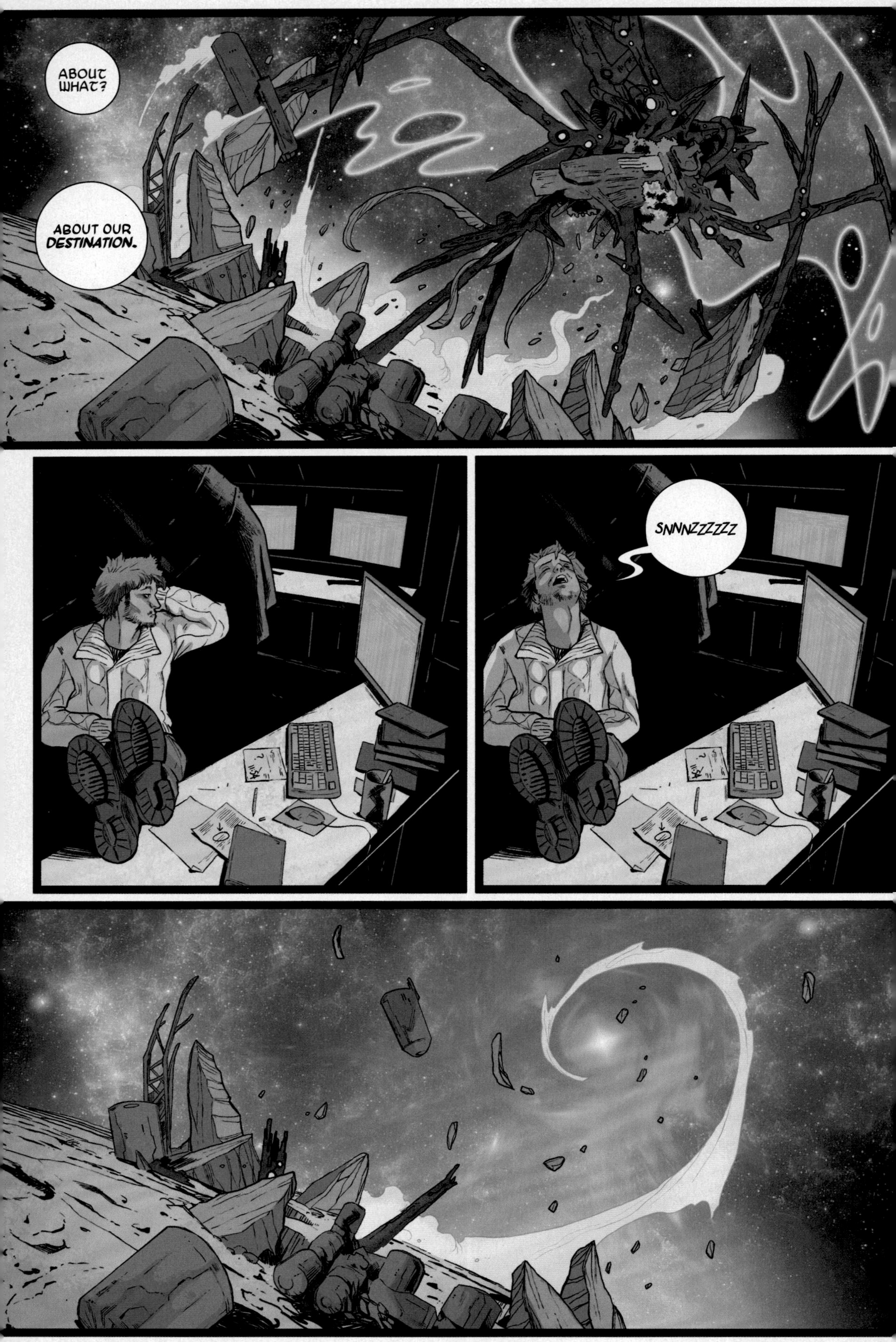
ABOUT WHAT?
ABOUT OUR DESTINATION.
SNNNZZZZZZ

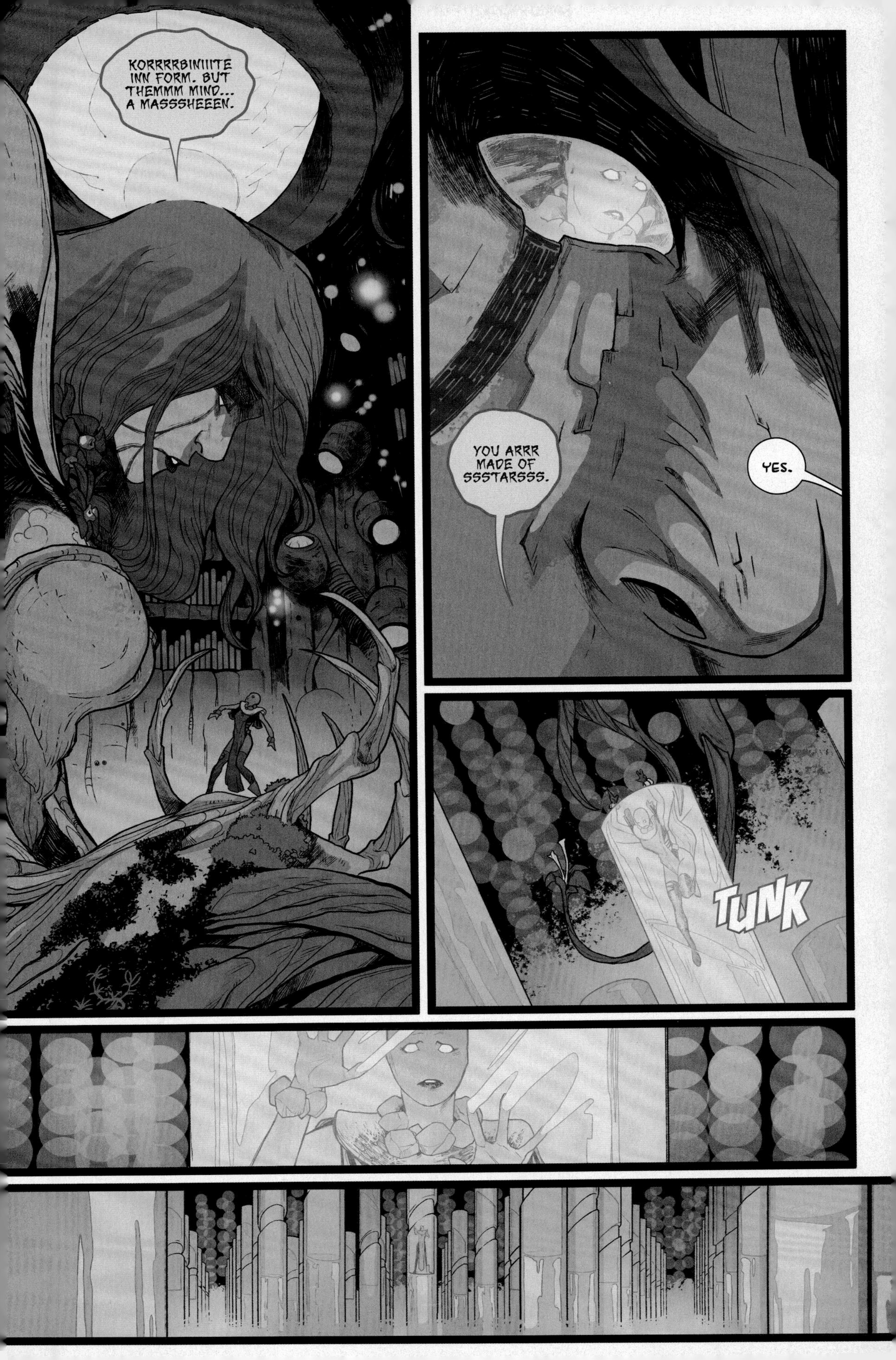
KORRRRBINIIITE INN FORM. BUT THEMMM MIND... A MASSSHEEEN.
YOU ARRR MADE OF SSSTARSSS.
YES.
TUNK

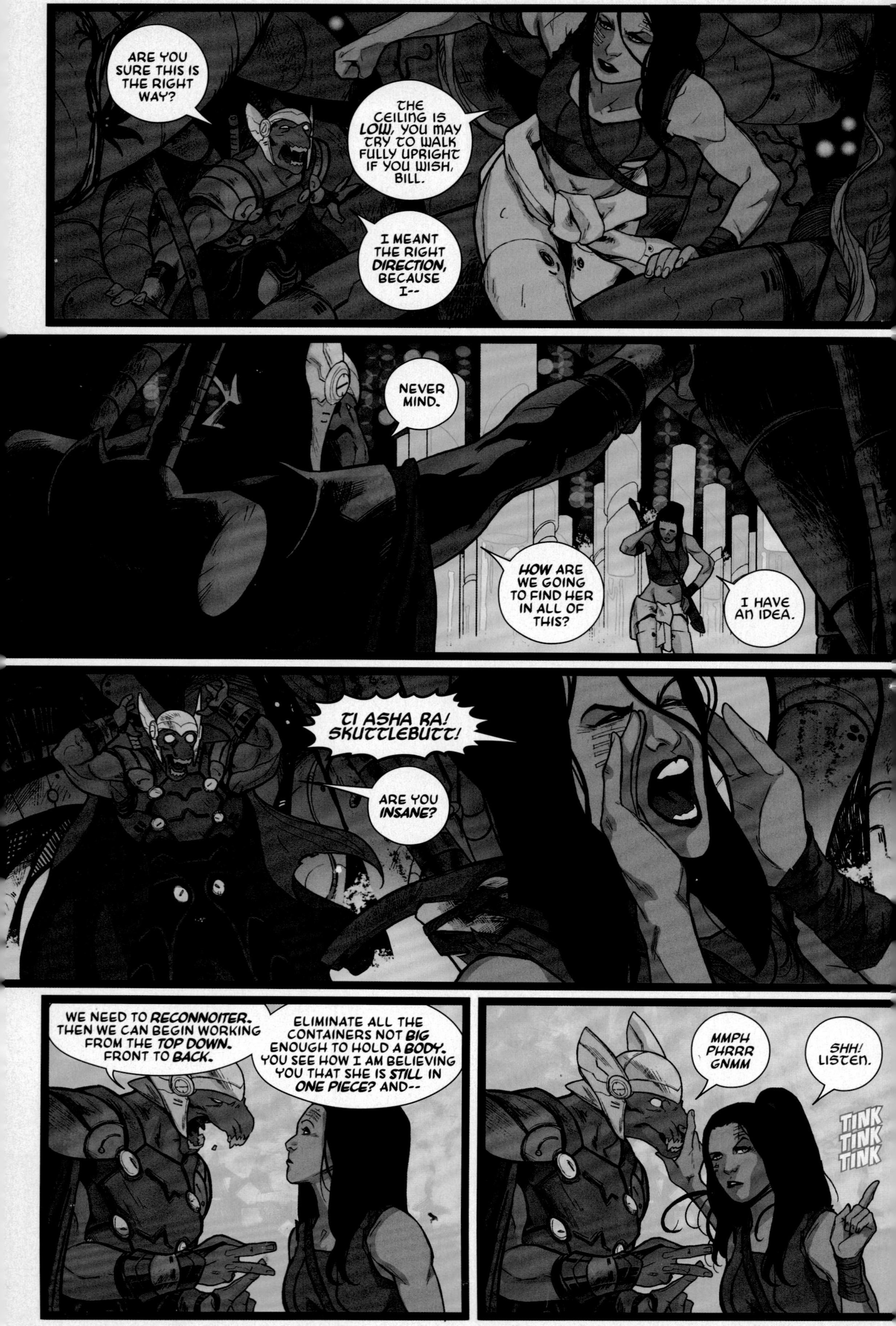
ARE YOU SURE THIS IS THE RIGHT WAY?
THE CEILING IS LOW, YOU MAY TRY TO WALK FULLY UPRIGHT IF YOU WISH, BILL.
I MEANT THE RIGHT DIRECTION, BECAUSE I--
NEVER MIND.
HOW ARE WE GOING TO FIND HER IN ALL OF THIS?
I HAVE AN IDEA.
TI ASHA RA! SKUTTLEBUTT!
ARE YOU INSANE?
WE NEED TO RECONNOITER. THEN WE CAN BEGIN WORKING FROM THE TOP DOWN. FRONT TO BACK.
ELIMINATE ALL THE CONTAINERS NOT BIG ENOUGH TO HOLD A BODY. YOU SEE HOW I AM BELIEVING YOU THAT SHE IS STILL IN ONE PIECE? AND--
MMPH PHRRR GNMM
SHH! LISTEN.
TINK TINK TINK

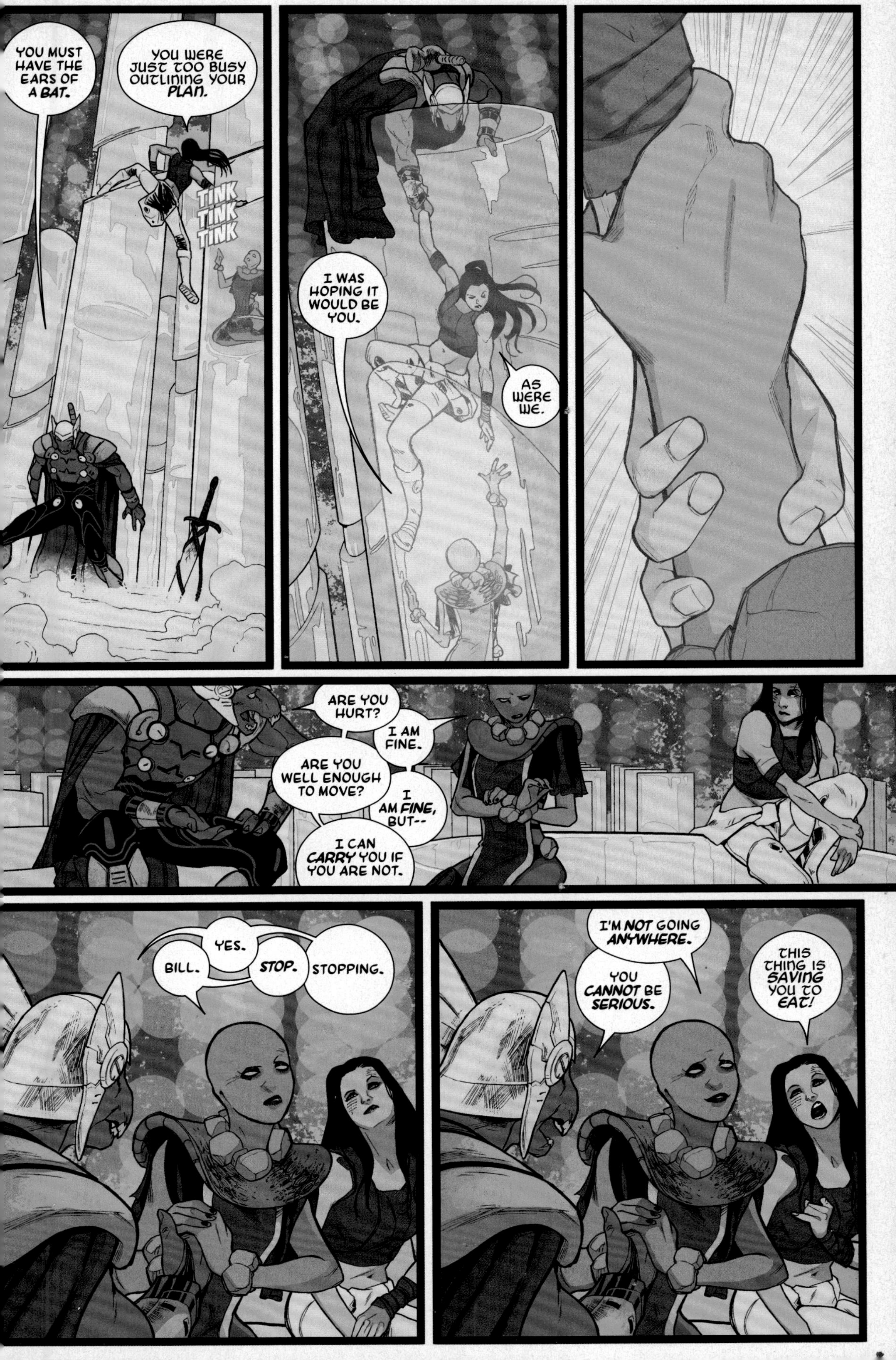
YOU MUST HAVE THE EARS OF A BAT.
YOU WERE JUST TOO BUSY OUTLINING YOUR PLAN.
TINK TINK TINK
I WAS HOPING IT WOULD BE YOU.
AS WERE WE.
ARE YOU HURT?
I AM FINE.
ARE YOU WELL ENOUGH TO MOVE?
I AM FINE, BUT--
I CAN CARRY YOU IF YOU ARE NOT.
BILL.
STOP.
YES.
STOPPING.
I'M NOT GOING ANYWHERE.
YOU CANNOT BE SERIOUS.
THIS THING IS SAVING YOU TO EAT!

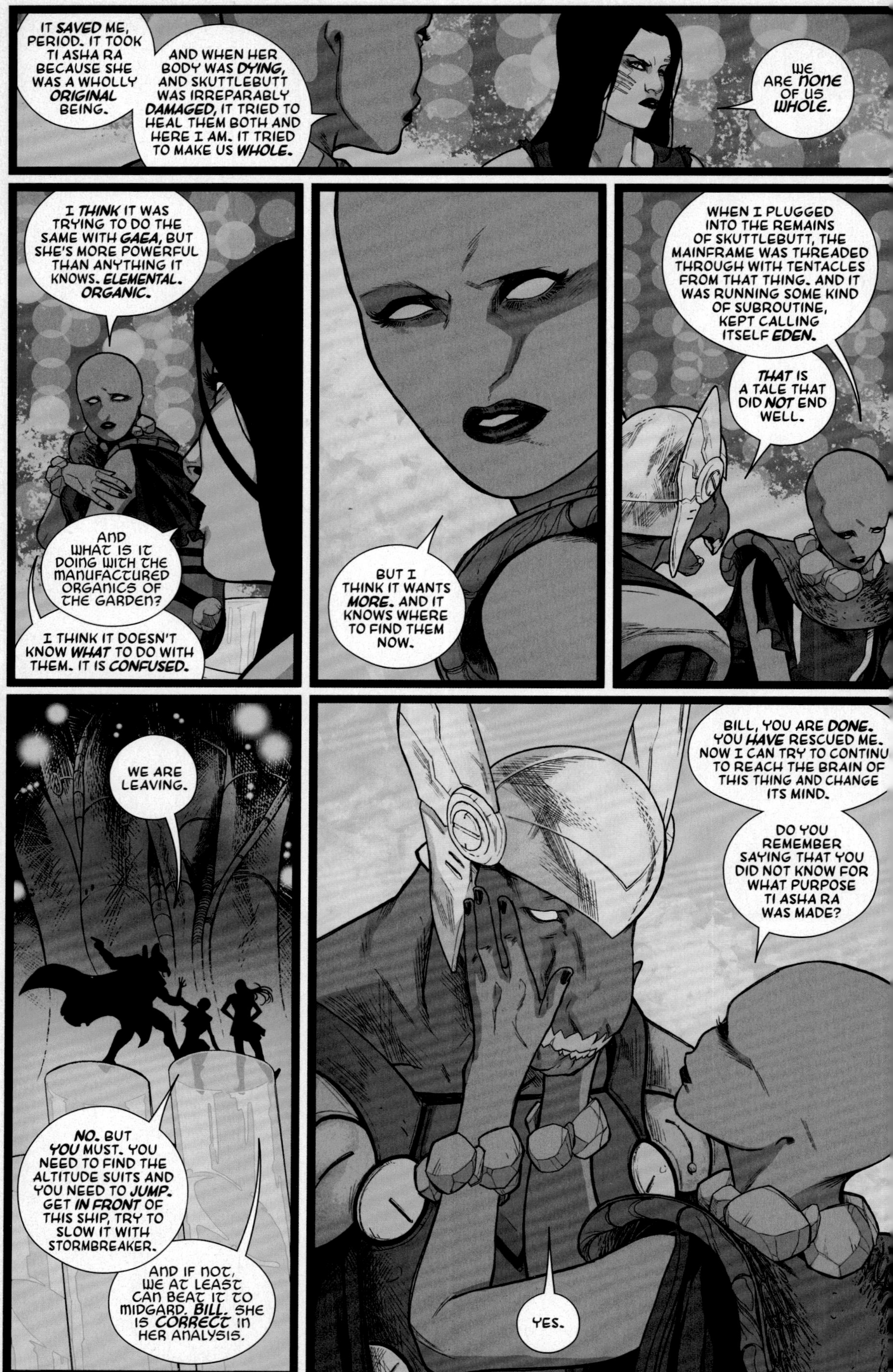
IT SAVED ME, PERIOD. IT TOOK TI ASHA RA BECAUSE SHE WAS A WHOLLY ORIGINAL BEING.
AND WHEN HER BODY WAS DYING, AND SKUTTLEBUTT WAS IRREPARABLY DAMAGED, IT TRIED TO HEAL THEM BOTH AND HERE I AM. IT TRIED TO MAKE US WHOLE.
WE ARE NONE OF US WHOLE.
I THINK IT WAS TRYING TO DO THE SAME WITH GAEA, BUT SHE'S MORE POWERFUL THAN ANYTHING IT KNOWS. ELEMENTAL. ORGANIC.
AND WHAT IS IT DOING WITH THE MANUFACTURED ORGANICS OF THE GARDEN?
I THINK IT DOESN'T KNOW WHAT TO DO WITH THEM. IT IS CONFUSED.
BUT I THINK IT WANTS MORE. AND IT KNOWS WHERE TO FIND THEM NOW.
WHEN I PLUGGED INTO THE REMAINS OF SKUTTLEBUTT, THE MAINFRAME WAS THREADED THROUGH WITH TENTACLES FROM THAT THING. AND IT WAS RUNNING SOME KIND OF SUBROUTINE, KEPT CALLING ITSELF EDEN.
THAT IS A TALE THAT DID NOT END WELL.
WE ARE LEAVING.
NO. BUT YOU MUST. YOU NEED TO FIND THE ALTITUDE SUITS AND YOU NEED TO JUMP. GET IN FRONT OF THIS SHIP, TRY TO SLOW IT WITH STORMBREAKER.
AND IF NOT, WE AT LEAST CAN BEAT IT TO MIDGARD. BILL. SHE IS CORRECT IN HER ANALYSIS.
BILL, YOU ARE DONE. YOU HAVE RESCUED ME. NOW I CAN TRY TO CONTINU TO REACH THE BRAIN OF THIS THING AND CHANGE ITS MIND.
DO YOU REMEMBER SAYING THAT YOU DID NOT KNOW FOR WHAT PURPOSE TI ASHA RA WAS MADE?
YES.

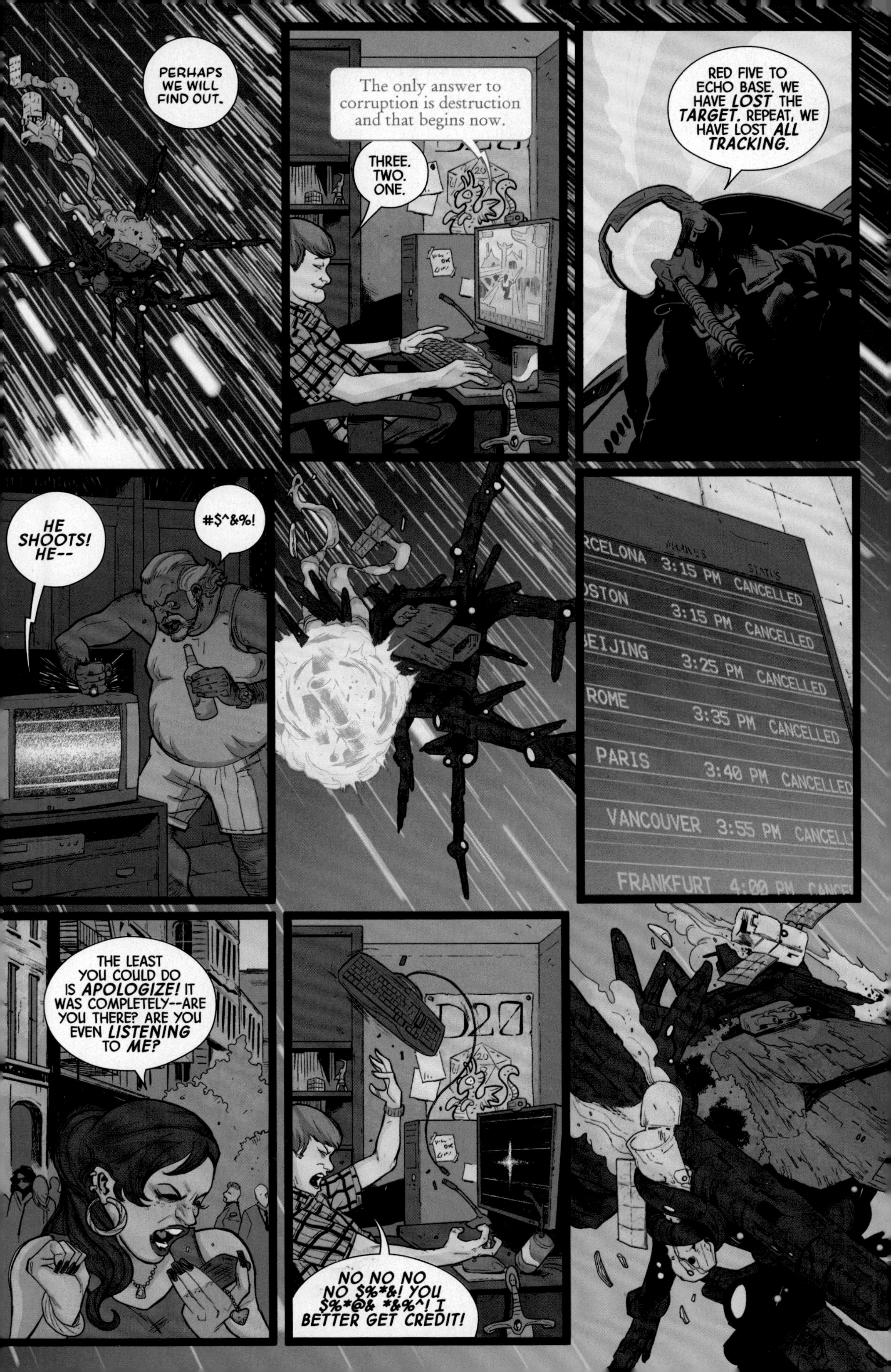
PERHAPS WE WILL FIND OUT.
The only answer to corruption is destruction and that begins now.
THREE. TWO. ONE.
D20
RED FIVE TO ECHO BASE. WE HAVE LOST THE TARGET. REPEAT, WE HAVE LOST ALL TRACKING.
HE SHOOTS! HE--
#$^&%!
BARCELONA 3:15 PM CANCELLED
BOSTON 3:15 PM CANCELLED
BEIJING 3:25 PM CANCELLED
ROME 3:35 PM CANCELLED
PARIS 3:40 PM CANCELLED
VANCOUVER 3:55 PM CANCELL
FRANKFURT 4:00 PM CANCEL
THE LEAST YOU COULD DO IS APOLOGIZE! IT WAS COMPLETELY--ARE YOU THERE? ARE YOU EVEN LISTENING TO ME?
D20
NO NO NO NO $%*&! YOU $%*@& *&%^! I BETTER GET CREDIT!

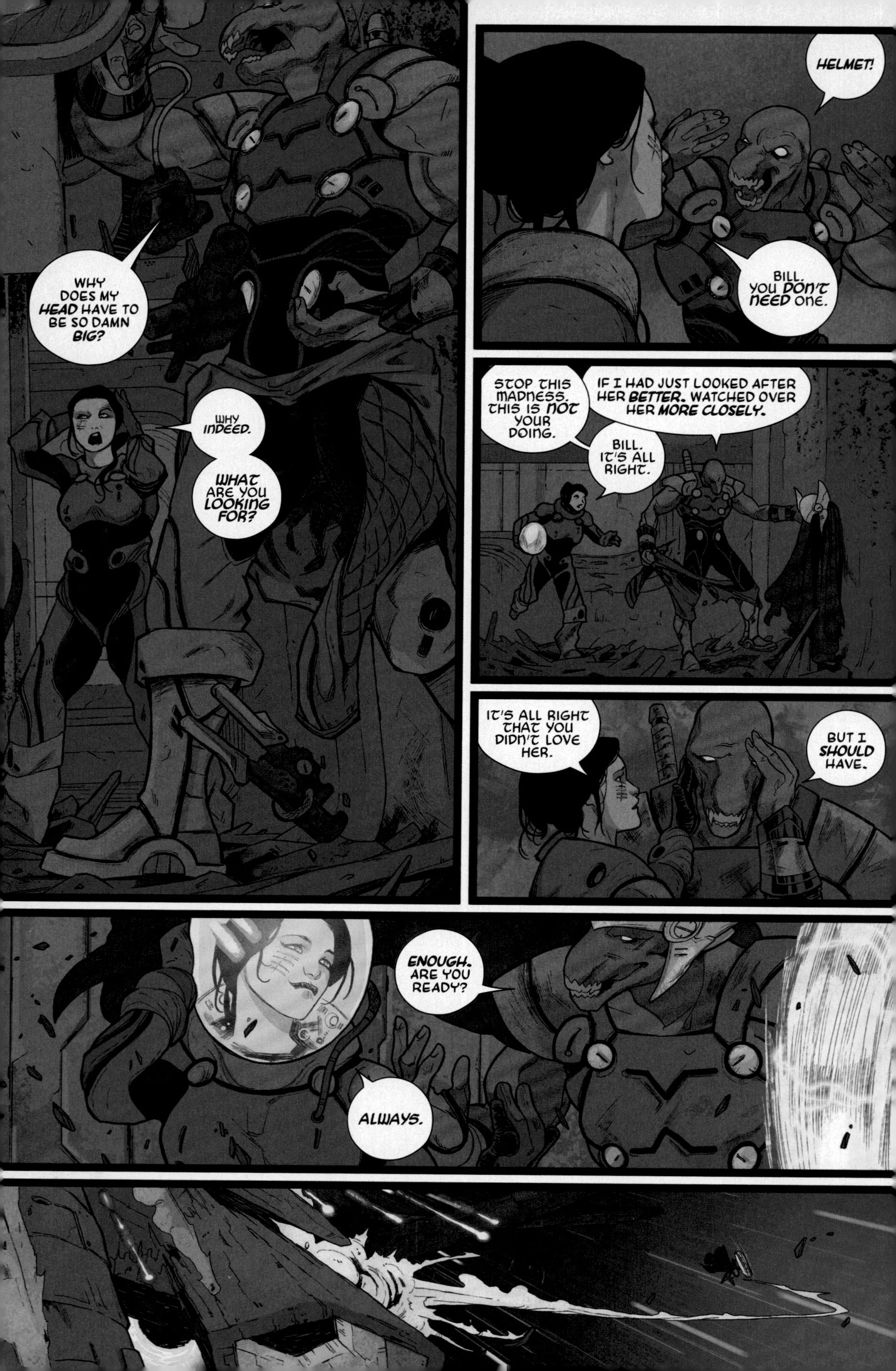
WHY DOES MY HEAD HAVE TO BE SO DAMN BIG?
WHY INDEED.
WHAT ARE YOU LOOKING FOR?
HELMET!
BILL. YOU DON'T NEED ONE.
STOP THIS MADNESS. THIS IS NOT YOUR DOING.
IF I HAD JUST LOOKED AFTER HER BETTER. WATCHED OVER HER MORE CLOSELY.
BILL. IT'S ALL RIGHT.
IT'S ALL RIGHT THAT YOU DIDN'T LOVE HER.
BUT I SHOULD HAVE.
ENOUGH. ARE YOU READY?
ALWAYS.

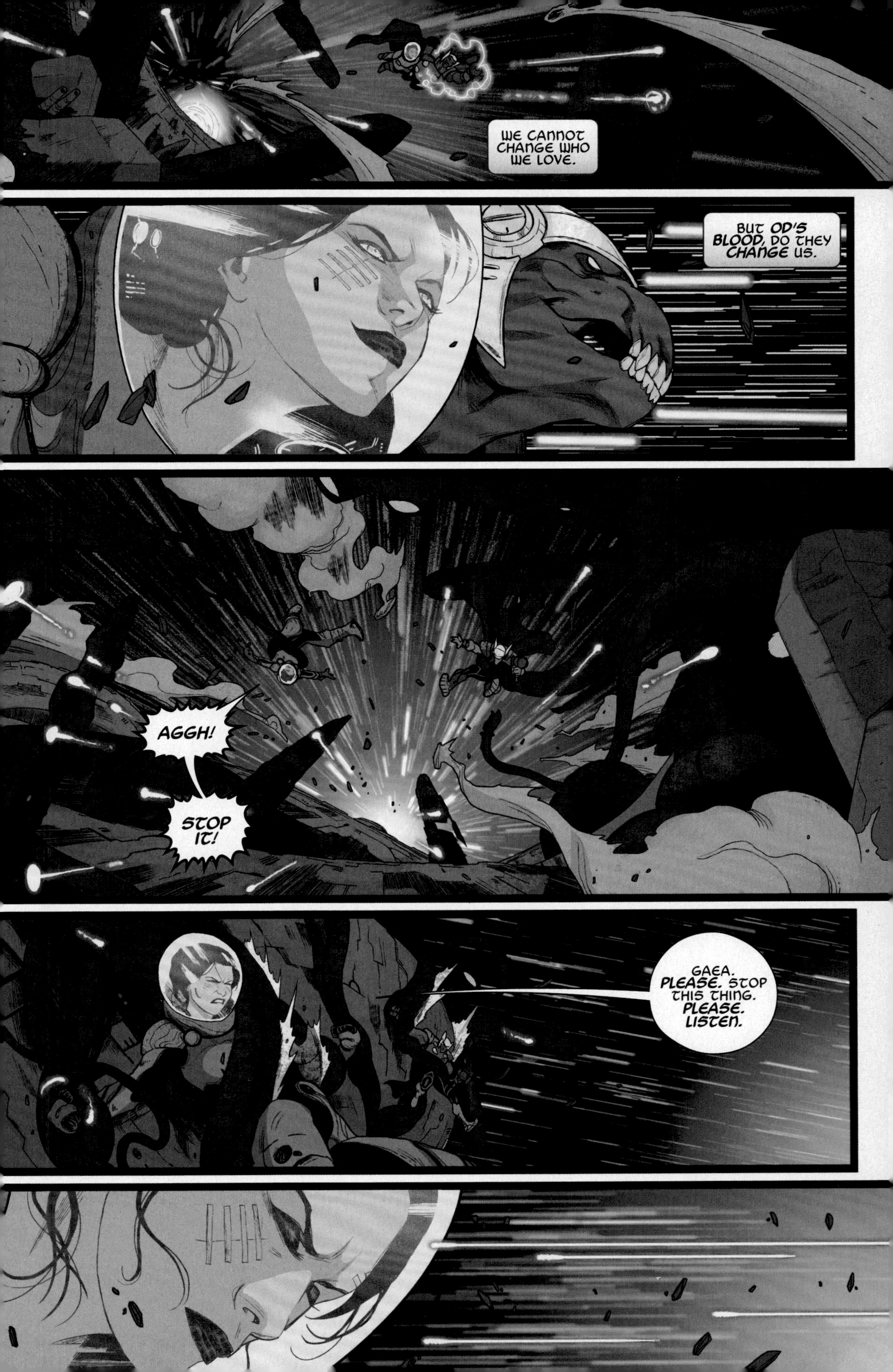
WE CANNOT CHANGE WHO WE LOVE.
BUT OD'S BLOOD, DO THEY CHANGE US.
AGGH!
STOP IT!
GAEA. PLEASE. STOP THIS THING. PLEASE. LISTEN.

YOU **MUST** HEAR ME. EARTH **NEEDS** YOUR MINISTRATIONS, NEEDS HEALING, BUT **NOT** THIS WAY!

YOU ARE **WASTING** YOUR TIME.

BILL, **HELP** ME. THERE IS **SOMETHING**, SOMEONE IS **LISTENING**! I-I CAN FEEL IT.

YOU CAN **FEEL** IT? SINCE **WHEN**? WHAT ARE **YOU** TURNING INTO?!

WE ARE **NOT** A PROBLEM TO BE **SOLVED**! JUST BECAUSE SOMETHING IS **INCOMPLETE** DOES NOT MEAN IT IS **BROKEN**!

KEEP TALKING, SIF. THEY HEAR YOU. THEY **HEAR** YOU.

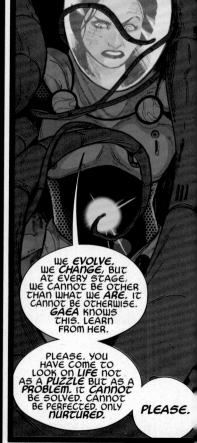

WE **EVOLVE**. WE **CHANGE**, BUT AT EVERY STAGE, WE CANNOT BE OTHER THAN WHAT WE **ARE**. IT CANNOT BE OTHERWISE. **GAEA** KNOWS THIS. LEARN FROM HER.

PLEASE. YOU HAVE COME TO LOOK ON **LIFE** NOT AS A **PUZZLE** BUT AS A **PROBLEM**. IT CANNOT BE SOLVED. CANNOT BE PERFECTED, ONLY **NURTURED**.

PLEASE.

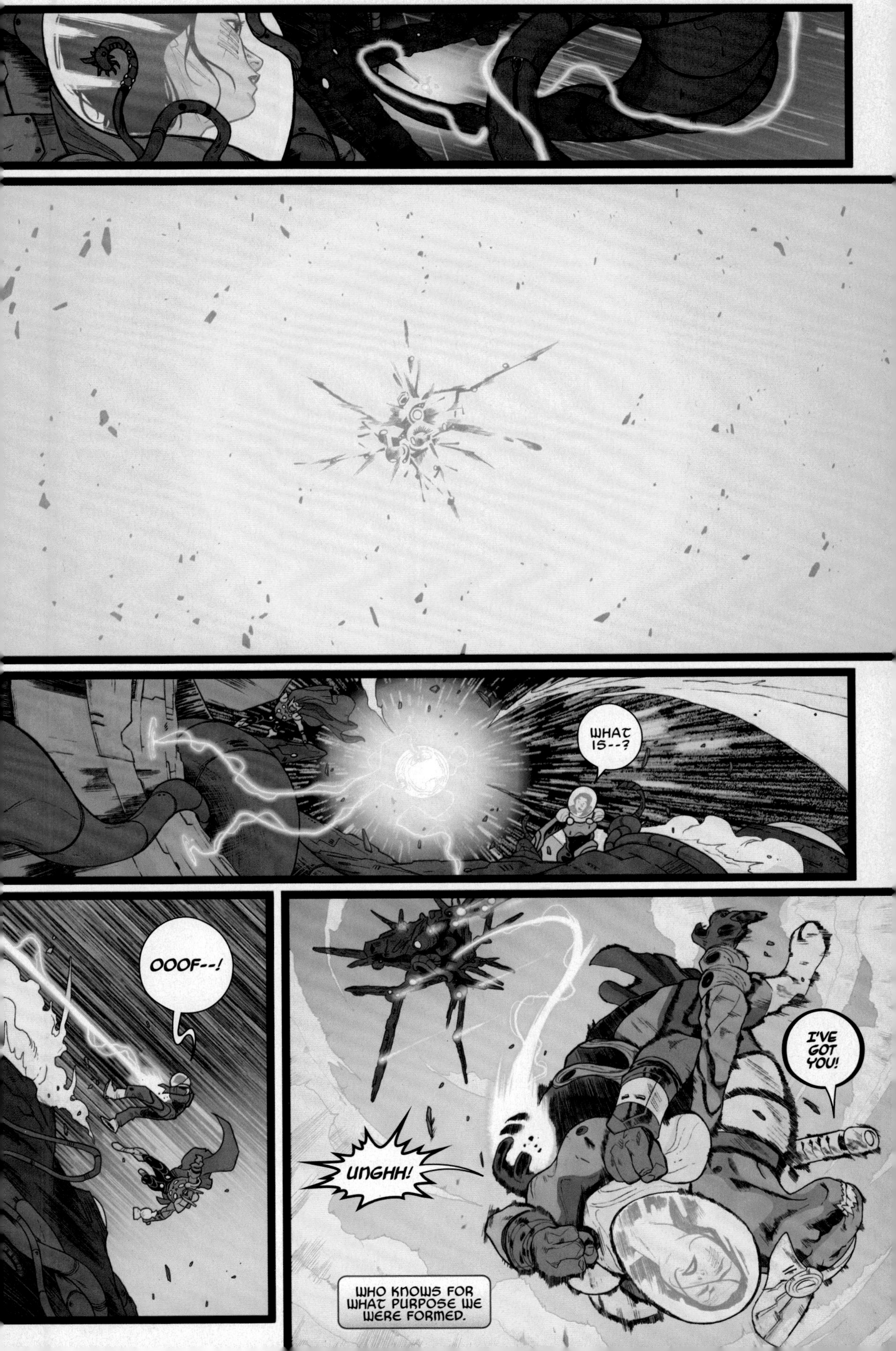
WHAT IS--?
OOOF--!
I'VE GOT YOU!
UNGHH!
WHO KNOWS FOR WHAT PURPOSE WE WERE FORMED.

Asgardia, hovering outside Broxton, OK

FALLING STARS?

WHOMP-P-P-P-P

AND FOR WHAT END.

≩GASP≩

KA-THODOOM

BEHOLD.

FROM AN ARK, A BIRTH. FROM A SEED, A BEGINNING.

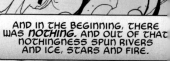

AND IN THE BEGINNING, THERE WAS NOTHING. AND OUT OF THAT NOTHINGNESS SPUN RIVERS AND ICE, STARS AND FIRE.

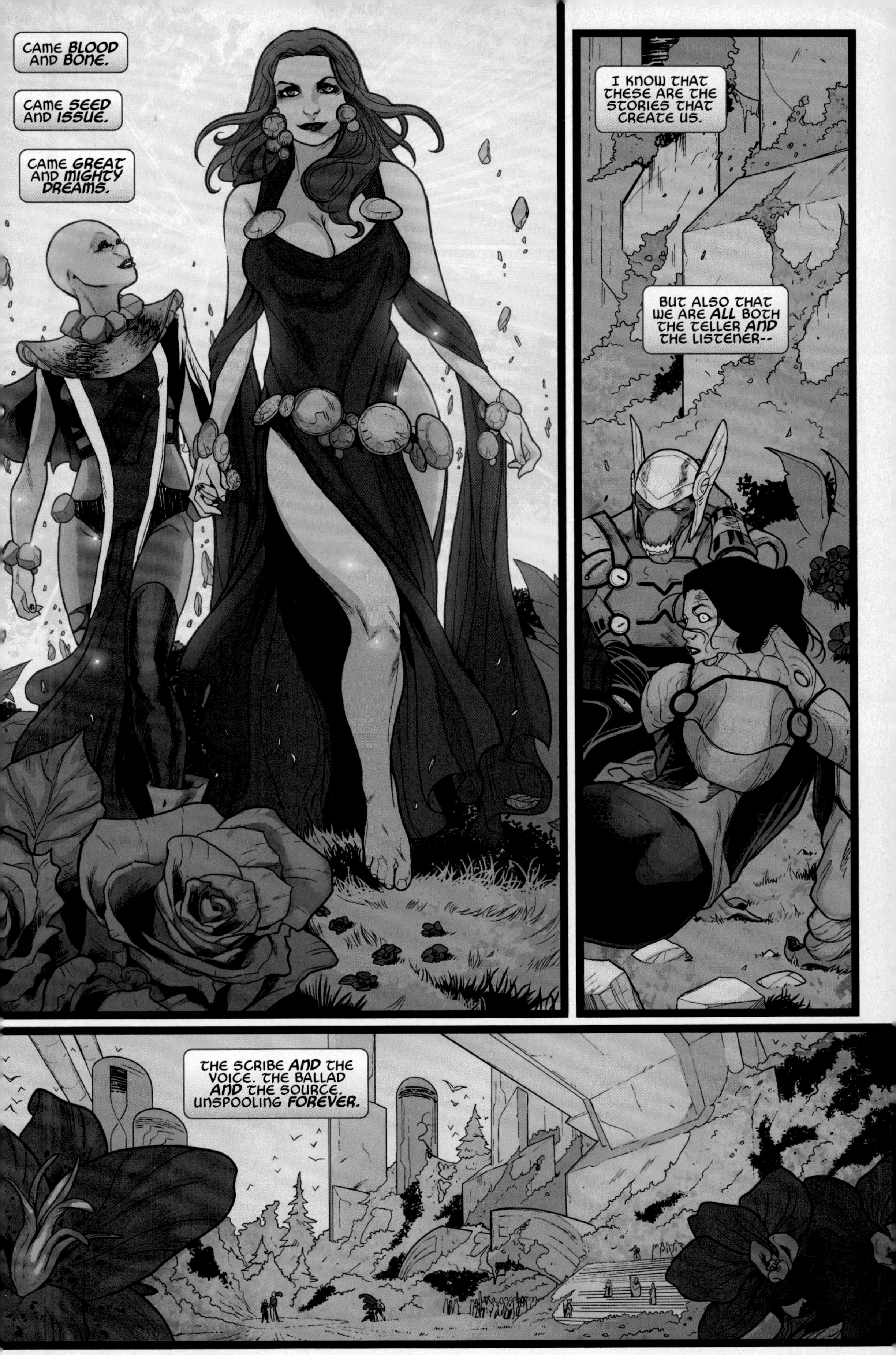
CAME BLOOD AND BONE.
CAME SEED AND ISSUE.
CAME GREAT AND MIGHTY DREAMS.
I KNOW THAT THESE ARE THE STORIES THAT CREATE US.
BUT ALSO THAT WE ARE ALL BOTH THE TELLER AND THE LISTENER--
THE SCRIBE AND THE VOICE. THE BALLAD AND THE SOURCE. UNSPOOLING FOREVER.

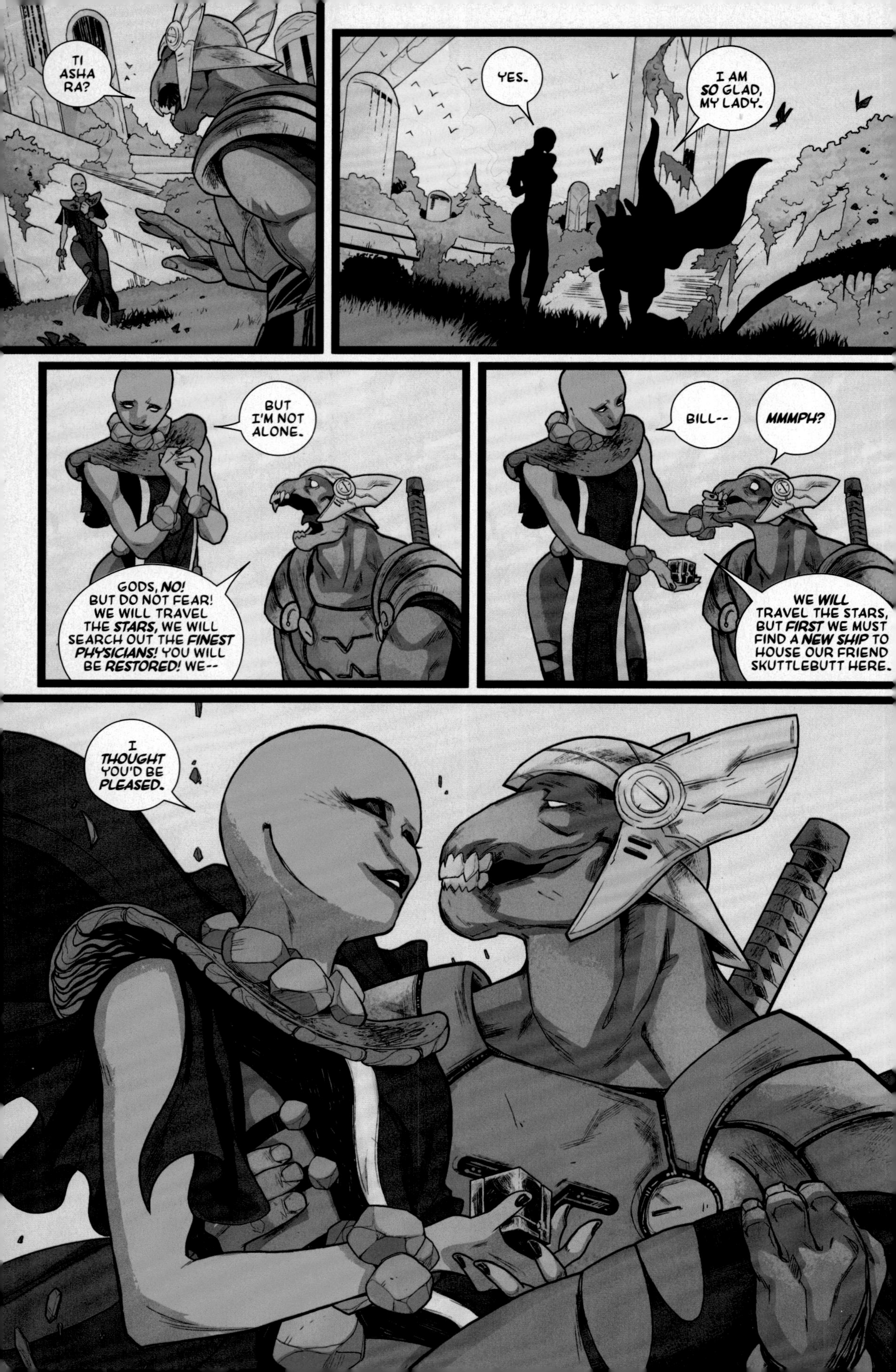
TI ASHA RA?
YES.
I AM SO GLAD, MY LADY.
BUT I'M NOT ALONE.
GODS, NO! BUT DO NOT FEAR! WE WILL TRAVEL THE STARS, WE WILL SEARCH OUT THE FINEST PHYSICIANS! YOU WILL BE RESTORED! WE--
BILL--
MMMPH?
WE WILL TRAVEL THE STARS, BUT FIRST WE MUST FIND A NEW SHIP TO HOUSE OUR FRIEND SKUTTLEBUTT HERE.
I THOUGHT YOU'D BE PLEASED.

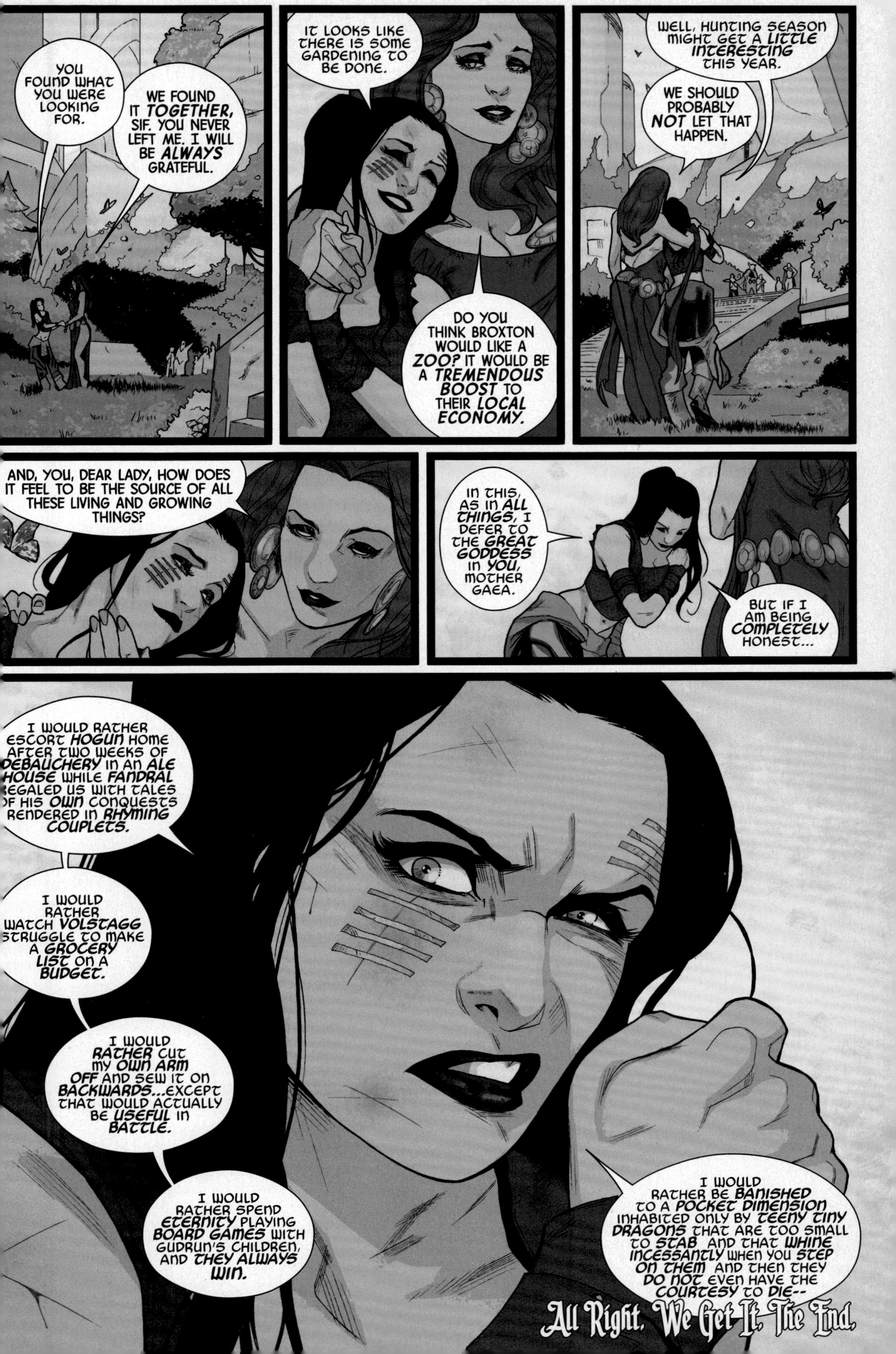

YOU FOUND WHAT YOU WERE LOOKING FOR.
WE FOUND IT TOGETHER, SIF. YOU NEVER LEFT ME. I WILL BE ALWAYS GRATEFUL.
IT LOOKS LIKE THERE IS SOME GARDENING TO BE DONE.
DO YOU THINK BROXTON WOULD LIKE A ZOO? IT WOULD BE A TREMENDOUS BOOST TO THEIR LOCAL ECONOMY.
WELL, HUNTING SEASON MIGHT GET A LITTLE INTERESTING THIS YEAR.
WE SHOULD PROBABLY NOT LET THAT HAPPEN.
AND, YOU, DEAR LADY, HOW DOES IT FEEL TO BE THE SOURCE OF ALL THESE LIVING AND GROWING THINGS?
IN THIS, AS IN ALL THINGS, I DEFER TO THE GREAT GODDESS IN YOU, MOTHER GAEA.
BUT IF I AM BEING COMPLETELY HONEST...
I WOULD RATHER ESCORT HOGUN HOME AFTER TWO WEEKS OF DEBAUCHERY IN AN ALE HOUSE WHILE FANDRAL REGALED US WITH TALES OF HIS OWN CONQUESTS RENDERED IN RHYMING COUPLETS.
I WOULD RATHER WATCH VOLSTAGG STRUGGLE TO MAKE A GROCERY LIST ON A BUDGET.
I WOULD RATHER CUT MY OWN ARM OFF AND SEW IT ON BACKWARDS...EXCEPT THAT WOULD ACTUALLY BE USEFUL IN BATTLE.
I WOULD RATHER SPEND ETERNITY PLAYING BOARD GAMES WITH GUDRUN'S CHILDREN, AND THEY ALWAYS WIN.
I WOULD RATHER BE BANISHED TO A POCKET DIMENSION INHABITED ONLY BY TEENY TINY DRAGONS THAT ARE TOO SMALL TO STAB AND THAT WHINE INCESSANTLY WHEN YOU STEP ON THEM AND THEN THEY DO NOT EVEN HAVE THE COURTESY TO DIE--
All Right. We Get It. The End.

JOURNEY INTO STATIONERY

Vhat farewell column would be :omplete without a salute from he creators themselves? (pull out your hankies, gang!) Take it iway, Kathryn! -JT

As Sif and her pals punch and stab their vay to the finish line, the rest of us seem o be trying to murder each other with chmaltz (not delicious chicken fat... the ther thing.) But if there's one thing I've earned from Sif, it's that you've got to go with your gut and lead with something ointy (that's two things... I digress.) These ten issues have been such a good ime and, as I've said before, if all they lid was boost Valerio to even greater eights, that would have been enough. But that's not all that happened. Jordie nade every page sing and glow and do a ittle dance and what can you say about Clayton that does not include words like masterful' and 'seamless.' Thank you to our fearless leaders, thank you to Pepe arraz for being the best relief pitcher inyone could ask for, and most of all, hanks to you, our fearless readers who ut no slack and came along for the ride inyway. All of you make me want to nake every single panel better than the one that preceded it.

SEMPER ADORKABLE.

-Kathryn

loved this book but believe me when I ay that it was very hard work, so the est that I can do is to thank the people hat supported me during this real-life 'JOURNEY INTO MYSTERY". Of course 'm talking of the team, Lauren, Jake, Kathryn, Jordie, Clayton, Jeff and Pepe: hank you guys for this great run, I wish or even greater things for you all in the uture. Thanks to my close support, my jirlfriend Vega, because there's a lot of ter in my Lady Sif. And thanks to you, the erson holding this book: I ride so far for ou...without you, there is nothing.

Thanks,
Valerio

My list of fictional crushes is short: a edheaded FBI agent, a pointy-eared cience officer, a masked bounty hunter with a jet pack...and Sif. They are all logical, calculating creatures who do what they do best while taking zero lip. Thank you, Kathryn, for writing a character that didn't know the burden of "Women? Pfft, they can't do that!" and to Valerio who drew a character so effortlessly. For a Goddess she was more than approachable to anyone! And to my BFF Clayton who managed to make my colors look like they could tell a story after all! But mostly, thank you so much Lauren and Jake for bringing us all together and thank you, true believer, for picking up this title!

<3 <3 <3
-Jordie

One time I was lettering this book and I said, "Valerio Schiti draws a really cute Jane Foster." Then Jake and Lauren made fun of me for, like, an hour. I'm sorry, I would have written something really kind and sentimental, but everyone else already did, and I can't beat or match anything they said. Thank you Kathryn, Valerio, Jordie, Jake, Lauren, and Pepe Larraz for all the good times; and goodbye, JOURNEY INTO MYSTERY. I will truly miss you.

-Clayton

I had a great time doing these JIM covers. I want to thank everyone who enjoyed them, everyone who stopped at my table at conventions to let me know they enjoyed them, and Lauren for giving me a shot at 'em. I'm happy to have been part of a great team.

-Jeff Dekal

Obviously, I love super heroes, but there's very few I'd actually want to be friends with. Tony Stark's cool and all, but partying with that guy? It'd be exhausting, and he'd probably hit on your girlfriend. Cap's like hanging out with your grandpa. Captain Marvel's super competitive, Hawkeye's moody, Black Widow's too intense. But Sif? Holy smokes. I want to be Sif's best friend. I want to get silly on mead with this warrior goddess and cause a ruckus! It's no mystery why this Sif has captured our hearts, she's a brilliant composite of all the personalities that went into making her: Kathryn the Great, Valerio, Pepe, Jordie, Clayton, Lauren, and who wouldn't want to get crazy with that motley crew? It's been a blast, and the recap to JiM #652 is taped up at my desk to remind me. Thanks for the great run, all, and thanks for reading!

How did all this sand get into our office, and why is it all suddenly in my eyes? I'll just...give me minute...

-Jake T.

NELSON & MURDOCK
ATTORNEYS AT LAW

August 28, 2013

Hullo!

I'm told this is the final issue of JOURNEY INTO MYSTERY. Really? This is of some surprise. I was under the impression that JOURNEY INTO MYSTERY would have ended – oooooh – ten issues ago? Something like that, anyway. I'm not sure what's going on.

Anyway! A hearty congratulations on the run of your fine comics publication, and you'll be hearing from my lawyers.

Yours,

Loki Laufeyson

Loki Laufeyson

(Or Kieron Gillen. Who can tell the difference?)

And that, ladies, gents, ethereal beings, is that. I can't thank you all enough for such a rich and wonderful experience you have made this book, readers and creators alike. We were The Book That Could...we are now The Book That Did (And Rocked Many Socks Off In The Process).

So...who's in for a group hug? C'mere you.... mmmmmmMMMM!!

Until the next adventure, eat lots of chocolate and NEVER. STOP. DOING. YOUR. THING.

-LS

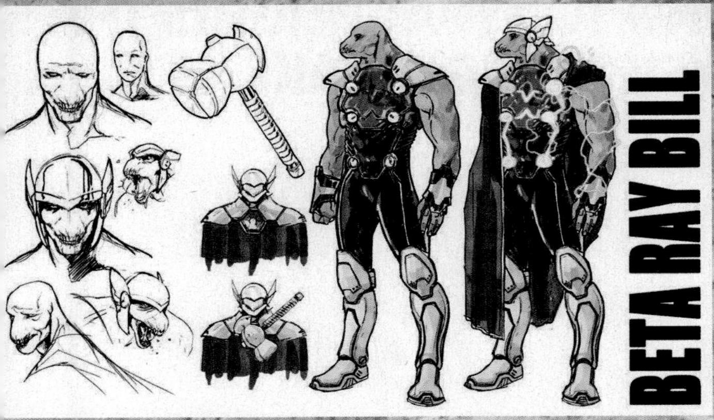
BETA RAY BILL

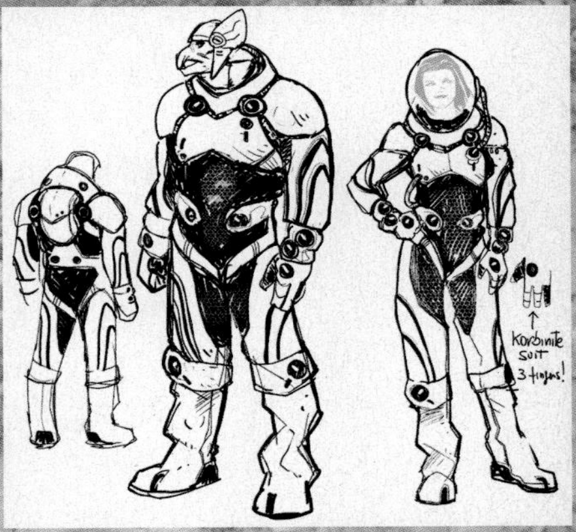
Korbinite suit
3 fingers!

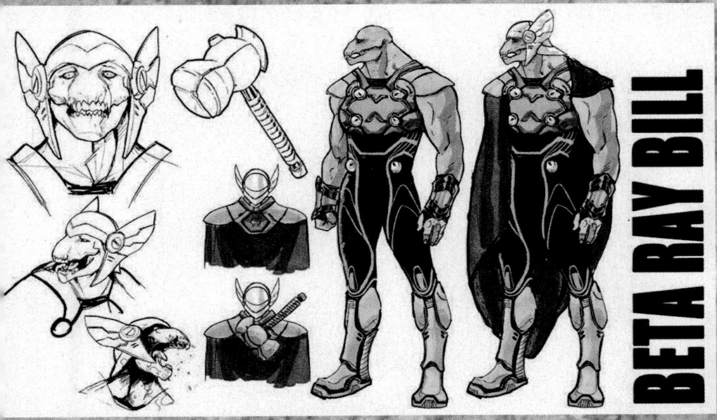
BETA RAY BILL

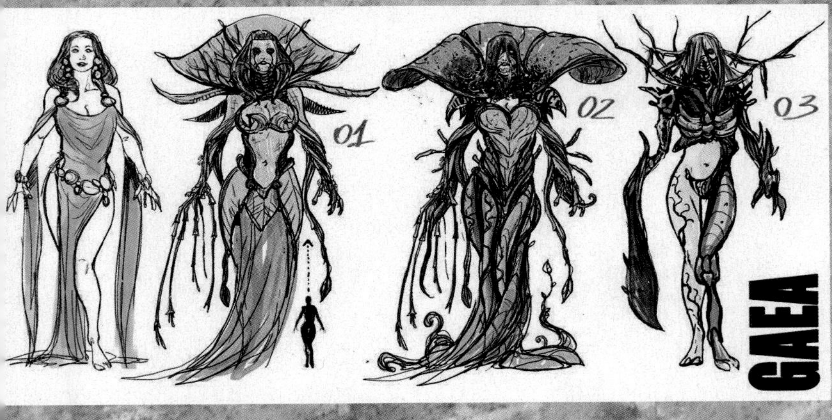
01
02
03
GAEA

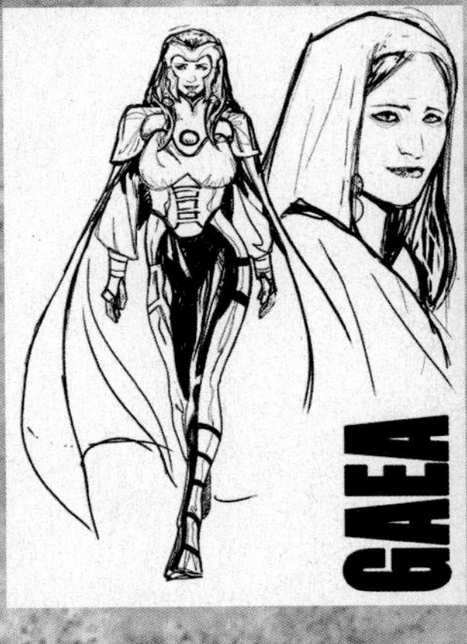
GAEA

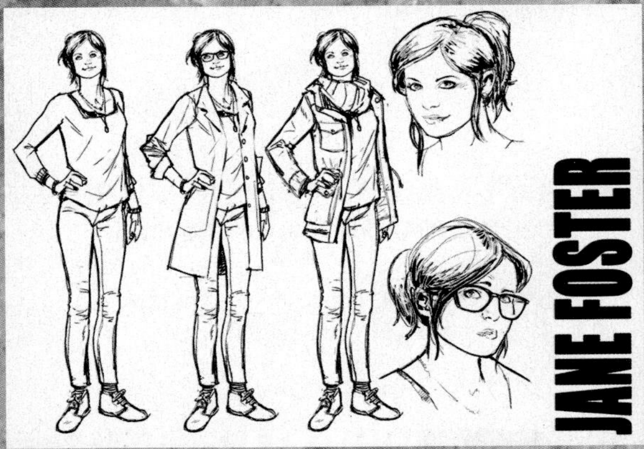
JANE FOSTER

CHARACTER SKETCHES BY VALERIO SCHITI

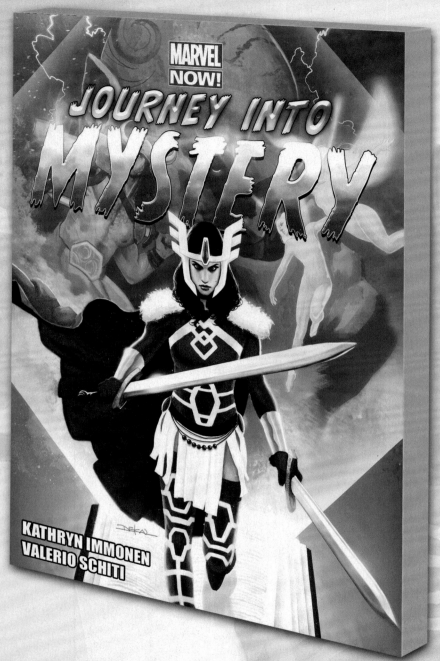